In 20 Years, We've Covered a Lot of Country Together

By Jerry Wiebel, Editor

AS EDITOR of *Country* and *Country EXTRA*, I figure I've got one of the best jobs a country kid could hope to have.

I grew up on an Iowa farm, and I'd thought about becoming a veterinarian. But my mom submitted a scholarship application along with some of my high school writings to a farm magazine, and I was awarded a $300 college scholarship. You know what they say about a bird in hand...so I figured I'd give agricultural journalism a try. (Plus, I was a bit nervous about all the chemistry those smart veterinary students had to take.)

Then, through some twists and turns in my career path, I eventually hooked up with Roy Reiman, and I've been working on *Country* for 8 of its 20-year history. Amazing how things work out.

Part of my "job" is selecting the breathtaking photos that appear in the magazine. I put that in quotes because I can't really call it work with a straight face—although I do look at some *10,000* professional photos a year just to come up with the hundred or so that appear in each issue.

Sometimes I find myself daydreaming about the photo I'm looking at—just wishing I was there. That tells me it's a winner, because if it makes me feel that way, chances are it'll make readers feel the same.

Then there's all of the mail from subscribers that the staff and I get to read every day. Just imagine your own mailbox crammed full of interesting letters, stories and snapshots from your family and friends every day. That's how we feel about reading the heartwarming mail we get from readers.

Upbeat, Wholesome Reading

But the thing I appreciate most of all is the upbeat, positive and wholesome tone Roy set for *Country* when he launched it. I've often thought about

the stories I'd be writing if I were still a farm reporter—reporting mostly on the tough times farmers and ranchers have faced in the 30-some years since I've been in this business.

For me, that'd be about as depressing as the morning after a hailstorm that riddled my wheat crop. But in *Country*, we can set aside all of the cares of the day and simply celebrate the joys of life in the country.

I once saw a sign that read, "A good rain and a baby calf are always welcome." That about sums up a good day in the country—and the kind of smiles we try to bring you in each issue of *Country* and *Country EXTRA*.

Book Was a Bonus

As fun as my job is, editing *The Best of Country* was a bonus for me—like getting a baby calf *and* a healthy litter of 3-pound baby pigs to boot! That's because I could relive all of the memorable stories and breathtaking photos of my 8 years as editor...plus go back to the very beginning.

No doubt about it, we've covered a lot of country together over those 20 years...and we hope you enjoy this "trip" back over the last 2 decades as much as our staff did putting *The Best of Country* together.

We've included some of our very

best "Now This Is God's Country" features (that was a tough decision) as well as dozens of heartwarming reader photos of rural people, farm animals and country kids. Interspersed among them are stories from readers that'll put a smile on your face on one page and a lump in your throat on the next.

Remember Cora Holmes? There's a whole chapter about her adventures as she moved from a high-stress job in Boise, Idaho to a 152,000-acre sheep ranch in Alaska's remote Aleutian Islands. We talked to Cora before going to press and added an update on what she and husband Milt are doing today.

Then there's our Amish friend Elsa. Readers first got to know her several years ago when she was engaged, through the "Week in the Country" diary she kept. There was so much interest that we asked Elsa to do a follow-up story about her Amish wedding...and another on her first wedding anniversary. Some readers even sent anniversary cards to her and husband Allen!

Our Top 10 Covers

Subscribers have always marveled at how vivid and lifelike our covers are. So our editors selected what they considered the top 10 covers of the past 20 years. Then we asked our 350 Field Editors to vote on their favorite of all time. See the chapter beginning on page 16 to see what they decided.

Longtime subscribers will recall *Country's Reminisce Hitch* and the coast-to-coast trek of those six champion Belgian draft horses as they "pulled for seniors." We've included reports from the road they traveled, along with comments from Roy on why he put the hitch together, in a chapter called "Memories of My Favorite Horse."

We'd also like to invite you to an "Editors' Potluck." Like all country folks, members of our editorial staff love to eat. So we asked them to select some of their favorite recipes from the "Taste of the Country" section. We can't promise that all of these foods "go together," but we had more fun than a church picnic doing it!

So dig in and enjoy *The Best of Country*.

The Best of
Country

Travel Back Through Our First 20 Years

Now *This* Is God's Country

C'mon, Let's Head for the Country

A Week in the Country

A Taste of the Country— Editors' Potluck

Dilly Cucumber Salad, Teriyaki
Salmon, Golden Mashed Potato Bake,
Sunshine Coconut Pineapple Cake
and more!

Editor Jerry Wiebel; **Managing Editor** Robin Hoffman; **Senior Art Director** Sandra Ploy; **Contributing Editor** Paula Wiebel; **Editorial Assistant** Maxine Burak; **Copy Editor** Susan Uphill; **Photo Coordinator** Trudi Bellin; **Assistant Photo Coordinator** Mary Ann Koebernik; **Photography** Jim Wieland; **Set Stylist** Jennifer Bradley Vent; **Food Stylist** Joylyn Trickel; **Graphic Art Associates** Ellen Lloyd, Catherine Fletcher; **President** Barbara Newton; **Senior Vice President, Editor in Chief** Catherine Cassidy; **Creative Director** Ardyth Cope; **Chairman and Founder** Roy Reiman

Country Books

©2005 Reiman Media Group, Inc. 5400 South 60th St., Greendale WI 53129

International Standard Book Number: 0-89821-464-5   /   Library of Congress Control Number: 2005934308

How *Country* Came About

REALLY? *Really?* Can it already be *20 years* since we started *Country* magazine? For me, those 2 decades have breezed by like a hummingbird headed for a hollyhock.

Part of the reason, I'm sure, is the fun we've had sorting through thousands of beautiful rural photos and warm reader letters as we've put all those issues together. And now, as we sorted through those back issues to share with you the *best features* in this special edition, we've had the fun of rereading and revisiting those enjoyable experiences all over again.

Before you move on to see which features and photos we chose to include (it wasn't easy!), I thought you might like to know how and when *Country* began. So here's a brief version of its origin:

By the early 1980s, we'd decided that veering from "farm" to "country" would be a good direction for our small publishing company. The farm economy was still in the doldrums, and we felt a country-oriented publication would have a much broader appeal.

Confirming that opinion was a study we'd come across which showed that, given the choice, nearly 50% of the people living in the city would prefer to live in the country or in a small town.

Cures Concrete Claustrophobia

The reason? It appeared many metropolitan people were beginning to feel a bit of concrete claustrophobia, brought on by the crowds, traffic, noise and pollution of urban living. Yet, the majority just didn't have the choice of moving to the country.

We felt we had the solution: The magazine we had in mind would take them there…vicariously.

After a good deal more thought and planning, we decided to make our move and began gearing up for the launch.

When we settled on a name for this new magazine, we were amazed during the trademark search to learn that other publishers had come up with everything from *Country Living* to *Country Journal* and from *Country People* to *Coun-*

try Place…but no one had used just plain *Country*!

That's exactly what we wanted; for us, that one word said it all. And that's the name we quickly registered, with our art director's capital "R" making our *CountRy* logo unique.

We printed the Premiere Issue on the highest quality paper we could find. We used full-color photos on every page, screening as many 5,000 photos to select 100 for that first issue.

Then we used the two things that had by now become our company's "formula"—we included no advertising, and we basically had the readers write the articles for us.

We edited and reworked and reworded and reworked that Premiere Issue over and over (see the cover at left). When we finally finished it, we sent a free sample of it to a test list of 100,000 prospects. Then we waited.

What a Winner!

The wait wasn't long. Response was immediate and huge. Subscriptions *poured* in. It was just unbelievable!

The launch of *Country* was better than anything we'd experienced before. For that matter, it was unlike anything any other magazine publishers had ever heard of, either.

The normal goal for mailings touting a new magazine such of this is a 2% response. With *Country*, we received an _18%_ response to the first 100,000 copies! To this day, that kind of response has been unheard of anywhere in the magazine industry.

We kept putting more sample issues in the mail to larger lists of prospects, and by the end of the first year, we had topped a *half million subscribers*. What's more, a high percentage of those folks requested and paid for *2 years* right off the bat.

Why was this magazine so "hot" from the start? We discussed this at length and came to several conclusions:

Likely it was because a high percentage of our society is only one or two generations away from Grandpa's farm, and in today's fast-paced world, they long to go back there now and then…to the way things were in those happy uncomplicated days of their youth.

That's what subscribers tell us. They say *Country* takes them "home" again, and that each issue offers them a 2-hour escape from the reality of their lives.

We've even received letters from subscribers in office towers in New York City who tell us they enjoy reading *Country* while having lunch at their desks. You might be surprised at the state with *Country's* largest number of subscribers. It's California.

In other areas as well, we soon found this magazine appealed to cosmopolitan people as readily as to rural residents. Urbanites who aren't a tad "country" enjoy having this classy magazine on their coffee table.

The Pace Didn't Slow

Whatever was behind it, the circulation kept soaring from the outset. Subscribers liked *Country* so much that they gave well over 100,000 gift subscriptions to friends at Christmastime at the end of its first year.

By 1991, its fifth year, *Country* hit a circulation of 1.7

THINKING OUTSIDE THE BOX. Credit for *Country* goes to Roy Reiman, standing by the sign at our company headquarters.

million. It didn't stop there. In February of 1993—after we finished tallying an even bigger holiday gift subscription response—the circulation of *Country* reached *2,264,000*.

As that Russian comedian Yakov Smirnoff in Branson, Missouri is fond of saying, "What a country!" In this case, what a *Country*.

For whatever reasons, this magazine has been and continues to be a huge success. And since it's still supported solely by subscriptions, we owe that success to people like *you*.

So we thank you and millions of others for your support over these 20 wonderful years…and invite you to browse the following pages to see samples of what's made *Country* unique over the past 2 decades.

Enjoy!

Roy Reiman, Founder

Montana...Now *This* Is God's Country!

In each issue, we invite readers to tell us why they think a particular area is the best place to live. This time, Chuck Haney shares his love of Montana's Glacier Country.

Northwest Montana is known as Glacier Country. I also like to call it God's Country because our Creator showered it with an abundance of natural wonders, ranging from sparkling blue lakes and high mountain peaks to lush forested hills and endless plains.

I've made my home in this magnificent area for well over a decade now, and I'm still amazed by the beautiful landscapes and warmed by the friendliness of the people who live here.

The centerpiece of the region is Glacier National Park. The Continental Divide runs north and south through it, which is why the

THE BEST SPOT. Map shows the highlighted area author says is the country's *best* location.

Blackfeet Indians who live in the area call it "the backbone of the Earth."

The park is so vast that it has

"**BOOTS** are ready for work on the ranch of my friends Leo and Ellen Hargrave."

"**BEAR GRASS** blooms profusely every few years, and the white puffs (left) turn the mountains into scenes from a fairy tale. Last year's bloom was especially good on Big Mountain near where I live."

"**HARVEST** gets into high gear in August (below) as a combine gobbles up wheat and barley on a farm in the Flathead Valley."

"**SHORTLY** after I took this photograph of Little Therriault Lake in the Whitefish Range near Eureka (left), I broke the water's morning stillness with a canoe ride."

"**MY WIFE**, Diana, and I enjoy scenes like this one (below) while driving rural roads near our hometown of Whitefish."

two distinct ecosystems. On the east side, along the Rocky Mountain front, open vistas and grass prairies dominate, while to the west, a dense rain forest grows.

There are over 700 miles of hiking trails that lead to jaw-dropping sights, like thundering waterfalls spiraling downward past alpine meadows. Towering mountain peaks loom over verdant valleys teeming with wildlife. You'll often see mountain goats, bighorn sheep, moose and even grizzly bears along the majestic Going-to-the-Sun Highway.

We share Glacier National Park with our friends from Canada, where it spills across the border and becomes Waterton Lakes National Park. The two parks became the first International Peace Park in 1932.

The spirit of Glacier Country seems to rub off on the people, making them just as wonderful as the scenery. During my travels on photo assignments through the region, I'll often strike up a conversation with farmers and ranchers ↻

"**SPRING ROUNDUP** and branding are always exciting times at the Hargrave Ranch near Marion."

"**ONE** of my favorite photo opportunities presented itself as the calm, glassy surface of Maskinonge Lake reflected the majestic mountains in Waterton Lakes National Park in Alberta, Canada."

"**THESE** are some ripe Flathead cherries. I can almost smell a pie cooling on the windowsill!"

"**THE SPARKLING WATERS** of Montana's mountain streams are world-famous for blue-ribbon trout fishing. This fly fisherman is trying his luck on Ninemile Creek near Huson (left)."

"**HILLSIDES** in the National Bison Range near Moiese are colored with arrowleaf balsam root in late spring (right). Some 400 head of bison graze on the 19,000-acre refuge."

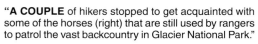

"**A MONTANA COWBOY** needs to be ready for any type of weather, as evidenced by the gear on these horseshoe hooks at the Whitetail Ranch near Ovando."

"**A COUPLE** of hikers stopped to get acquainted with some of the horses (right) that are still used by rangers to patrol the vast backcountry in Glacier National Park."

I've never met. Before I know it, they'll invite me in for a cup of coffee. There's always a helping hand available, no matter what the situation.

Spring is my favorite time of the year in Glacier Country. Fields in the Flathead and Mission valleys turn green with freshly sprouted crops of barley, potatoes and peppermint. Lofty mountain peaks still covered in snow pierce the blue skies and tower over lush meadows accented by fragrant wildflowers.

Creeks and streams roar with runoff from melting mountain snow. Newborn calves kick up their heels in pastures where cowboys work the herd on well-trained horses.

As spring deepens into summer, the huckleberries ripen, and folks head to secret locations in the mountain woods to pick this sweet-tasting treat. Bears like 'em, too, and you never know when you might have to share your huckleberry patch with one!

It's also the time when succulent Flathead cherries are harvested from manicured orchards along the shores of Flathead Lake, the largest natural freshwater lake in

"THE SIGHTS, sounds and aromas of the Flathead County Fair in Kalispell fill the summer evening air with excitement. It's an annual event that my family and I wouldn't dream of missing."

"THE SETTING is timeless as mares and foals graze by a pond at Fire Creek Ranch near Huson."

"**I SPOTTED** this couple enjoying the serenity of a canoe ride on one of the many small lakes in Glacier Country (left). Autumn was turning the larch trees on the shore to a golden hue."

"**FALL COLORS** and Montana's famous Big Sky frame Mt. Jackson and Jackson Glacier. There are approximately 50 active glaciers within the boundaries of Glacier National Park."

the West. Both the berries and the cherries are great with a scoop of homemade ice cream at summer family picnics.

The brisk days of September herald the beginning of autumn. Ranchers bring their cattle down from the high country, and in the valleys, farmers are busy harvesting their crops.

We have two distinct autumn seasons for a double-barreled blast of color. First, stands of aspen trees illuminate the mountain foothills with their golden leaves. Several weeks later, we get a second helping of color as tamaracks, or larch trees as they are also known, dapple the hillsides with green and gold. They are among the few conifer trees to shed their needles each fall.

Winters are long, and the snow in the high country is deep enough to cover all but the tallest trees. But we don't mind, for it's a time to strap on snowshoes or skis and get a different perspective on the landscape—like the "snow ghosts" that form when mist freezes on the pine trees in the Whitefish Mountains.

No doubt about it, the Creator really outdid Himself here in Glacier Country. I sometimes have to look twice at the grand setting in which I live and pinch myself to make sure it's all real.

This truly is God's Country. ✹

"**HIGH SCHOOL FOOTBALL** is spirited—and sometimes muddy. A few years ago, our team and fans from Whitefish rode buses 500 miles across the state for a state play-off game against the Miles City Cowboys (above right).

"**THE PILOT** of a paraplane has a bird's-eye view as he soars above farm fields (right) in Flathead Valley on a calm summer evening."

"**TURN THE PAGE** for a glimpse of paradise as wildflowers bloom along Picnic Creek in the Swan Mountains Jewel Basin. All of Glacier Country is beautiful, but this place is a gem."

The First 20 Years

Our Top 10 Covers
From the Past 20 Years

SINCE WE STARTED publishing *Country* in 1987 and *Country EXTRA* in 1990, we've printed well over 200 covers…and that adds up to a lot of breathtaking country scenes and heartwarming "found moments." So we thought it would be interesting to look back over the years and select the very best of these covers. It was fun, but we had no idea how tough a job it would be!

But before we share the Top 10, here's a little background on how our editors go about selecting photos for the magazines:

We work with dozens of freelance rural photographers from around the country. They're topnotch professionals, and they don't just go to well-trod national parks to snap a few pictures. They travel the rural backroads to find down-home country scenes our subscribers can relate to.

That's why, even though it may be beautiful, you won't see a photo of an ocean shore in *Country*—or rarely even the Great Lakes, for that matter. We'd much rather print photos of a secluded farm pond that elicit memories of when our subscribers may have fished for bluegills off the dock or gone skinny-dipping on a hot summer night.

Our rural photographers understand this, and every season they send us some of the very best photos they've taken. We've never actually kept track,

but our editors probably study *over 10,000* of these pictures every year! The very best appear on the cover, and other good ones appear inside.

As a rule, we're looking for photos with colors so bright and vibrant that they look lifelike…and composition that makes you feel like you could step right into the scene. But most importantly, we're looking for photos that make readers say, "I want to be there!"

How We Picked the Top 10: The editorial staff for *Country* went back over the years, and among us, we identified 28 covers that we felt best represented what *Country* is all about.

Next, we laid these covers out on the counter and asked about a dozen other editors and artists at Reiman Publications to help us narrow it down further. We asked them to pick their top 10 choices in order, and the photos that garnered the most votes made our Top 10 list.

Finally, we printed copies of these Top 10, sent them to our 350 Field Editors and asked them to pick their favorite one. "This is by far the hardest job you've given us!" remarked Field Editor Cyndy Nesbit of Sacramento, New Mexico.

We tallied their votes, and here's the official list of the Top 10 *Country* and *Country EXTRA* covers from the past 20 years, along with a few comments from the Field Editors who voted for them.

10

April/May 1995 *Country*, by Sharon Eide/S&E Photo, of a worker harvesting tulips in Washington's Skagit Valley.

"Who could resist those beautiful red tulips?" asks Field Editor Shanna Campbell of Wyandotte, Oklahoma. "But the one unexpected yellow tulip is extraordinary—like the country!"

9

June/July 1996 *Country*, by Terry Donnelly, of a field of purple coneflowers near Trout Lake, Washington.

"I asked myself which scene I'd most like to be in if I could," writes Sandy Hartwick of Smith, Nevada. "It's tough to beat summer in a flower field with beautiful mountains all around."

8

October/November 1988 *Country*, by M. Thonig/Robertstock.com.

"This cover captures the very essence of the country—the gorgeous multicolored trees, peace and solitude of the sheep contentedly grazing. Only God could have planned this picture in its perfection," says Carolyn Jones Logan of Disputanta, Virginia.

Our Top 10 Covers

From the Past 20 Years

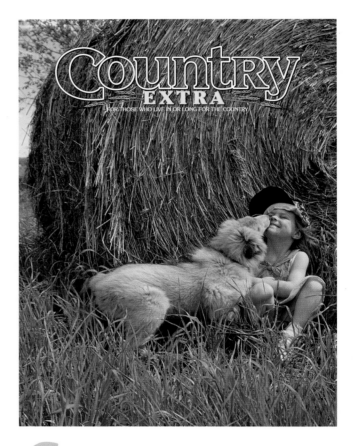

7

October/November 2002 *Country*, by Dugald Bremner, at Lake Placid, New York.

"There's just something special about a father spending time with his son," observes Caroline Kost of Powell, Wyoming.

6

March 2005 *Country EXTRA*, by Julie Habel, on à farm near Luxemburg, Iowa.

"This photo brings back memories of a dog I used to have as a child. And the setting is classic country. Love it!" notes Diana Eberling of Henderson, Nevada.

5

November 2004 *Country EXTRA*, taken by George Robinson, near Jericho, Vermont.

"This cover evoked so many sweet memories of our kids heading off to their wonderful country school on a crisp fall morning," says Eleanor Joyce of Leechburg, Pennsylvania.

4

June/July 2004 *Country*, by Stephen Schoof, of a lake in North Carolina.

"It reminds me of the 23rd Psalm... 'He leads me beside still waters,'" writes June Foster of East Waterboro, Maine.

Our Top 10 Covers

From the Past 20 Years

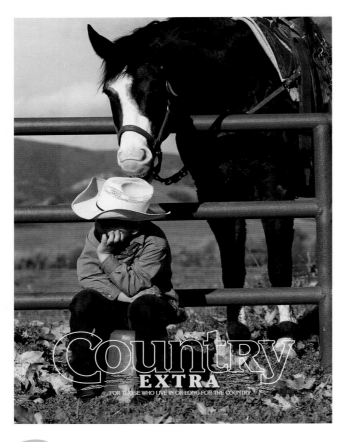

3

September 2003 *Country EXTRA*, by Londie Padelsky, at San Luis Obispo, California.

"This is something my horse would do!" notes Kathy Hayes of Farmington, Georgia.

2

February/March 2003 *Country*, by William Johnson, in the Virginia countryside.

"It was next to impossible to decide, but in the end, this one won out for me," writes Brenda VanHorn of Alexander, New York. "With the spring blossoms and young livestock, it perfectly portrays the promise that comes with living in the country."

Country

FOR THOSE WHO LIVE IN OR LONG FOR THE COUNTRY

1

April/May 1998 *Country*, by Stephen Gassman, on a farm near Martin, South Dakota.

"Country life is all about a slower and relaxed pace of life," says Cheryl Terrano of Buckhannon, West Virginia. "This photo is a reminder to us all to take a moment for ourselves now and then in our favorite special place."

Dear Editor,

It's time to be honest. It's time to come out. I am a "closet farmer."

I was raised in the '50s and '60s; I graduated from high school in 1972. Ours was a traditional farm with the full variety of crops, plus chickens, ducks, geese, cattle, pigs, horses, cats and dogs. My father was thrifty, so our equipment was neither shiny nor new, and we did many of our chores by hand.

When asked at an early age if I would follow in my father's footsteps, I answered in the confident tone only a teenager can possess: "Only a fool would work so hard for so little." No way! I would head for the bright lights.

I wonder...is it too late?

I have spent almost 20 years chasing the dollar at full throttle, working to pay for all those things we just couldn't live without. I'm almost 40 now, and when I drive past a farm with cattle in the pasture and fruit trees, I look on the scene longingly.

Is it too late?

I miss baling hay. I miss doing chores. I miss shelling corn. When we shelled the year's crop, all the neighbors came to help, and there were those wonderful snack breaks with sandwiches and pop. The men would sit and talk about the weather and the crops, and even though I was young I felt I belonged.

I miss playing in the creek. I miss making forts in the huge piles of snow my father created as he plowed out our lane. Before I had a driver's license, I rode my horse to town. I found it embarrassing then, but I would love to do that today.

My brother became ill one fall in the late '60s and had to be taken to a hospital in Iowa City. My parents spent the next several weeks there. I still remember that Saturday morning when a dozen or so combines and pickers rolled into our yard, followed by tractors and wagons.

It was an unforgettable scene as that army of neighbors harvested our crop. I sat on top of the barn and watched row after row of corn disappear. Those neighbors came from many miles away, and I knew every one of them by name. Today, I still don't know the names of the couple who lives across the street.

We have five television sets in our house, and on any given night at least three will be on at the same time. When I walk past my children sprawled in front of these tubes, fighting over which meaningless show they will watch next, I realize they miss the farm as well—**they just don't know it yet.**

I still have all the tools, and I almost cried when I sold my John Deere lawn tractor—it was the last hold I had on a time when I came in late from the field covered with dirt and full of a true sense of accomplishment.

Nowadays, I lie on the couch watching sports on Sunday, regretting that Monday will come too soon. I should be satisfied. After all, I could buy a house with my gold credit cards.

But I'm forced to face reality. I eat too much, I smoke too much and the muscle tone my body once had has slowly softened.

And so, I wonder...is it really too late for me to go back? Am I the only one who feels this way?

Sincerely,
Bruce Carrington
Ankeny, Iowa

When Bruce Carrington of Ankeny, Iowa wrote the letter at left to the *Des Moines Register*, he was satisfied just to see it in print. He had no idea of the reaction it was about to get.

"I wrote that letter to vent some personal frustrations," Bruce explains. "I had no preconceived notions as to what response there would be, if any at all.

"It started about 9 a.m. on the Sunday the letter was published. A woman showed up at our doorstep with the article in hand. She wanted to tell me how much she and her husband enjoyed that letter.

"Shortly after, the phone began to ring. It rang all day and continued to ring through the week.

"Two days later, I began to get let-ters in the mail, and I received about 50 that first week alone.

"Writing that letter to the editor has allowed me to step to the shoulder of the road. The hours I've spent since then talking to people on the phone and reading the open, honest feelings in their letters have been the most enjoyable times I've had for many, many years."

Others Felt the Same

"When I wrote the letter, I wondered if I was having some kind of mid-life crisis. But the wide variety of people who have called or written has convinced me that if I am, I'm not alone.

"I've heard from 20-year-olds and 80-year-olds, men and women, some who are still on the farm and many who wish they were. Some farmers called and told me I was longing for a time that no longer existed; yet others said the farm life and values I cherish are alive and well.

"I guess the main thing I've learned from all this is that there are a lot of people out there who have fond memories of a simpler time, and wish things were still like that.

"It seems my letter stirred some deep feelings in a lot of people. I don't take any real credit for this. I was just the one who put down on paper the thoughts a lot of people obviously share."

More than anything else, perhaps, Bruce's letter shows that the most eloquent writing is still something that's penned with the heart.

Lance Johnson

C'mon, Let's Head for the Country...

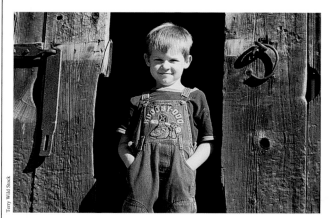

Terry Wild Stock

OVERALL COUNTRY KID. With his fancy britches, this youngster looks ready to help tackle spring chores around the farm.

EN-DEER-ING SCENE. A deer grazes peacefully (top) amid the colorful wildflowers in Washington's Mt. Rainier National Park.

Spring is on the wing. Let's celebrate with a photo tour of this big beautiful land of ours.

THERE'S just something exhilarating about springtime in the country. Maybe it's in the air. The breezes become balmy and laced with the scent of blossoms from the orchard.

Then again, maybe it's the sights that make this such a spectacular season…with poppies poppin' up in the meadow, wildflowers in the woods and lush green foliage everywhere you look.

Or it could be the gentle ring of spring…from birds chirping from the treetops to brooks babbling in the valley.

Our staff of rural photographers have hit the backroads and brought back photos so vivid you'll feel like you're there—taking in the scents, sights and sounds of this magical time of year.

So sit back, sip a cup of coffee and enjoy this issue's armchair tour of the countryside.

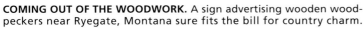

COMING OUT OF THE WOODWORK. A sign advertising wooden wood-peckers near Ryegate, Montana sure fits the bill for country charm.

EYE-POPPING PASTURE. Bright red poppies bloom under a brilliant blue sky and cotton-candy clouds (right) in a meadow in Teton County, Idaho.

TAKING THE BAIT of a sunny spring day is this fly fisherman trying his luck at Upper Rock Creek in the eastern Sierra Nevada of California.

The First 20 Years

DAZZLING DISPLAY. As other trees begin to leaf out, a redbud (left) steals the show as it blossoms along an old rail fence in Indiana.

EGGING US ON. A nestful of bird's eggs is cause for excitement—it's a sure sign that spring has finally arrived and is here to stay.

WELL-WEATHERED. An old barn stands in stark contrast to the green grass of the Zumwalt Prairie in Wallowa County, Oregon. That barn has seen many a spring come and go.

BATTER UP! In rural towns and even cow pastures, a spirited game of Little League baseball is a scene that's played out every spring. Looks like a bunch of all-stars on this team!

Michael Gadomski

WHAT A VIEW. There are forested mountains as far as the eye can see (left) on Skyline Drive in Virginia's Shenandoah National Park.

Lance Johnson

RASCALLY RODENTS. A pair of marmots frolic in the sun. Even though they see their shadows, winter's over for this year!

THEY'RE KEEPERS. Their fish aren't exactly whoppers, but they'll grow as these anglers share their fish tales at the general store.

Terry Wild Stock

Dennis Frates

Steven J. Korba

DOUBLE DELIGHT. Reflections make the sunrise over Bow Lake in Canada's Banff National Park look twice as nice.

AWESOME BLOSSOMS are a cheery welcome to an Amish farm in Ohio. Note the reflection of the barn in the gazing ball.

Mary Liz Austin; next page: George Robbins

A WONDER OF NATURE. Skunk cabbage may not smell great, but sure is pretty. Its odor attracts flies for pollination.

TURN THE PAGE to enjoy a rocky peak in Wyoming's Beartooth Mountains reflected in a mirror-smooth lake.

Photos: Julie Habel

How Auctioneers Learn to Talk So Fast

THE CHANT of an auctioneer at a farm or household sale is every bit as much a song of the country as the chirping of the birds and the rustling of the wind in the trees.

Like a pied piper, the auctioneer draws people from far and wide with his singsong cadence. Serious bidders gather almost spellbound in a tight circle around the treasures to be sold. Standing behind them are curious onlookers—folks who come to see what's for sale and how much it brings.

Still others stand on the outer fringes, sipping coffee from the lunch wagon while they visit with friends and neighbors and catch up on the latest news. After all, an auction is a community event as well as an efficient way of selling property.

Going once, going twice—sold! For excitement and fun, you can't beat a good old-fashioned auction.

Ever wonder how an auctioneer learns to talk so fast? We put that question to an instructor for an auctioneering school and had so much fun listening to his answer that we decided to make it the topic for this issue's Country Primer.

First, a bit of background: Auctions have been around at least since 500 B.C.

Back in the days of the Roman Empire, they were used to dispose of the spoils of wars.

In ancient China, the Chinese held auctions to sell surplus property to raise money for their religious leaders and temples—kind of like today's charity benefit auctions.

During our country's Civil War, troops often seized property from farmers and merchants as they marched through an area. The contraband was then sold at a public sale orchestrated by the commanding officer, often a colonel. That's why auctioneers are still frequently referred to as colonels.

Entertains the Crowd

There are two reasons for an auctioneer's fast-paced chant, according to Wendell Hanson, an instructor for the Nashville Auction School headquartered in Tullahoma, Tennessee.

"One is to entertain—to draw a crowd to a sale and keep them interest-

NUMBER *76* IN A SERIES

WHAT'LL YA BID? You can buy just about anything at a farm sale—from sleigh bells (above) to the horses that made them jingle (left). Far left: An auctioneer scans the crowd for bidders.

ed. The other reason is to sell things rapidly," he explains.

It's a lot like singing. Once you get into the rhythm of a song with a fast beat, you can sing the words a lot faster than you can speak them.

Wendell teaches his students to chant at two speeds—fast and faster!

"We have what's called a speed chant, and with it, we can sell 150 items an hour," he explains. "That's selling something every 24 seconds.

"But at estate auctions, where there may be a lot of inexperienced bidders in the audience, we slow down and use a rhythm chant. That way, folks who aren't completely attuned to this method of selling can hear what's going on."

Listen for Numbers

Actually, the auctioneer's chant isn't all that hard to understand, once you develop an ear for it. It's basically a series of numbers connected by "filler" words to give buyers time to think between bids. Here's an example:

One-dollar bid, now 2, now 2, will ya give me 2?

Two-dollar bid, now 3, now 3, will ya give me 3?

Three-dollar bid, now 4, now 4, will ya give me 4?

What's important is to listen for the numbers—the amount that's already been bid and the next dollar amount the auctioneer is calling for. You really don't need to understand the words in-between.

"We're an English teacher's worst nightmare," adds Wendell with a chuckle. "That's because we teach our students to shorten syllables and chop up words.

"Take the number 1-1/2. We say 'one naf' because it's two syllables instead of four.

"But as long as people understand the numbers, that's the main thing."

Another secret to becoming a fast-talking auctioneer is learning to breathe properly—using the diaphragm in your chest just like an opera singer does in order to produce a strong voice without running out of breath.

"At the beginning of the course, we ask students to count to 10 forward and backward as many times as they can without taking a breath," Wendell explains. "By the time the course is over 9 days later, they can double or triple their performance."

Tricky Tongue Twisters

Tongue twisters are another teaching tool. Here's one used to help control breathing:

Around the rough and rugged rock

the ragged rascal ran. Try repeating it several times without taking a breath!

Or test your tongue on this tricky verse. You can almost hear the auctioneer's rhythmic chant as you say it—*if* you can say it.

Betty Botter bought a bit of butter. "But," she said, "this butter's bitter. If I put this bitter butter in my batter, it will make my batter bitter. But a bit of better butter will make my batter better." So Betty Botter bought a bit of better butter, which made her batter better.

"Tongue twisters help stretch out the vocal chords and limber up the lips," Wendell notes. "It's like an athlete loosening up before a game."

Of course, there's a lot more to becoming an auctioneer than learning the chant. The typical curriculum also includes such topics as advertising, clerking sales, public speaking and the legal aspects of selling various types of merchandise and property.

"We give students the basics," says Wendell. "After that, it's a matter of practice and hard work to become a professional auctioneer."

Auction Etiquette

Auctions used to have the reputation of being "distress sales"—a quick way to dispose of property as a result of a bank foreclosure, for instance.

But, says Wendell, "They're becoming increasingly popular because sellers have found out they can get a better price for what they have to sell."

If you've never attended an auction, he offers these suggestions:

● Register ahead of time and get a bidding card. That way, the clerk has your name and address, and the auctioneer doesn't have to stop the sale to get this information if you buy something.

● Inspect merchandise carefully before the sale. Items are usually sold on an "as is—where is" basis, which means they're not guaranteed. They're yours if you're the winning bidder.

● Bid by holding up your card. It's a clear signal, and the auctioneer knows immediately who the successful bidder is from the number on the card.

● Pay for your purchases before you leave and take them with you.

One more rule—have fun!

Why Are Most Barns Red?

Ever think about that as you drive down a country road? There's a good reason... here's how it got started.

SURE, you're seeing a few new colors splashed on barns these days...especially the modern steel structures that sport pre-painted panels of green, greys, off-whites, golds, blues and beiges.

But that wasn't always the case. There was a time when it was hard to look at a barn without seeing red. In every rural neighborhood in every section of the country, the majority of barns were painted one color: red.

Even today, any old wood barn with any "character" to it proudly displays its red roots. One of our *Country* editors began wondering why recently as he made a swing through several states...and barn after barn on farm after farm flashed by in faded red, brilliant red and even brownish red. But always red.

Whetted Our Curiosity

After he got back and mentioned this curious red rampage to our staff, we decided to dig into the origin of this rural tradition.

Our research indicates barns weren't always painted red. In fact, in the earliest settlements, it was considered "showy" and vulgar to paint the barn at all. But in the late 1700s, farmers began to use homemade wood preservatives to protect their barns.

Then came paint. The Virginians used lampblack—it sank into the wood and it resulted in coloring the barn grey.

In the North, farmers mixed red iron oxide with skimmed milk and lime—and got a paint of sorts which hardened and coated the barn like a plastic. The mixture was a very red color and, obviously, so was the barn.

After a few years, red became the standard color. And once red got a firm foothold, it hung on year after year—red and barns became synonymous. Farmers, more than most other breeds of people, are reluctant to change, and tend to stay with the same thing once it's "working."

Did It Like Dad

So it was then with barns—Dad and Granddad had painted their barns red, so rather than shake up the neighborhood the next time a new barn went up, it likewise was painted red.

That long-run role of red along sideroads continued until the last decade or two, when farmers began to learn how the color of the outside of a building can help control the temperature inside.

Therefore, in colder areas of the country, you'll now see more new livestock shelters exhibiting darker colors—green, blue, brown (and red, still a favorite)—and in warmer parts of the country, you'll see lighter colors—grey, off-white, gold and beige.

Yet, even today, when you come across an old wood barn that someone's grandpa likely put up, nine out of 10 chances, it's going to be as red as a ripe tomato. ✺

Norman McConnell

We Love Mail!

And we read every single letter, postcard and E-mail you send us.

WITH 13 MAGAZINES written mainly by our readers, "We get an average of 22 tubs, 30 flats and three bundles of mail a week," says Bonnie Anderson, who supervises the mail department here at Reiman Publications. "That's nearly 70,000 pieces of mail each week."

Add in E-mail, which is beginning to rival the volume we get through the post office, and this avalanche of correspondence would bury most folks. But not *Country* Editorial Assistant Maxine "Max" Burak (pictured above).

Max bears the brunt of the initial wave as it hits *Country*, sorting the "My Favorite Horse" stories from "Animal Tales," and "Country Kids" from "Candidly Country."

She files the "Can You Help Me?" requests and separates the compliments from the "gotcha" notes. ("If a honey stand isn't on the Minnesota backroad exactly where the photographer said it was, we'll hear about it," Max explains with a wry grin. "You don't slip anything past our readers.")

"And for anyone who has ever wondered, every letter, every E-mail gets read," she adds.

Early Christmas

Just like you, we laugh at the jokes for "Little Humor" and "Country Cafe." We marvel at the clever captions readers write for "If Only They Could Talk." And we get lumps in our throats when somebody takes that last walk with their trusty dog or favorite horse.

In late November and early December, the boxes in Max's office begin piling especially high as the deadline for our Rural Photography Contest nears. With 4,000 entries in four categories each year, it's like an early Christmas.

We're consistently amazed at the quality, creativity and warmth of these amateur photos. In fact, the best professional photographers in the world couldn't duplicate our favorite "found moments" in these pictures.

Perhaps our favorite letters, though, are like this one from Doris Onken from New Boston, Illinois: "I was a city girl and registered nurse when I married my husband, Gene, and moved to this farm 56 years ago. We raised three sons and three daughters here. We have 10 grandchildren, and are expecting our first great-grandchild in December.

"Our youngest son recently took over the farming operation after Gene 'retired.' Of course, he's still out there every day doing all he can to help. We both love the feel and smell of the country: freshly turned soil, new-mown hay, and the sweet smell of corn in the field on a summer night. We were blessed with the opportunity to live in the country."

And we feel blessed every time the mailman shows up with a fresh batch of letters, photos and even "gotcha" notes from great country folks like Doris. Your mail keeps us in touch with our country roots, and lets us keep you in touch with each other through *Country*.

SPECIAL DELIVERY. Imagine the fun of getting this much mail from readers every day, adding up to approximately 70,000 pieces a week!

The Week I Fed the Banker's Pig

I WASN'T SURPRISED when my son, Jeff, a suit-wearing banker, announced he was going to raise a pig.

I had seen it coming. Our family lineage is filled with Maine farmers (I'm not one of them), and no doubt to satisfy an ancestral yearning, Jeff had bought a dilapidated 200-year-old farmhouse a year ago.

Lots of hard work went into fixing up the place, including the barn. After some months, he declared the barn fit for a pig. I couldn't disagree, but I certainly wasn't going to encourage it.

Besides, my brother Paul provided all of the encouragement Jeff needed. Easy for him. After all, my brother was

By Earl Smith, Belgrade Lakes, Maine

in town for only a brief visit and soon returned to Texas—hundreds of miles from any pig-raising responsibilities.

As spring blossomed, the farm became home not only to a pig, but to two goats. Fine with me—I live 6 miles away. I thought that was a reasonably safe distance until the banker and his family decided to take a vacation.

Left Written Instructions

"Would you mind feeding the animals?" he asked. "After all, it's on your way to work."

I reported for the first feeding early Monday morning. Jeff had carefully

written instructions on two pages of a yellow legal pad—far more detailed than anything we ever left for his baby-sitter.

On top of the grain bin was the food …portioned in plastic bags like individual microwave dinners. The bags were marked "pig" and "goat."

Both the goat yard and the pigpen are attached to the back of the barn. For even greater economy of fencing, the thrifty banker made the front of the pigpen common with the back of the goat yard. That meant I had to pass by the goats on the way to feed the pig.

The goats clearly liked this arrangement and were bleating cheers when I approached with a bag of their food in one hand and a bucket of pig food, softened with water from the rain barrel, in the other. The instant I lifted the hook on the gate, the goats butted it open and romped joyously past me into the open pasture.

Visions of missing goats and the banker's crying children flashed before my eyes. But I had no more than put the food on the ground inside the fence to give chase when the goats reversed direction. They raced back into the pen and bore down on the pig's feed bucket—upending it on the grass.

When I bent to scoop what pig mush I could back into the bucket, the goats were on me in a flash…alternately munching on the spillage and the lower half of my 30-dollar necktie.

Pleased Porker

Meanwhile, the pig was up on his hind legs, hanging what I would call his elbows over the top rail of the fence and watching the scene with an honest-to-goodness grin. I know it was a grin because I have some experience reading animal expressions.

We once had a cat that stuck her tongue out at me when no one else was looking (the feeling was mutual). And we now have a golden retriever with several faces—"I love you completely," "Feed me" and "Let's play ball".

A pig's repertoire is much broader. No mistake about it, he was plainly enjoying my troubles.

I stuck out my tongue at him and dumped what was left of his breakfast into the feed trough. Then I replenished his water and left, taking care to fasten the gate.

At work a half hour later, I was adjusting a borrowed necktie when the phone rang. The only sounds from the other end were a loud pig-like snort and a giggle. It was the banker calling from somewhere on the road to make sure I'd remembered my chores. He hung up before I could express my current feelings about the joys of fatherhood.

I was a bit late reporting to the farm on Tuesday morning, and the goats were impatiently bleating from the top of their wooden house. They were proba-

bly anticipating another chance to get at the pig's food. The pig himself was leaning over the fence—frowning. If he'd had a watch, he would have pointed at it.

The feeding was carried out without incident. Getting water for the pig was another matter.

Thus far, I had been able to tend to the pig without entering his pen. I found this a most agreeable method and had no intention of straying from it—even though the pig had pushed the watering pan well beyond my reach that morning. So I filled the bucket from the rain barrel and took careful aim at the pan.

Either the splash or a natural aversion to clean water startled the pig something awful…sending him spinning around the pen and throwing splat-

> *"If he'd had a watch, he would have pointed at it…"*

ters of mud onto the front of my shirt. When I got to work, I took a sponge bath in the men's room.

It rained Tuesday night. By Wednesday morning, the ground in the pigpen, already the color of chocolate pudding, had achieved a consistency to match. Worse, the pig had further rearranged his furniture. The feeding trough was upside down, although still close enough to the fence that I could reach it. But the water pan had been shoved 3 feet farther to the back of the pen.

The pig had a smug look…his beady eyes inquiring what I planned to do about getting him water. I found a long stick and turned the feed trough right side up. It was on a bit of a slant, but good enough. I put the food in the top end of the trough and the water in the bottom. It was my turn to be smug. The pig looked stumped.

On Thursday, the water pan was three-quarters buried and upside down on the far side of the pen. He must have been up all night burying it.

Maybe, I thought, both the pig and I could survive the 1 remaining day before the banker returned if I just added lots more water to his food. I'd seen

the stuff this guy drinks; mineral spring water it wasn't. The heavily watered-down slop prompted a snooty sneer of disapproval from the pig. But I left for work anyway.

The sun blazed all day and my guilt rose with the temperature as I thought about the pig without fresh water.

When I finally drove up the gravel driveway to the barn early Friday morning, I sighed in relief. Dehydrated pigs don't stand on their hind legs and lean over fence railings with twitching curly tails and disgusted looks on their faces like this pig was doing.

Glad to See Him

It was a little embarrassing to realize how glad I was to see him, and I managed a warm hello. He ignored me.

This morning's furniture configuration suggested he was thinking of moving out. The trough and the water pan were overturned and stacked upside down on top of each other against the back of the barn, and I knew in an instant I was going to have to get inside that pen or the pig was done for.

Opening the pen door gingerly, I took a tentative squishy step toward the pig. He seemed a great deal bigger than he appeared from outside the rail. "Shoo," I said, trying to sound authoritative, but certainly not threatening. (It was sort of a loud "shoo" with a question mark after it.)

My shoes made a sucking sound as I approached the furniture. Finally, I was able to grab the filthy trough and, carefully, with two fingers, squeeze one end and ever-so-gently drag it to the front of the pen.

The pig followed these proceedings closely and seemed to be snorting encouragement. I'd have been happier if he had waited in the corner for me to get everything in order. But no, he had to lean against my legs as I retraced my steps to retrieve the water pan.

The rest was easy—clean water in the pan and fresh slop in the trough. The pig watched admiringly. The goats seemed pleased as well.

As I went around the corner of the barn, I looked back. The pig was slurping water like a sump pump. But he paused for a brief second to look up and smile. I felt a bit foolish, but I waved.

I'm pretty sure that pig loves me.

A Lazy Stream Is a Country Kid's Dream

This farm boy is awash with memories of swimmin' and fishin' in the creek.

By Murl Black, Field Editor, Lohrville, Iowa

WHEN I was turning 11 on our little farm in Wapello County, Iowa, my mother decided to give me a birthday party. The invitees were boys from surrounding farms. Her intention was to gather in our house yard, play a few games and then eat cake and homemade ice cream.

The first guests to arrive were my two close friends from the neighboring farm. The three of us often went fishing for bullheads and panfish in Honey Creek, which ran through our pasture. Since we had an hour and a half before the party was supposed to start, we decided to go fishing.

Our fishing gear consisted of a couple of homemade seines—sticks attached to gunnysacks—that we dragged through the water. We also took a large bucket for the fish. (You must think positive when you go fishing.)

We were having a good time when another neighbor boy came to join us. He had stopped at the house, and Mom told him to go get us for the birthday party.

Of course, he, too, became a part of the fishing party. Like the rest of us, he took off his shoes and socks and rolled up his pant legs in a vain attempt to keep his pants dry.

Soon another person came along, and instead of taking us back to the house, he also joined in the fun. Eventually, everyone invited to the party found his way out to the pasture and waded into the water to reduce the fish population of Honey Creek ever so slightly.

Mom was the last one to come out to the pasture—but not to do any fishing. She was less than elated with the turn my birthday party had taken.

Mom Wasn't Happy

We were summarily evicted from the creek. We rolled down our pant legs so they could dry, and with Mom following closely behind, we walked back to the house. There, we had birthday cake and ice cream. Mom was angry with me for quite a while. But I had a great time at my birthday party, and as far as I knew, so did my guests. How could she be so unhappy with a party that was a roaring success…even though it didn't follow the conventional route she had in mind? Moms can surely be difficult to train properly.

The following summer, the two neighbor boys and I con-

WHOPPER. "My grandsons Shay and Tanner caught this trout in our pond," says Carol Gianinetti of Carbondale, Colo. At right, Kellan Foster and friend Seth dive in. Kellan's mom, Lynnette, of Nevada, Mo. snapped the photo.

tinued to entertain ourselves down at Honey Creek whenever we got a break from our farm chores. Although never as often as we'd have liked, we spent many hours there swimming and fishing.

The problem was finding a spot deep enough and large enough for our aquatic activities. There was one particularly long stretch of the creek that was just too shallow for swimming or fishing. That seemed like wasted creek to us.

Built a Dam

Then we came up with the idea of building a dam to raise the water level. Never mind that a dam would most likely wash out with the first big rain. While we may have been short on dam-building knowledge, we were long on ambition, so we gathered shovels and tools necessary to undertake our task.

First, we devised a plan for fortifying the dam. We built a solid wood frame—a rectangular box-like affair—to set in the water. Then we dug dirt from the surrounding area to fill the middle of our frame and create a rather large earthen dam. It was quite a structure.

The water quickly started to build up behind our dam.

Following the first big rain, we couldn't wait to get back there and see what had happened. We were apprehensive when we came over the little rise and could see our dam. But to our surprise and delight, it had held, and the water had backed up a half mile…clear onto the neighbor's property.

The neighbor didn't mind because it provided a good source of drinking water for his herd of cattle. We were happy, too, because we had a wonderful new place to swim as well as a habitat for fish.

We fished the lower parts of the creek and tossed our catch behind the dam to stock our newly created lake. Before long, the fish were multiplying, and we had great fishing in addition to a swimming hole.

Beginner's Luck

The dam withstood several years of spring floods, and the pond behind it became a part of the landscape. It provided untold hours of summertime fun.

It was amazing, considering it was built by three farm kids with no prior knowledge or background in dam building. Definitely beginner's luck.

A perfect ending to this story would be to say that we went on to become civil engineers who built some of the world's great dams. That's not the case. One of us became a college writing professor, another an agribusiness executive and the third a farmer.

But we all carried with us fond memories of summer days spent swimming and fishing down in the pasture on Honey Creek.

A KEEPER. "Dustin was so proud of the fish he caught," says Grandma Lea Ann Brown, Mt. Pleasant, Texas. "The size didn't matter."

REELLY FUN. "As a child, I fished for hours—just as my son Robert and nephew Greg do now," says Callie Lansdell, Auburn, Wash.

After City Life, She's Home on the Range

PROFILE: Necel Golden lives on a 20,000-acre ranch near Weston, Wyoming, where she and her husband, Travis Hakert, take care of 800 beef cows, 50 bulls and 100 yearling heifers …not to mention horses, cats, orphan lambs and a Border collie named "Pete."

Sunday, July 28—Greetings from the Laurel Leaf Ranch, on the banks of the Little Powder River near Weston, Wyoming.

The Laurel Leaf, which is where my husband, Travis, and I live, is part of the 20,000-acre Shippy ranch. Larry and Sue Shippy have 800 beef cows, 50 bulls and 100 yearling replacement heifers. Travis hired on as a ranch hand, and we moved here last October.

Travis is a fourth-generation rancher and grew up in the shadow of the Big Horn Mountains near Buffalo, where his parents still raise sheep and cattle.

LOTSA ROOM TO ROAM. Necel, Travis and Tyler head out on horseback (above) to check on the cattle in a pasture that stretches clear to the horizon. Talk about wide-open spaces!

Come along for a "visit" as Necel Golden keeps a weeklong diary of life on a Wyoming cattle ranch.

He's a great conversationalist, and I love to hear him recount childhood memories of trailing sheep to the mountains.

I grew up in southeastern Texas in an area known as The Big Thicket. On our small farm, we gardened, sold fresh eggs and had pigs, cows, sheep, horses, goats, dogs, cats, ducks and geese. I was involved in the FHA, FFA and 4-H during my school years. One year, I baked the prize-winning, blue ribbon pound cake for our local fair.

At age 25, I left my country home for Virginia, where I became the office manager of a busy real estate firm. Although successful in my career, I was eternally homesick during my 9 years in the city. Eventually, the stressful lifestyle and the conviction to return to the country became overpowering, and I wound up in Travis' hometown of Buffalo.

I lived and worked at a guest ranch near scenic Crazy Woman Canyon. Days at this working cattle ranch were long, and the work was often exhausting. But each night before retiring to my cabin, I'd take a deep breath of fresh air, look up at the millions of stars twinkling in the sky and know in my heart that the decision to move from the city had been a good one.

Here at the Shippy operation, the cattle are gathered in the fall, and the calves shipped to market. The cows and bulls are trucked to river pastures, where the steep banks of the river, lined with cottonwood trees, provide good protection against the Wyoming winters. We feed the cattle in winter and continue through the spring calving season. It's fun summoning the cattle with a cattle call—the most popular one being "C'mon boss"—and watch them come running to the feed truck.

In June, near the end of calving season, we begin the first of six weekly brandings and relocate the cows and calves to northern pastures until fall. The reason we do it over 6 weeks is that there are just too many calves to sort, brand, vaccinate, ear-tag and then truck with their mothers at once.

This time of year, with the cows all situated until fall, our main activities include checking to be sure the livestock have water, fencing and repairs. In a year with rain, we'd also be putting up hay for winter, but this part of the country is experiencing a severe drought, and there's no hay to be made.

Regardless of the season, you never know when a few cows will go searching for greener pastures and break through a fence. That goes double for the bulls. On more than one morning, I've found myself chasing escapees in my nightgown.

I spent this weekend with my friend Kathy, who lives 2-1/2 hours away in Whitewood, South Dakota. I first met her in Virginia, where we boarded our horses at the same stable. Originally from South Dakota, she returned there only months after I moved to Wyoming.

When I arrived home this evening, Pete came running over to greet me. Before I could get out of the car, a rabbit hopped across the yard, and poor Pete couldn't decide whether to come say hello to me or chase the rabbit.

To help with his doggy dilema, I told Pete it was okay to chase the rabbit, and off he went in hot pursuit. It's incredibly funny to watch him chase something because, when he gets too close, he slows down to ensure that he won't catch it.

SMITTEN WITH A KITTEN. Tyler plays with one of the new ranch kittens named "Slinky."

Travis' 11-year-old son, Tyler, is visiting us, and together they went to Buffalo. Travis has been practicing his heeling lately as he will be team roping with his friend Paul at an upcoming county fair and rodeo. They practiced until dark, and he and Ty didn't get home until late tonight.

After feeding the lambs, Pete and the kittens, I took advantage of the quiet house to call my mother, Nelda, in Texas. I've been considering a trip home as it has been over 3 years since I have seen my family.

Monday, July 29—We slept a little later than usual this morning because we were all worn out from the past few days. Plus Pete woke us up in the middle of the night with his barking. Whenever he raises a ruckus, it usually means there's a coyote or some other critter out in the yard.

First thing each morning, Pete and I head out to feed, water and turn out the lambs. Two members of my woolly quartet are registered Targhee ewes, "Spring" and "Ivy," who have been here since they were only 2 days old. "Pip" and "Phyllis" are twins that I adopted when they were 6 weeks old. We got them from Travis' parents, when their mother became unable to care for them.

Each lamb has its own personality. Spring is the leader of the bunch and very curious, brave and independent. Ivy, always wanting to be by my side, is a little sweetheart. While the others are off grazing, she will rest her head on my lap and fall sound asleep.

Pip is quiet and demure, and closes his eyes and appears to smile as I scratch him behind the ears. Phyllis is skittish of people and doesn't like to be touched. She loves Pete, however, often patiently standing in front of him with her head bowed for him to lick her ear.

On the way back to the house, I moved the sprinklers. We have a stock tank that is continuously fed by an artesian well. Because there are no cattle in this pasture right now, we are able to divert the water to our lawn. It's nice to have green grass around the house, even when everything else has turned brown.

Most mornings are spent tidying up the house, but today I opted to let most of my indoor chores wait until the afternoon. I started a load of laundry before riding along with Travis to check the stock tanks in the northern pastures where we summer about 550 cow-calf pairs.

The peaceful, 17-mile drive winds through pretty countryside with the terrain slowly changing from rolling, grassy plains to hilly, pine-covered ridges. On a clear day, you can see the Big Horns, 100 miles away.

Much to our dismay, we discovered there was no water at three of six tanks, which are fed by a pipeline. After a couple of hours spent bouncing in the pickup from tank to tank through sagebrush and over rough, steep trails, the problem was solved with the flip of a switch. Somehow the circuit breaker to the well had been turned off. Travis breathed a sigh of relief as it would have been catastrophic to lose water.

We recently butchered a hog and have a freezer full of fresh pork. So for dinner, I fried sausage, potatoes and onions, which we ate on flour tortillas with sour cream.

Just before I left for South Dakota, we had a hailstorm with severe winds. So after we ate, we cleaned up the yard and picked up the limbs blown down by the storm.

Around 3:30, we came inside for a cold drink and to cool off in the air-conditioning. We polish off a gallon of iced tea and a gallon of lemonade each

TIME TO SADDLE UP. Necel slips a halter on "Howdy" in preparation for moving cattle.

A Week in the Country...

BOARD MEETING. A rail fence is a perfect place for Tyler, Necel and Travis to gather and catch up on the day's activities. Of course, wherever they are, you'll also find their old Border collie "Pete."

day, so Ty made a fresh jug of each, putting the tea in the warm sun to brew.

Then Travis went to check the yearling heifers at the Spring Creek pasture, and I mowed the lawn. It took 3 hours instead of the usual 5, since there isn't nearly as much to mow because of the dry weather.

The evening cooled off quickly, so we took the lambs up on Dead Man's Hill and watched the sunset. We jokingly named it this because there is a steep cliff on one side, which Ty likes to climb. We kid him that if he falls, he'll be a dead man.

There's a wonderful view of the entire valley from atop the hill. The sunsets here are spectacular and, although the colors are most vivid over the hills to the west, the sky turns a beautiful pale pink in every direction. It's as if we have a 360-degree sunset.

The cool evening breeze had all of the animals feeling frisky. The lambs were frolicking on the hillside, and we could see the horses bucking and kicking as they loped across the meadow. Pete, acting much like his tail was on fire, ran large circles around the hill at lightning speed.

Since it was so cool, it was nice to go to bed with the windows open tonight.

Tuesday, July 30—We woke up to a beautiful cool morning, just 60° with a light breeze. The temperature rose to around 90° in the afternoon—still warm,

but a lot better than when the thermometer soared to over 100° for a couple of weeks.

I didn't go with Travis this morning to check cows, because he went on to Larry's place to unload a truck of alfalfa hay that was delivered. Because of the drought, we'll need to buy about 25 truckloads—900 tons or so—to get through the winter.

Travis's mother, Donna, and I E-mail several times a week. She's a very funny lady, and I enjoy corresponding with her. This morning she invited us to raid their garden, which is running wild with cucumbers, beets and Swiss chard.

When Travis got home, I made a late dinner of barbecued pork chops and macaroni and cheese. While I was cooking, I watched our gray tabby kittens, "Slinky," "Smooches" and "Fluffy," playing with a leaf on the back steps.

This afternoon I organized and cleaned our mudroom, which we currently use for storage. We hope to do some repairs to it before next winter, so we can use it for its intended purpose—keeping mud out of the rest of the house. With the drought, that hasn't been a problem here lately.

Later, I accompanied Travis to the Hatfield pasture, which is about 8 miles to the south. He needed to put out salt blocks and check the cows.

I was happy to see one of my favorite cows, "Pencils." I named her that be-

cause she has two straight, skinny horns that resemble pencils. I grew accustomed to seeing many of the same cows every day while feeding them last winter and gave some of them names. It was good to see Pencils looking so sleek and fat.

On the way home, we stopped at the reservoir to let Pete cool off with a swim. Then Travis helped Ty hang a tire swing from a big cottonwood in the backyard.

Wednesday, July 31—It was cool again this morning, so I put a roast in the oven to slow cook for 5 or 6 hours. It'll give us sandwiches to munch on for several days.

Travis and Ty made the 35-mile trip to Gillette this morning to run errands and buy lumber to repair our front porch. While in town, Travis got a much needed haircut and picked up a few things for me from the grocery store. I'm very much the procrastinator when it comes to going town, so my cupboards often resemble those of Old Mother Hubbard.

While the boys were gone, I took advantage of the empty house to clean it from top to bottom. By the time they got home, things were sparkling.

What with the drought, cattle and gravel roads, dusting is a never-ending chore. I like things spotless, but have been trying really hard to relax a little about the housework. One day while discussing housekeeping with Travis's mother, she offered me new insight when she said a house should be clean enough to be healthy and dirty enough to be happy. What a great motto!

Upon returning from town, Travis and Ty started repairing the front porch. Before they could rip it apart, they had to remove Pete's chair. There was an old, broken recliner in the house when we first moved in. We set it outside with every intention of hauling it away until Pete discovered it, claiming it for his own. Because he was so attached to it and slept on it day and night, this eyesore has remained until now.

We needed to move cows this evening after it cooled off, so Ty rounded up the horses. We have four horses here—"Crazy Alice," "Barbie," "Ginger" and "Howdy." Back when Travis was breaking Crazy Alice, she bucked him off into the side of the corral and broke his arm. Nine times out of 10, Alice doesn't buck anymore, but the tenth time is usually a humdinger.

Barbie is Alice's daughter. I named her after the Barbie doll because she has two tall white socks like the white go-go boots Barbie used to wear when I was a girl. Despite Travis's objections, the name stuck. He said he'd be embarrassed to tell the guys he rode a horse named Barbie, so I told him to call her Barb—as in wire—for short.

We finished moving the cows in the nick of time because a terrible windstorm came whipping out of the north. We arrived home to find the laundry blowing off the clothesline and all over the yard. Ty and I scrambled to retrieve it.

We pulled up the comforters tonight because the temperature was expected to drop into the 40s.

Thursday, Aug. 1—None of us got much sleep last night. Shortly after we turned in, Pete began to bark. Travis finally got up and brought him in the house in order to quiet him down. After settling back into bed, we soon became very aware of the reason for the commotion. In through the open window drifted the unmistakable fragrance of a skunk. Fortunately, Pete managed to avoid the line of fire.

The whole gang went up north this morning, where we spent the better part of the day fencing. There was a long section in need of repair, so Ty and I laid out the steel posts while Travis followed behind, pounding them into the ground and stretching the wires.

Tyler and I went in search of some wild plums. We did not find any, but we did find hoards of wild chokecherry trees loaded with berries. When they

DAY'S END. Necel and Travis sit on a bluff overlooking the ranch to watch a glorious sunset.

ripen, I think I'll pick some and try my hand at making jelly. I'll swap some for the delicious mayhaw jelly my mother makes from the mayhaws that grow in swampy, wet areas where she lives.

This afternoon when we returned home, I decided to read a bit. The house was so nice and cool and the bed was so comfortable that I accidentally dozed off. An hour later when I awoke, I felt guilty for napping on such an exquisite day and hurried back outside to enjoy the blue skies and fine weather.

Never wanting to take for granted the things with which I have been blessed, I often take time to reflect. Today, I found myself in awe of the wonderful views from most of our windows. From our bedroom, I can watch the horses and cattle as they graze on the hillsides. I have a nice view of the pond, full of cattails and migrating geese and ducks in spring and fall. I'm able to lie in bed each morning and see gorgeous, colorful sunrises.

My favorite window is in the kitchen. From here, I can see the backyard activities and admire the lambs. Wild turkey, antelope and deer are abundant and can be seen daily, foraging with their young in the meadow beyond the sheep pasture. Snow-covered in winter, green in spring and a pale shade of yellow summer through fall, this meadow is my favorite place to walk.

Friday, Aug. 2—The boys left bright and early this morning to mend fences. Pete didn't make a peep all night, so, gratefully, we all slept really well.

I left for town just before dinnertime as we were in dire need of provisions. Being a big fan of classic country music, I took advantage of the 45-minute drive to listen to some CDs. The countryside was pretty, and the only traffic between here and town were a few deer.

This evening we went fishing for bullheads in the reservoir. We didn't catch any, probably because the dog's splashing scared away the fish. But I was glad to see Pete acting perky because he'd been moping around over the loss of his beloved chair.

Saturday, Aug. 3—After feeding the lambs, Travis and I hopped in the pickup to make the rounds of the cattle pastures. On the ideal

DOWN TO THE WIRE. Travis does some fence mending before the cattle try to get out.

ranch outing, you'd take a peaceful drive through the countryside and find the stock tanks full of water and the cattle on the right side of the fence.

On a typical ranch outing, however, anything can go wrong and often does. I'm learning the hard way to follow certain rules before leaving home. It's no fun trailing cows 2 miles in the blazing sun through rattlesnake-infested sagebrush. It's even worse if you're wearing sandals. So rule No. 1 is to always wear appropriate footwear.

Rule No. 2 is to always have a full tank of gas, so when you break the first rule, you can drive home and change shoes. Rule No. 3 is to take a full water jug and a snack because you never know how long you'll be gone.

Today, as I often do as when driving through the hills, I hung my head out the window, admiring the vivid blue sky and inhaling the sweet aroma of pine that hung in the air. (Pete and I argue daily over who has the rights to the window seat.) I exchanged pleasantries with each cow that we passed. I know they don't understand, but I like talking to them anyway.

Tonight we're headed to the county fair. We'll be late getting home, so I'll take time now to say good-bye to you.

If you're like I was—a person working in the city, but yearning for the simple country life—I hope my story has been an inspiration to you to maybe make a move. The country is a great place to live.

Pennsylvania...Now *This* Is God's Country!

In each issue, we invite readers to tell us why they think a particular area is the best place to live. This time, Jerry Irwin shares his love of Pennsylvania.

If I had just one word to describe Pennsylvania, that word would be valleys.

The topography consists of many soft green valleys created by the Appalachian, Allegheny and Blue Ridge Mountains, which sweep diagonally, ridge after ridge, from the southwest to the northeast corners of the state.

I was born and raised in Pennsylvania and lived in Lancaster County for many years. Although I recently moved to Delaware, I still consider Pennsylvania my home. In fact, I live just 100 yards from the border and can walk there anytime I want. As far as I'm con-

THE BEST SPOT. Map shows the highlighted area author says is the country's *best* location.

cerned, Pennsylvania is God's Country, and you won't find me straying too far away from it.

The valleys in the south-cen-

"**PENNSYLVANIA'S GRAND CANYON** runs 40 miles through Tioga and Clinton counties and is 1,000 feet deep in places. The view of the canyon from Mt. Gillespie is spectacular."

"**TRAFFIC JAMS** take on a different form when you travel the backroads. This photo of a farmer driving his cows down the road in rural Berks County (far left) is one of my favorites."

"**MY MOUTH WATERS** over these goodies from an Amish housewife's larder in Lancaster County."

"**I SPOTTED** these canoeists taking a leisurely trip on the Brandywine River in Chester County in southeastern Pennsylvania. Chester County is also known as horse country."

"**WELLSBORO** is a town of about 3,500 people not far from the Grand Canyon of Pennsylvania. Its quiet streets are quite a contrast to the big industrial centers like Philadelphia."

"**THE REMOTE LOCATION** and covered bridge create a bucolic setting for this well-kept German farmstead in Lancaster County. There are many family farms tucked away in valleys like this one."

"**THE COMBINATION** of woodlands and farms is perfect habitat for deer, and Pennsylvania has an abundance of them. Isn't this fella a beauty?"

"**RURAL FOLKS,** like Lloyd and Virginia Weaver, are so friendly. They planted thousands of tulips and invite visitors to enjoy them. Retired farmers, the couple came by their green thumbs naturally."

tral part of the state are endowed with rich soil, making agriculture an important industry. In fact, the land supports one of the highest concentrations of small family-owned farms in the country.

These farms, many of them Amish, average 70 acres. But don't dismiss them because of their small size—they are highly productive.

Many of the older German farming settlements in this area date back more than 275 years. Lancaster County, which boasts some of the most productive and beautiful farmland on Earth, is considered a national treasure by many people.

Half of the state is covered by dense hardwood and conifer forests. There are 50 natural lakes and 45,000 miles of rivers and streams, which add to the tranquility and beauty of the land.

While folks in a hurry take the Pennsylvania Turnpike to whiz across the state, I prefer the backroads. That's how to see Pennsyl- ♂

"FROM its earliest days, Pennsylvania was a refuge for people suffering religious persecution. You still see evidence of that from the many lovely country churches that grace the landscape."

"THE MILLERSBURG FERRY is the nation's last wooden stern-wheel ferry and takes folks across the Susquehanna River. The Susquehanna is as pretty as its beautiful-sounding name."

"**CELEBRATING** her heritage, a woman gears up to ride in a tractor parade at the Pennsylvania Dutch Festival in Summit Station."

"**YOU'LL** find lots of treasures at an auction in Pennsylvania's Amish Country. It's an exciting event."

vania up close. On one photo-gathering assignment, I traveled 5,000 miles and never left the state's borders.

One of my favorite drives is Route 6, a 310-mile stretch of road without a foot of superhighway or interstate along its length. It winds its way through small towns and some of the most remote and sparsely populated areas of north-central and northeastern Pennsylvania.

As I've crisscrossed the state, I've gained an appreciation for the sturdy old barns that dot the landscape, including the classic Pennsylvania bank barns and others made of native fieldstones. They are often adorned with colorful hex signs, which were originally intended to ward off evil spirits, but now add to the charm of the countryside.

The post-and-beam construction of these 18th- and 19th-century masterpieces was patterned after the techniques used to build the great sailing ships of the day. I often marvel at the labor it must have taken to raise them without modern power tools.

My backroads trips sometimes lead me to diverse community festivals that celebrate the German ♂

"**BERKS COUNTY** was famous for its decorated barns. Some farmers continue the tradition."

"**A PILOT** joyfully soars over the land in a home-built plane. It's a grand day for flying!"

"**AS I** was wandering the backroads in Tioga County, I discovered a farmstead hidden from the rest of the world in an isolated valley (left)."

"**THIS** 1930s-era motel along Route 6 in northern Pennsylvania is still in business. I've never stayed there, but with such peaceful surroundings, I'll bet you can get a great night's sleep."

"**AT SUNRISE** in their cemetery, the residents of Churchtown observe Memorial Day. They've done so for over 100 years."

"**ON** Wednesday mornings, farmers from miles around bring produce to sell at the farmers' market in Belleville. Livestock and hay are sold in the afternoon."

The Best of COUNTRY

and other ethnic heritages of the state. There are farm auctions, too, with a couple hundred people showing up for the lively bidding, good food and fellowship.

And, of course, you never know when you'll discover a covered bridge around the next bend in the road. Pennsylvania has over 200 of these inviting spans, the most of any state. Built in the 1800s, they're a testimony to old-fashioned craftsmanship and to a time when life was lived in the slow lane.

One of my most memorable experiences was a day in May when I surveyed the patchwork fields of Lancaster County from the window of a small Cessna airplane. Amish and Mennonite farmers were working the land with their teams of horses and mules. Some teams consisted of as many as seven animals in harness together.

Even from the air, I could smell the distinctive scent of the freshly tilled soil as I passed overhead. What a glorious time it was!

But then again, divine times like these are not uncommon in Pennsylvania. After all, this is God's Country. ➳

"**QUIET** country roads, lazy streams and green valleys epitomize the Pennsylvania countryside."

"**TURN THE PAGE** for a bird's-eye view of Lancaster County in the springtime. People consider the county a national treasure because it has some of the most beautiful farms on Earth."

"**AMISH CHILDREN** line the banks of a stream for a fishing derby that's held every spring. It's a popular event. For many youngsters, it's their first experience dropping a line in the water."

Newfangled Addresses Take the Fun Out of Giving Directions

Guiding folks down country roads just isn't the same anymore.

By Al Batt, Hartland, Minnesota

THERE'S been a change at our place. For years, our address was R.R.1, Box 56A. It was a substantial, rural-sounding address, one that gave me a sense of belonging.

Now, I live at 71622-325th Street. No, I haven't moved to town—I'm still on the same farm where I've always lived.

The county has instituted a rural addressing system and presented me with yet another long number to remember. I'm sure it will be a good thing. It will help ambulance, police, fire, pizza delivery and other emergency services find us.

The signed streets, avenues and house numbers make navigating our rural roads a piece of cake. But I'm not completely happy with the new system. It has taken something away from us—the art of giving creative directions is a thing of the past.

Just the other day, I was fixing the lawn mower, when a fellow driving a Volvo pulled into my yard and asked, "How do I get to the home of Alfie Dodin?" He was wearing a beret. We don't get many berets in Hartland.

Turn at the Cottonwood

Imagine the fun I could have had back before we had this new numbering system. "Do you want to get to the Dodins' new home or their old home?" I'd have asked him for starters.

"Well, their new residence, of course!" Beret wearers are a touchy lot.

"Excellent choice," would have been my reply. "They don't live in their old place anymore. Somebody named Hawkins or Haskins or Higgins lives there now.

"Whoever it is, they paid way too much for it. The Dodins moved to the old Johnny Johnson place. You know it?"

"No, that is why I am asking you," I can almost hear the fellow say. Beret wearers are an impatient bunch.

"Okay, head right down this road here. Take a right where the biggest cottonwood in the township used to be. Keep going down the rough road until you pass the spot where the old schoolhouse was, before it was moved.

"Turn left and keep heading down that road until you come to a bridge. You should have turned north about a mile before that bridge.

"You have got to pay more attention, unless you want to be like that poor Boy Scout troop that was lost for about a week after asking me for directions. So you turn before you get to the bridge, and you'll go right by the old Sorenson farm.

"Look for a place with nothing there. That will be the Sorenson farm. The buildings all burned down in 1971.

Beware of the Pothole

"Next, you need to avoid that bottomless pothole on what we call Hamster Trail. If you make it past the pothole—there might be a Mazda in it—start looking for a big brown cow on your left. That will be Oscar Olson's cow. Make sure you wave at her—she likes that. I think being a cow can get kind of boring.

"Then keep driving down the washboard road until you're sure you are lost, or until your license plates fall off. The Dodin place is the next driveway on the left.

"Here, let me draw you a map on the instruction manual for my lawn mower. I'll never use it anyway."

Now, I'd just tell the guy in the beret that the Dodins live on 12345-999th Avenue. Where's the fun in that?

Change is necessary, but it isn't always easy. Oh, I'll get used to living at 71622-325th Street, but I sure will miss watching someone drive past my place over and over again after I've given him directions.

Memories of My Favorite Horse

COLT STRICK will be the first to tell you there's nothing quite like the feel of a trusty horse under saddle. In a photo taken by Jean Armstrong of Wray, Colorado, he's shown crossing the south fork of the Republican River.

If you love horses, this chapter will put a smile on your face on one page…and a lump in your throat on another…as readers share the strong-as-harness-leather bond between them and their favorite horse.

We'll take the lead with memories of our own special team—*Country's Reminisce Hitch* that pulled a wagon across the country from Maine to California in 1993.

THEY'RE OFF!

After a weather-delayed start, our cross-country hitch splashed through the Atlantic surf and is now on the road.

AS this piece is being written, *Country's Reminisce Hitch* has crossed the lower corner of Maine and is most of the way across New Hampshire and gradually nearing Massachusetts.

Things are now going smoothly, but that wasn't the case in the beginning. We'd told ourselves again and again that this cross-country trip would be hard to schedule, because we'd be dealing with three unpredictable elements— horses, road conditions and weather.

Well, we have already confirmed we are right about the latter. The weather in Maine was so bad at the onset that it delayed the start of the trip by more than a week.

But on Tuesday, April 13, 1993, the hitch trotted through the Atlantic surf at Kennebunkport, Maine (see photo above) and officially got under way.

Likely, it will be more than a year before these beautiful Belgians touch their feet in the Pacific Ocean near San Diego, California.

In fact, if crowds continue to swarm the hitch like they did when the horses were stabled at a farm next to the beach at Kennebunkport, the trip may take much longer! Hundreds of our subscribers brought their families to see *their* hitch.

One chamber of commerce official there told us the appearance of this hitch caused a greater stir than usual visits by President George Bush! (His summer home is less than a mile up the road from where the above picture was taken.)

That's just one of the reports from the road as *Country's Reminisce Hitch* high-stepped its way across the country—10 miles a day and stopping to

give rides to subscribers and visit senior centers along the way.

"We're making good progress, and everything's going great," said driver David Helmuth in another report as they crossed western New York. "The people along the way have been fantastic! They are still bringing us food, from home-made cookies to homegrown apples and even a couple of home-baked apple pies!

"Most people—especially the seniors—really get excited to see their hitch. Some folks get downright emotional when they see us coming."

Touched Her Heart—and Ours

Especially touching was the reaction of an elderly woman who was sitting in a wheelchair beside the road along Highway 2. She smiled and waved, excited because this hitch she'd read about was passing right by her place on its trek from Maine to California.

She seemed even more pleased when David reined in the horses and stopped the wagon right beside her. What followed next nearly overwhelmed her. "Would you like to ride with us for a while?" he called down to her.

And then, hardly waiting for an an-

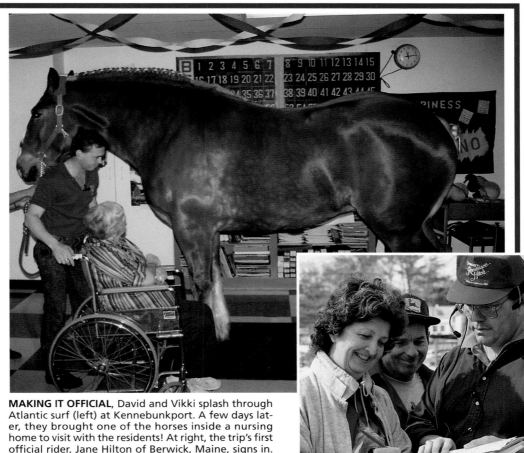

MAKING IT OFFICIAL, David and Vikki splash through Atlantic surf (left) at Kennebunkport. A few days later, they brought one of the horses inside a nursing home to visit with the residents! At right, the trip's first official rider, Jane Hilton of Berwick, Maine, signs in.

swer, two burly crewmen loaded the lady—wheelchair and all—onto the wagon. The expression on that lady's face and the delight in her eyes was nearly enough in itself to make this whole trip worthwhile.

Why We're Doing It
By Roy Reiman, Founder

I'VE always loved horses. Especially draft horses. *Especially* Belgians. It stems from growing up on an Iowa farm.

I was a kid during the "in-between" years of agriculture—that is, in between horses and tractors. When I was a little squirt, my dad often let me ride up there in front of the wagon with him when he drove our team, "Dan" and "Mabel." And now and then, he handed me the lines.

I've been holding on to them ever since…and with the memories that go with them. In fact, one of the main reasons I'm doing all of this—organizing and carrying out this first-ever six-horse trek across 18 states—is the memory of my father.

If he were still alive, he'd think this was a wild and wonderful adventure, and it would have been hard to keep him from coming along. And he wouldn't have been just one of the "riders;" he would have insisted on being one of the *crew*—he would have been brushing, braiding, harnessing and helping with this hitch every day.

I, too, wish I could be with the hitch every step of the way. Unfortunately, I'll only be able to be with the horses now and then during this journey. Still, when I'm there, helping get these champion Belgians ready for their day on the road…smelling the sweat and the harnesses…busting up bales of hay and feeling the lines…all this will take me back to those days with Dad that I so fondly remember.

And it will likely do the same for thousands of people along the route. There's something about draft horses that brings back those "kinder, gentler days" that George Bush used to talk about.

If *Country's Reminisce Hitch* can have the same effect on thousands of retired farmers (I predict it will) who will come to our cross-country route to see them, and can bring about a better understanding and appreciation of early agriculture to thousands of others, then I feel this trip is worth doing.

Likewise, if these horses can give a lift to thousands of senior citizens (we plan to take the hitch—or at least "Firestone," our most famous horse—to senior centers all along the route) for just a day here and there, then this trip is worth doing. The "We're Pulling for Seniors" slogan on the hitch wagon has meaning.

And, in the face of all the crime and graft and negative news that seems to dominate the nation's newspapers and TV screens these days, if the "personal appearance" of these beautiful Belgians in hundreds of small communities along our 3,000-mile rural route can add a bright note to a dull day, then this trip is worth doing.

Lastly, my dad taught me more than just how to drive draft horses. He and my mother instilled certain val- ♂

ues that still linger. They taught me there were just certain things that were "the right thing to do."

One of those values was that, if you're blessed with success, you have an obligation to share part of your good fortune with those who are less fortunate. In other words, you "give back" to the community that helped you get where you are. So that's what I've decided to do—to give back something to the community of millions of people who now subscribe to our magazines.

As I see it, since we've used part of their subscription payments to buy this champion hitch, that makes them "part owners" of these beautiful Belgians. And I can't think of a better way to show our appreciation for their support and loyalty than to bring *their* hitch to them to see, meet and pet.

If this gives thousands of them a good deal of satisfaction...if this "sharing" experience makes them feel closer to us and to other members of our subscriber "family"...and if this cross-country trek allows our hitch crew and me to look many of them in the eye,

shake hands and say, "Thank you," then this trip is worth doing.

They're Off Again—
This Time from West to East

AS WE mentioned earlier, no matter how hard you try, not everything goes according to plan, especially when your plan is limited by weather and horses.

And with a summer and fall that were more pleasing to ducks than a six-horse hitch on its way from Maine to California, inclement weather forced us to make a change in our plans.

The six champion Belgians in *Country's Reminisce Hitch* splashed their huge hooves in the Atlantic Ocean on April 13, 1993 and headed west, bent on splashing in the Pacific Ocean off the coast of California sometime next year.

The route took them through Maine, New Hampshire, Massachusetts, New York, Pennsylvania, Ohio, Indiana and Illinois. On Friday, Oct. 15, after walking over 1,300 miles, they crossed the Mississippi River at Fort Madison, Iowa

and continued west along Highway 2.

But the continuous rainy weather that plagued the Midwest much of the summer put the hitch well behind schedule, and driver David Helmuth yelled his last "Whoa!" for a while when he reached Centerville, Iowa on Oct. 23.

We'd hoped we would get to Kansas and start heading south by mid-November. But we said from the onset that we would never do anything on this trip that would be asking too much of the horses or the crew, and the steady run of chilly breezy days in mid-October was becoming a challenge for the crew as well as the riders. We began getting concerned about the chances of having cold weather close in on them or—worse—having the hitch get caught in a freak early blizzard.

So reluctantly, we decided we had no choice but to put our contingency plan into effect. Here it is:

When the champion team reached Centerville on Oct. 23, we officially stopped our east-to-west trek, and a ceremony was held. There, a la the days of the "Golden Spike," the crew implanted a "Golden Horseshoe" in the road to mark the point reached by the team.

Then, after resting the team and crew for several weeks, we loaded the horses on our special semi and hauled them all the way to the finish of our planned route at San Diego.

On Monday, December 13, *Country's Reminisce Hitch* got back on the road, only this time headed east.

Early that morning the horses splashed through the surf of the Pacific Ocean at San Diego, just as they'd splashed in the surf at Kennebunkport, Maine on April 13. By doing so, they made the trek an official ocean-to-ocean effort.

Now the team is walking back along the same route in the opposite direction. This puts the hitch and crew in the southern part of Arizona and New Mexico during the best time of the year there—December through February—and will have them headed north through Texas, Oklahoma, Colorado and Kansas as spring moves north with them.

5000 PEOPLE crowded Centerville, Iowa's town square to welcome the hitch and watch the laying of the "Golden Horseshoe."

HAPPY HOMECOMING. At the trail's end, driver David Helmuth greeted our subscribers as Roy and Bobbi Reiman look on.

"The weather's great down here," David reported by phone after several days on the road. "But the mountains just east of San Diego were really something the first few days!

"We're now back on level land, and it'll be that way for a good piece of our route now until we get well beyond Yuma."

David, his assistant and wife, Vikki, (they got married on the trip) and the other seven members of the crew were glad to be back on the road again after the extended respite. "I can tell the horses are glad to be back in harness, too," David said.

"Remember, these are Belgian draft horses, and they'd rather work or pull something any day than ride on a truck or relax in a pasture. So when we hitched them up in San Diego and headed for the beach to get the return trip under way, they seemed to know we were going back on the road for our 10 miles a day, and they pranced like young geldings."

You might say *Country's Reminisce*

Hitch "peaked out" when it camped overnight at Mountainair, New Mexico. The scenic mountain town has an elevation of 6,500 feet, making it the highest point on the entire cross-country route.

Downhill from Here!

"I was a little concerned about how the horses would handle the climb, but actually the roads weren't too steep, and they made it in fine shape. And it was pretty along this stretch," said David in another report.

Although the hitch was traveling through sparsely populated desert, they still had lots of company. "We're seeing and giving rides to quite a few 'snowbirds' on their way home back north—many are following the same route we are," he observed. "We've had riders from as far away as Ontario, many Midwestern states and even a busload of kids from a school in North Carolina."

The weather turned warm in late May and early June, as the team made its way across the plains of southern Kansas. So was the reception as hundreds of well-wishers turned out in towns along the way.

The hitch spent one weekend in Kinsley, Kansas, which is also known as "Midway USA," because it is located in the exact center of the country—1,561 miles from New York City, and an equal distance from San Francisco. One visitor that weekend was a San Francisco resident who drove all 1,561 miles just to see the hitch!

"We Did It!"

"Give 'em a little room please—these horses want to see that horseshoe! They've walked a long, *long* way to get here!"

These were the words jokingly called out to the excited crowd by hitch driver David Helmuth on the afternoon of Friday, August 12, 1994 as he "Whoa'ed" *Country's Reminisce Hitch* and faced them right at the Golden Horseshoe on the edge of the town square in Centerville, Iowa.

The enthusiastic onlookers, numbering around 5,000 and representing at least 20 states, responded with laughter and a rousing cheer. David handed the lines to Vikki, stood up on the wagon seat, swung his hat overhead and let out a loud yell. Then he bowed deeply to the large crowd as they applauded.

"We're absolutely delighted to be here," David said. "I have to admit there were some days when we wondered if we'd actually make it. But these horses proved they're the champions we've said they were, and with your support and the grace of God, we did it!"

After Roy Reiman and several Centerville dignitaries appeared on stage to welcome the hitch home, a second Golden Horseshoe was implanted in the pavement.

And so ended the epic 16-month journey of 3,800 miles...with visits to hundreds of senior centers along the way, rides to tens of thousands, and smiles from countless more who came out to see *their* hitch.

Afterward, the horses were stabled at David and Vikki's Paradise Acres farm near Waverly, Iowa. But they continued to make the rounds of fairs and horse shows for the next 2 years, where other subscribers could get a first ↷

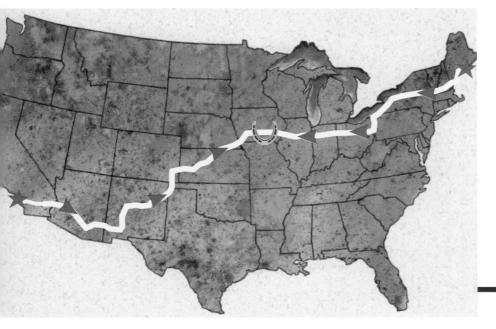

hand look at these beautiful animals.

Then, in 1996, Roy announced that it was "time to hang up the harness. They've accomplished their mission...they walked clear across the country at 10 miles a day, covering 3,800 miles in 16 months...they've honored *thousands* of seniors and given them memories they'll never forget...and they've given more than a *million* of our subscribers a chance to see, meet and pet them firsthand."

With that, Roy transferred ownership of the hitch to David and Vikki in appreciation for the care they gave the horses...and *Country's Reminsce Hitch* eased into retirement at Paradise Acres.

Rest easy, our old friends. You've earned it.

How This 'Hitch of All Hitches' Was Assembled

The search and training took over 3 years.

DRAFT HORSES by nature are very willing workers. Most of them would rather pull something than stand in a pasture.

Yet, they still require a lot of patient training before they fully cooperate with the driver...and the rest of the team.

They have to do their job individually, and also function as part of a smooth-working unit that moves almost as one.

These things are true even if you have a two-horse hitch. Making six horses perform as a unit is a formidable challenge.

The Lead Team

A lead team in a six-horse hitch must be willing to go wherever the driver wants them to go—and do it with style.

The Swing Team

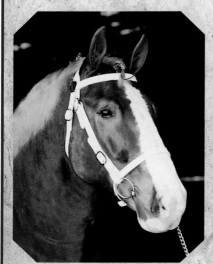

"Chip"
Height: 18 hands
Weight: 2,000 pounds
Age: 7 years
Awards: Eight times first place in Men's Cart competition, 10 times first place in six-horse hitch.

"CHIP was the second horse acquired in the hitch," says David, "and in many ways, he's the real leader of the team. No other horse can 'out-proud' him. He simply will not allow it."

"Magic"
Height: 18 hands
Weight: 2,000 pounds.
Age: 4 years
Awards: Grand Champion Stallion, four times first place in Men's Cart competition, eight times first place in six-horse hitch competition.

"IT TOOK us 3 years to find a horse to keep up with Chip," notes David. "Magic seems determined to give Chip a run for his money, and a healthy competition and respect has developed between them."

"Firestone"
Height: 18.2 hands
Weight: 2,200 pounds
Age: 7 years
Awards: Eight times Grand Champion at major shows, 19 times first place in cart competitions.

"FIRESTONE was the first horse we acquired and was already a legend," says David. "At age 7, he'd won more awards than many horses win in a lifetime. He also has the best disposition you'll ever find."

In addition, in order to win on the show circuit, each individual horse in the hitch must be an outstanding animal to pass the judges' exacting criteria of physical appearance, breed characteristics and markings. Each horse has to exhibit muscle quality, alertness, proper carriage and an eagerness to perform.

David Helmuth, the trainer and driver of *Country's Reminisce Hitch*, had all of this in mind as he set out in 1989 to put together "the hitch of all hitches." The team is the result of a 3-year search for just the right horses.

In that time, David changed his starting lineup almost continually. Dozens of horses were bought and sold, shuffled in and out of the hitch as he struggled to create that ideal team.

He constantly looked beyond an individual horse's characteristics—and kept in mind how the horse would fit in with the others. To give you an idea of how much attention he paid to that detail, there was only a *1-inch difference* in height between the lead team and the swing team. (The lead team is, obviously, the two horses up front, and the swing team is the two horses in the middle of the hitch.)

Likewise, there is a 1-inch difference in height between the swing team and the wheel team. What's more, there's only a *1/2-inch difference* between the height of each pair of horses in each of the hitch positions.

There's a host of other physical factors an experienced driver/trainer like

David looks for when assembling a great team. The feet of draft horses are given high priority, because they measure a horse's usefulness. "No foot, no horse," draft horse experts say.

Good long hocks, a strong well-shaped back and withers, a nicely shaped head with alert eyes: all these are desirable characteristics.

Next, David begins talking about the disposition of a horse, and his voice gets even more enthusiastic. He likes to refer to disposition as "heart."

"If a horse has a big heart, I can train him,' he says. "He has to have a fire in his belly. The best feet and head and marks in the world don't mean a thing if he doesn't have the desire to perform."

Horses in a swing team must be even tempered to perform in the middle slot with horses in front and behind.

"J.R."
Height: 18.1 hands
Weight: 2,100 pounds
Age: 3 years
Claim to Fame: He's a full-blood brother to Firestone.

"BECAUSE Firestone is such an outstanding horse, finding a mate for him was really a chore," notes David. "Every other horse paled by comparison. Then along came J.R., his full brother."

The Wheel Team

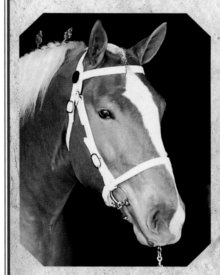

"Bobby"
Height: 18.2 hands
Weight: 2,400 pounds
Age: 5 years
Awards: Grand Champion Gelding, three times first place in Men's Cart competition, eight times first place in six-horse hitch.

"BOBBY is the best wheel horse in the country," says David. "He has the quickness and agility of a lead horse, but the size and strength of a wheel horse. He's the second smartest horse in the hitch."

The wheel horses are the largest and strongest because they tow the biggest portion of the load.

"Jack"
Height: 18.2 hands
Weight: 2,350 pounds
Age: 8 years
Awards: Grand Champion Gelding, seven times first place in Men's Cart competition, eight times first place in six-horse hitch.

"JACK'S a major key to our success," notes David. "He's a real competitor. The tremendous leg action of Jack and Bobby is one of the things that distinguishes our hitch from the rest."

HORSES became our daughter Linda's favorite topic of conversation from about the time she was 6 years old. Owning a horse became an obsession. But because of her age and small size, my husband and I were concerned about her safety.

For 2 years, the family listened to her incessant chatter about horses. Finally, in hopes of satisfying her, we bought "Speedy," a neighbor's donkey, believing the smaller animal would be safer than a full-size horse. Our purchase thrilled Linda and gave the rest of the family some relief.

The acre of land that served as Speedy's new home was enclosed by two sides of our house and a fence. Linda's bedroom overlooked Speedy's pasture, with her two windows the same height as the donkey's head.

Wake-Up Call

Early on summer mornings when Speedy wanted food or company, he stuck his nose in her open window and brayed. The raucous sound bounced off the walls and wooden floors, echoing through the eight-room house. Awakening to that sound from a peaceful sleep is not the best way to start the day.

The first time our 6-year-old son, Mike, heard Speedy bray, he panicked. Running to me with tears in his eyes, he yelled, "Mom, come quick! Speedy's strangling!"

Speedy quickly developed an amusing habit. When Linda approached him holding a bridle, he knew this thing she carried meant he would be taken from his beloved shady pasture. He also figured out it might involve some work—like carrying a small girl on his back.

So he'd dash to the top of the hill, as far from her as the fence permitted. Then he put his head behind a large tree trunk and stood there, motionless. He seemed to think that if he couldn't see Linda, she couldn't see him. Surprised each time Linda "found" him, he'd throw his head in the air and trot away from her.

First Ride Was Memorable

It was hot the day of Linda's first solo ride outside the pasture. She insisted on saddling up without help. Willing to assist, but not knowing one end of a saddle from the other, I felt relieved at her show of independence.

She barely had the stature or strength to throw the heavy saddle over Speedy's back. Wet with perspiration after completing the grueling task, she mounted and proudly started down the driveway to the gravel road.

DONKEY'S DILEMMA. "Sammy," a miniature donkey owned by reader Debbie Bradshaw, Crestwood, Kentucky, has a mischievous nature like "Speedy," the donkey in the story.

She Got a Quick Lesson in 'Donkey Language'

Learning to understand her pet donkey was no problem for this youngster.

By Betty Lou Nease, Lakebay, Washington

Watching from the seclusion of the embankment over the road, I played the role of mother hen. To my relief, Speedy chose a slow, reluctant pace. No amount of urging changed his low gear. Satisfied with what I saw, I returned to the house.

About 20 minutes later, I heard Linda crying. I ran out to meet her.

A miserable sight awaited me. Linda was walking, leading Speedy. To my amazement, she was carrying the heavy saddle. Tears from red puffed eyes made clean stripes through the dust on her face. Mud covered parts of her face where she had wiped the tears and perspiration with her grimy hands.

Speedy was limping with every step. In addition, he was coughing and wheezing, head hanging nearly to the ground.

Got Message Across

As I ran to them, it appeared Speedy had thrown her off—along with the saddle.

"What happened?" I shouted, already afraid of the answer. "Oh, Mom. Speedy's dying."

I reached her, took the saddle from her aching arms and set it on the grass. "Are you hurt? Did he throw you off? Why are you carrying the saddle?" I asked.

I inspected her for blood and found none. Her short curly hair was saturated with sweat and dust. Her soiled clothes looked as if she had rolled in dirt.

"No, I didn't fall off. Speedy started limping and coughing and it got worse and worse. I took the saddle off to make it easier for him. Mom, I'm sure he's dying!"

Linda sobbed as we led the pitiful staggering animal to the pasture gate. I decided to call the vet, hoping Speedy would live long enough to receive proper medical attention.

Inside the gate, Linda took the bridle off. The simple action created a medical miracle. Speedy's head came up smartly, the cough and wheeze were instantly cured and he trotted rapidly across the pasture, small feet a blur, with no hint of the limp. Linda and I watched in astonishment.

Silently thinking this over awhile, Linda said, "Mom, I think he tried to tell me it was too hot to go for a ride."

Like the braying in the window and hiding behind a tree, Linda had received another lesson in "Donkey Language."

Dad Couldn't Part with His Old Mare

He walked 16 miles to bring the aging plow horse back home again.

By Irmagene Nelson
West Union, Illinois

IN THE SUMMER of 1938—when I was 10 years old—I lived on a small farm in Illinois. During that era, almost everyone farmed with horses, and so did we. We owned four work horses, one of which was an old black mare named "Jane."

On several occasions, I heard my parents' hushed voices as they whispered concern over Jane's failing health. She had become too slow for working in the fields, always lagging behind the other horses.

Jane would have to be retired, my father said. Then I heard my mother mutter, "Poor old soul." In those days, most old horses met their fates at the rendering plant. Farmers had a hard enough time providing for their families during the 1930s, let alone a horse that could not pull its weight.

On a particularly steamy July afternoon, I heard crunching gravel in our barnyard, and when I looked out the window, I saw a large, rickety truck lumbering up near the barn.

A wrinkled-faced old man in sweat-stained bib overalls and a shapeless dirty cap got out of the truck. Instantly, I knew who he was, and why he had come. He was the man who came to collect old animals.

Sold Her for $10

Watching and listening through the open window, I heard as he asked my father about buying Jane. My father removed his straw hat, wiped the liner and his forehead with his blue bandana and said, "Well, sir, I just don't know."

"If not now…when?" the man asked.

To my surprise, when the man offered my father $10 for Jane, Dad accepted. Turning quickly, he disappeared into the barn. Then I saw Jane plodding from the barn, guided by my father's tender hand.

Dad removed Jane's halter, clutched it in his hand and reached forward to stroke the white stripe that marked her face. I turned away as tears trailed down my cheeks.

Taking one last glance at Jane, I no-

ticed that as she stood in the truck, she was looking directly at my father. Then I heard the rev of the truck engine, and Jane and the man where gone.

My father ambled back to the barn, and I didn't see him again until supper-time. Eyes averted, no one said anything as we ate. But I knew Dad was thinking of the fate of the old mare…and haunted by the fact that she'd been such an obliging coworker and companion for so many years.

A Change of Heart

Later, in the wee hours of the morning, I was awakened by footsteps coming from my parents' bedroom. My father was padding around the room, and I heard Mother ask him what he was doing.

Dad announced that he was getting dressed and walking to town and—if Jane was still there—he was buying her back. It was 3:30 a.m. when he grabbed his weather-beaten straw hat and a halter and headed out the door.

We didn't own a car. So he proceeded to the nearby railroad tracks and walked alongside them the 8 miles to town.

The day passed slowly as I sat in the living room and tried to read. I looked

at the clock, wandered to the battery-operated Zenith radio and flipped the dial until I heard some music. Even though I wasn't hungry, I fixed some lunch to distract myself from a growing sense of dread.

A question flitted through my mind. What if Jane had already been shipped out to the rendering plant? Again and again, I looked at the clock.

Many hours later, in the late-afternoon dusk, I went outside and scanned the gravel road. I spotted two distant figures heading toward me and knew my father had found Jane. My heart started pounding, and I shouted the good news to my mother and sister.

As Jane and my father turned into our yard after their 8-mile walk from town, she lifted her head, pricked her ears forward and whinnied.

Dad pampered Jane until she passed away 10 years later. She died on our farm, where she had spent her entire life.

After we retired, my husband and I moved back to the farm that's been in my family since 1856. Living here, I often think of that day when my father walked 16 miles to and from town to save the old black mare he loved so much.

Your Turn to Saddle Up. If you have some recollections of a horse, or a team of horses, that was special to you, we'd like to hear from you. Send your story and photos to "Memories of My Favorite Horse," *Country*, 5925 Country Lane, Greendale WI 53129.

GENTLE GIANT. Like the mare in the author's story, the big fella in this photo by Zelda Rowley from Lancaster, Pennsylvania has no doubt been a loyal and faithful worker.

He Went Down Many a Trail with This Mare

She was as smart as they come and saved his life more than once.

By Roy Garcia, San Luis Obispo, California

AS A SCHOOLBOY, I read a book about "Justin Morgan," the founding horse of the Morgan breed, and how much strength, stamina and intelligence these horses exhibited.

So years later, when a dentist friend of mine gave me a Morgan brood mare in foal, I was excited. I raised her filly "Muffet" from day one, and I'm here to say Muffet saved my life more than once.

The first time was when I was leading my son, two daughters and two brothers home from a fishing trip in the Sierra National Forest in central California.

Muffet was a fast walker and could follow a trail. As we approached the Courtright Dam, I saw a trail going to the left, but I missed the one hidden in the shadows that went to the right.

I reined Muffet to the left and, from the sound of her hooves, I knew we were walking on solid granite. We walked about 40 feet, when all of a sudden, Muffet reared up, whirled around and proceeded to walk briskly—and with determination—back to the trail I'd missed.

Suddenly it dawned on me what had happened—we had walked out to the edge of a huge cliff that dropped straight down about 400 feet. I never knew how close we came to stepping off that cliff. But I felt as if I was hanging over it when Muffet raised her front feet and whirled around.

Every once in a while, I still have nightmares about that day and a shiver will run down my spine. I thank God for Muffet every time I think about it.

Caught in Snowstorm

Another time, I was near Delta, Colorado, helping a rancher gather his cattle in the high country. Riding alone, I had crossed over a couple of peaks looking for strays when it started to snow. Pretty soon, the flakes were coming down so hard I couldn't see Muffet's ears in front of me.

Getting cold, I decided I'd better get back to the rest of the crew, so I spurred Muffet ahead. We walked a ways, but then Muffet wanted to turn left. I was sure I knew which direction to move in, so I kept her going my way.

It was now getting colder and snowing even harder. The ground was white. Muffet slowed her pace, letting me know she didn't want to go the way I had her headed.

Finally, I decided to let Muffet have her way. I loosened up on the reins, and she immediately made a 90-degree turn and picked up her pace to a good brisk walk.

SITTING TALL IN THE SADDLE. Roy Garcia and Muffet the Morgan mare (above) shared many adventures during their mountain rides.

I was sure she knew where she was going. But how she did, I couldn't say. Within minutes, we found the rest of the crew, huddled around a fire they had just built to warm up.

Knew Way to Camp

Muffet had an incredible sense of direction. Once, when I was hunting up in Oregon, I left camp early in the morning and rode up over several mountains, covering lots of ground.

When it started getting dark, I decided I'd better head back to camp. Muffet seemed a little tired, but now that I think about it, I guess she was wondering why I was riding away from—rather than to—our camp so late in the day.

After riding a couple of hours, I ran into a sheepherder's camp. I braved his dogs and tried to get up to his wagon. I hollered a couple of times, but no one answered. It was cold and nearly midnight, so I figured he wasn't about to stick his head out. So I spurred Muffet on.

Finally, we came to a spot where we could descend the table mountain we were on. We went down and found a dirt road to follow. Then we came to a fork, and I chose the road that turned to the left…despite Muffet's efforts to go right.

By now, it was really getting late, and I didn't know where I was going. Muffet still wanted to go right, which would have taken us straight up a mountain.

I finally gave her free rein and up we went through the brush and trees. It was so dark, I couldn't even see the tree limbs, but Muffet never took me under one that was low enough for me to hit my head on.

Never hesitating or faltering, Muffet moved with strength and power I couldn't believe she possessed, carrying me straight up that mountain and into camp. I was so thankful, I could have kissed her. But I rewarded her with a drink of water and a bucket of grain instead. She was so easy to satisfy.

Spotted Large Buck

I remember another time when I was hunting in Utah. I had walked Muffet down a long canyon of aspens, when all of a sudden, she stopped and came to a point, just like an English setter does when it spies a game bird. Her ears were pointed straight ahead, and she stood like a wooden statue.

I looked between Muffet's ears, attempting to see what she was pointing at, but I couldn't see a thing. I stared for what seemed like 5 minutes. Then I saw this big wave of movement through the aspens, and out jumped the biggest deer I'd ever seen in my life. It was only 50 feet away, but I wouldn't have spotted it if hadn't been for Muffet.

Every summer, I'd trailer Muffet up to the top of a mountain in the Los Padres National Forest in California. I'd saddle her up and tie my sleeping bag on back over my saddlebags, which were stuffed with provisions for a few days of hunting.

Then I'd mount up and ride all day, stopping just before dark to set up camp for the night. The next day, I'd hunt from dawn to dusk. On the third day, I'd load my buck on my saddle, and Muffet and I would walk out to where I'd left my pickup and horse trailer.

Those 3-day hunting trips weren't hard on Muffet at all. In fact, by the end of the season, she would be in such good condition that we could make the trip in 1 day.

I'd ride into camp, hunt all day, load a buck on the back of my saddle and ride out that evening. Muffet carried me with strength, stamina and alertness that was hard to believe.

Learned by Her Example

Muffet taught me many things, including what a difference being in shape makes. I'm 77, and last summer I bucked 1,000 bales of hay from the field to the haystack with my pickup. My son wanted to help me, but I wouldn't let him because I needed the workout.

Two summers ago, a hay hauler couldn't get into my barn with his trailer, so he dumped the bales in my corral. My son suggested I hire someone with a loader to put the hay in the barn. But I decided it would be good exercise for me, so I got my 12-year-old grandson, and we started working.

It took us almost 3 weeks to get all 20 loads in the barn, but I felt like I had acquired the same gusto Muffet had when she was in top condition.

Besides stacking hay, I also still rope in competition, and I feel I owe that to Muffet. She taught me the value of being in shape mentally and physically.

Your Turn to Saddle Up. If you have memories of a horse or pony that was special to you, we'd like to hear from you. Send your story and photos to "Memories of My Favorite Horse," *Country*, 5925 Country Lane, Greendale WI 53129. Enclose a self-addressed stamped envelope if you'd like your photos returned. ✹

REMAINS ACTIVE. Now 77, Roy still enjoys going on mountain camping trips whenever he has a chance.

Londie G. Padelsky

Ill-Tempered Horse Was a
Saint Under Saddle

A circuit-riding preacher rode the goosey gelding clear across the country.

By Dick Downey, Westcliffe, Colorado

IT WAS 10 years ago this spring that my brother, Rev. Ken Downey, set out on a ride across America to commemorate the work of the old-time circuit-riding preachers.

Ken made the 3,300-mile trip on horseback, riding the entire way on just one horse, a frightened and mishandled gelding appropriately named "Jeremiah." This is the miraculous story of that very special animal.

At the time, Ken was on the staff of Oak Hills Bible College in Bemidji, Minnesota. He had been planning the cross-country trip for 2 years, and put 10,000 miles on the family car checking out highways and county roads where he could ride his Quarter Horse mare.

MAN ON A MISSION. Riding Jeremiah, Rev. Ken Downey traveled 3,300 miles to share his message. Here, the pair are shown crossing Idaho.

old Quarter Horse was anything but easy to handle.

Ken learned that Jeremiah had been seriously injured in a highway accident while being transported in a trailer. The other horse in the trailer with Jeremiah was killed.

Although Jeremiah recovered from his physical wounds, he trusted no one after the accident and was spooked by just about everything.

Despite Jeremiah's skittishness, Ken decided to see if the gelding could be trained to make the arduous journey.

From the beginning, Jeremiah made it known that he had no intention of going along with this man who wanted to ride him across the country. He bucked and carried on in such a manner that would discourage most men, especially one on so tight a schedule.

Then, just a couple months before the ride was to begin, Ken's mare suffered a serious wire cut on her leg. It was doubtful she would heal completely before Ken's scheduled departure date. And even if the wound did heal, there wouldn't be time to get her in shape for the difficult trip ahead.

Trusted No One

The only other horse Ken had was Jeremiah, a renegade gelding he had owned only a few months. Ken bought the horse cheap from a young rodeo rider who had acquired the gelding in a trade. The rodeo cowboy quickly discovered that the 6-year-

Rode in Deep Snow

It was the middle of winter, and the snow was deep on Ken's farm in the northwoods of Minnesota. So he started Jeremiah's training by riding him in the deep snow to tire him to the point that he would listen to his determined rider. After several days, Jeremiah did begin to listen and eventually learned to trust the tall slim man with the gray beard.

It was tough on Jeremiah to be reintroduced to so many

MILE AFTER MILE. Ken and Jeremiah passed through the Ohio countryside (left) and were greeted by a crowd (above) in Camby, Ind.

things that had been painful in his past. Just traveling beside the highway and seeing an oncoming pickup caused old memories to rush forward and made him panic.

But the day finally came—and none too soon—when Jeremiah could handle the stress of his appointed mission.

Ken and Jeremiah left Philadelphia, Pennsylvania on March 21, 1994. It didn't take many days on the trail for Jeremiah to settle down and—once he quieted—he stayed that way for the entire trip.

Cool with Kids

I joined Ken in Ohio and rode with him partway across Ohio and into Indiana on my Quarter Horse. While my horse was good for traveling, he wasn't easy with people. When we'd stop somewhere for Ken to speak, the little kids would come up and want to pet the horses.

Well, my horse was pretty skittish. But when people gathered around Jeremiah, he'd just stand there—and you know how excited kids can get around a horse. But that ol' horse was as calm as you please. It was amazing to see the transformation that had taken place in him.

The theme of Ken's trek was "One Nation Under God." Riding from church to church and house to house, he preached sermons, encouraging people to relate to the Lord on a personal level, and to remember another time when folks had few belongings but were rich in spirit.

Ken and Jeremiah covered anywhere from 20 to 45 miles a day. There was no support crew accompanying them. Instead, the trip was planned so that when they arrived at their next stop, there would be a place for Ken to sleep, and a bale of hay and 15 pounds of oats for Jeremiah.

When the pair crossed Wyoming, Montana and Idaho, where towns and people are few and far between, they camped out.

In all, they made 117 scheduled stops—and dozens more unofficial ones—for Ken to preach in churches, homes and even around a few campfires.

Braved the Elements

The two traveled in all kinds of weather, from winter snowstorms to summer heat of over 100°. Jeremiah braved windstorms and climbed high mountain passes with never a lame step.

Ken and Jeremiah averaged about 25 miles per day. Taking Sundays off for Ken to preach, the pair ended their ride 6-1/2 months later in Everett, Washington.

Jeremiah wore out five sets of horseshoes. Meanwhile Ken, who was attired in 19th-century clothing, went through four pairs of pants.

Some say Jeremiah was blessed by God to make such a journey. I can't argue with that, but it was also evident that folks were blessed by the message brought to them by the circuit-riding pastor perched on his back.

Many of those who heard Ken speak were encouraged by his message. They were equally amazed by the sight of the big black horse who carried his rider across America.

Your Turn to Saddle Up. If you have memories of a special horse, or a team of horses, we'd like to hear from you. Send your story to "Memories of My Favorite Horse," *Country*, 5925 Country Lane, Greendale WI 53129. Enclose a self-addressed stamped envelope if you'd like your photos returned.

HOMECOMING CELEBRATION. Ken and his wife, Carolyn, marked Ken's return with a get-together for friends at Oak Hills Bible College.

SHARING THE WORD. During his trek, Ken preached at many churches, including Ark Springs Baptist Church in Cumberland, Ohio.

Hardworking Country Girl Is Ridin' High

*She earned the money to buy a horse…
and learned about the satisfaction
that comes from a job well done.*

By Margaret Gold, Tullahoma, Tennessee

JENNY JO is the youngest of our four daughters. She's 11 years old and loves animals. Her menagerie includes eight cats, two dogs, two sheep, seven goats and two horses.

Jen started begging for a horse when she was about 8. She was so persistent for the next year that my husband, Barry, finally told her she could have one—provided she earned the money to buy it.

We never dreamed a 9-year-old would take up that challenge so seriously. She started saving any money she got for gifts, sold aluminum cans she picked up and got others to save cans for her. She was so determined.

Jenny had saved about $200, but right before her 11th birthday, we noticed she was becoming discouraged.

Then she heard a family talk about gathering walnuts. A feed store in a nearby town was paying $10 per 100 pounds for them. Jenny Jo saw this as an opportunity to earn some *big* money. It's not the easiest work, but she was fired up about it.

She picked up 450 pounds in two afternoons. Her dad drove her to the feed store on Saturday, and they sold the pickup load for $45.

Saw Dollar Signs

Now, the dollar signs were really flashing before her eyes. By Monday, she had gathered another 450 pounds…and by Thursday, still another load worth $45.

The ladies at the feed store kept encouraging Jenny Jo to keep working. They were pulling for her.

She went to our neighbors and friends and asked if she could pick up their walnuts…explaining that she was trying to earn enough money to buy a horse. As is often the case, the youngest child in the family is a charmer, and Jenny Jo is no exception. Some of these friends even paid her to pick up their walnuts, and they gave her their aluminum cans, too!

In just a few weeks, Jenny had $500, and we took her to the bank to open a savings account. She was so cute.

When the teller inquired whether she had any questions, she asked, "What would happen to my money if the bank burned down?" After a good laugh, the teller explained that her deposit was insured.

One day while she was picking up walnuts at her teacher's farm, the teacher told Jen that her son had lost interest in his mare and might want to sell her. She was a 4-year-old half Quarter Horse and half Paint named "Bree."

Jenny was very excited. She'd make us slow down every time we drove by so she could see Bree out in the pasture. She fell in love with her before she even knew whether the mare was for sale.

Several weeks went by and we didn't hear anything from Bree's owner. Meanwhile, the price of walnuts started dropping, and one day the ladies at the feed store told Jenny Jo they wouldn't be buying any more.

By this time, she had $635.75 in her bank account.

The week before Thanksgiving, the teacher's son called and offered to sell Bree for $800. Jenny's heart was broken—she'd worked so hard, but didn't have enough money.

Barry and I convinced Jen she ought to look at Bree anyway and make the boy an offer. A cousin who barrel-races horses offered to go along to check her out.

So we set up a time and looked at the mare. The young man rode her, our cousin rode her and then Jenny climbed in the saddle. She was in heaven!

Wheeling and Dealing

Then came the wheeling and dealing. Jenny offered $500 cash on the spot. But the boy insisted on $800, and once again, Jenny was heartbroken.

Finally, the young man said he'd take $500 in cash, and Jenny could pay him the balance as she earned it. He'd even throw Bree's saddle in on the deal. I'll always remember the big smile that came across her face—she had finally achieved her dream.

It was November 17 when Jenny Jo bought Bree. By the end of January, she had the mare paid for.

She still works to pay for Bree's feed and supplies. In addition, she's working to pay for a 6-month-old Paint colt named "Lucky." She "bought" him in exchange for 80 hours of cleaning stalls and doing chores from a man she met while looking for her first horse. We are also boarding a horse for my brother, and he pays Jenny to feed and care for it.

This may seem like a lot of work for a young girl, but Jenny Jo will be the first to tell you that if you want something bad enough, it's worth all the long hours.

We're proud of our children and hope we can teach each of them to take pride in a job well done and to hold up their end of any bargain they make.

It's all part of our country way of life.

TALL IN THE SADDLE. Jenny Gold sports a smile atop Bree, a horse she bought with her hard-earned money.

All 'Jewel' Needed Was A Child's Love

By Delmer Odell, Harrodsburg, Kentucky

I'VE LOVED HORSES for as long as I can remember. Maybe it came from my grandfather, who could tell his life story by recounting all the horses and mules he had ever owned.

Whatever the reason, I've always been fascinated with the beautiful horse farms of Kentucky and dreamed of raising Thoroughbreds.

I owned a couple of nondescript brood mares, but they were a far cry from the kind of horses Kentucky is famous for. Then one day a friend called about a mare someone wanted to give away.

Her name was "Airman's Jewel," and she was a full sister to a champion Thoroughbred. But she had fertility problems and was also unruly, so the owner wanted to get rid of her.

When she came to live with us, Jewel was as advertised—she snorted and tried to intimidate me every time I turned her in or out of the barn. When I tried to handle her, she acted more like a stallion than a mare.

Our little children liked to ride their tricycles up and down the alleyway of the barn. Whenever Jewel would see them coming, she'd stick her head out the door of her stall, bare her teeth, lay back her ears and snap at them.

She was hardly the farm favorite. We hoped we could put up with her bad behavior long enough to get one foal out of her, then sell her or give her away.

CORRAL PALS. "Our horse just loves kids, but our granddaughter, Angela, wasn't sure she wanted to pet him," comments Rita Furrer of Walcott, Indiana. "So her brother, Joshua, gave her some encouragement."

Miraculous Change

One day, I was having trouble latching the gate while turning Jewel out. Our 7-year-old son, Jeri, was tagging along with me as usual, so I asked him to hold Jewel for a second while I wrestled with the gate.

Jewel's response was amazing. The moment Jeri took hold of her lead rope, she lowered her head and calmed down.

Against my better judgment, Jeri persuaded me to let him lead her around the barn. I walked nervously by his side, but it wasn't necessary—she acted like a pet with him.

From that day on, Jewel was Jeri's horse. It was heart-warming to watch this big, rawboned and high-strung mare respond to the gentle touch of a child.

Before long, Jewel conceived and had a beautiful foal. More importantly, she became the queen of our hearts. She eventually came to trust the rest of our family, too, and lived out her life peacefully on our farm.

Occasionally horses are cantankerous because they are afraid. People can be like that, too. Sometimes all they need to change their disposition is to be shown some childlike love and gentleness.

He Hightailed It for the Backcountry

Alone in the mountains for 2 years, this dude ranch horse finally came back home.

By Jane Van Berkum, Antonito, Colorado

OUR FAMILY operates Rainbow Trout Ranch, a guest ranch set in a picturesque river valley in the San Juan Mountains, a range of the southern Colorado Rockies.

Standing in the shade of the massive porch that hugs the main lodge, we can look south across the horse pasture toward the mountains that drift down toward New Mexico.

Behind us, the mountains rise once more to a plateau of meadows and aspen groves. It's there that we take all-day rides as well as overnight rides.

Getting to the plateau is a steep climb, and both riders and horses get a workout. But the effort is well worth it once we reach what we call the backcountry.

Imagine, if you will, a 70-mile view across the vast San Luis Valley to the Sangre de Cristo Mountains and Mt. Blanca, Colorado's fourth highest peak. This is the backdrop for a unique story that took place several years ago.

The Tale Begins

Although the ranch itself has been in operation since the 1920s, we were just starting our second summer running it. On this particular week in June, seven guests and a wrangler headed up into the backcountry for an overnight ride.

One of the guests was riding a relatively new horse, a splendid roan with a "Z" brand on his hip, which led us to name him "Zorro."

The next morning, the seven guests returned with six hors-

es…and a rather shamefaced wrangler. Sometime in the night, Zorro had apparently spooked and pulled out the metal stake to which his long picket line had been tied.

Having that stake clattering along behind him, in effect chasing him, sent poor Zorro off in a blind rush through the trees and into the heart of the backcountry.

The wrangler didn't discover Zorro's absence until morning and, after a futile search, he and the guests returned to the ranch without him.

Hunted for Horse

That evening, after the guest rides were done for the day, David, my husband, Marc, one of our wranglers, and I went up to the backcountry and searched for Zorro.

In several places we found marks left by the tie-down

SPECTACULAR SCENERY. Guests at the Rainbow Trout Ranch (above) enjoy views like this on overnight rides into the high country.

STRETCHING THEIR LEGS. Horses and their riders (right) take a midmorning break during an all-day trail ride. Is the coffee ready yet?

stake as it was dragged along the ground, but—other than that—there was no sign of our lost horse.

All that summer, we'd search when we could in the evenings, on Sundays and on subsequent overnight trips. Once in a while, we'd hear a neigh, or one of the horses we were riding would prick its ears as though it heard something. But still no Zorro.

In the fall, the cowboys moving the cattle down for the winter spotted Zorro, but he evaded any attempts to herd him down and vanished into the aspens and pines.

Still later, hunters saw him and tried to capture him. But Zorro had gone wild and wasn't looking back.

Horses are very herd-oriented animals and need the company of other horses. We figured that Zorro would eventually make his way down to one of the ranches in the foothills and find some friends for himself. But although we put the word out, we never heard anything.

Cold, Hard Winter

That year, we had a cold, hard winter, and we feared Zorro might not survive on his own. But the following summer—on our very first overnight trip—we spotted a very thin and bedraggled Zorro grazing in a meadow.

He waited until we were quite close before disappearing over a ridge. By this time, he was as wild as an elk and even ran like one.

All that summer, we looked for him whenever we were up in the backcountry, but other than seeing a fleeting glimpse here or there, we didn't find him.

Zorro became legendary. Forest Service officials told us that Zorro couldn't remain running wild as we didn't have a permit to loose-graze horses on federally owned land. But neither they—nor we—could do much about it.

We let it be known that anyone who could catch Zorro could have him. But no one could even find him, let alone corral him. So Zorro remained on the loose.

Refused to Return

Fall blew in and the cowboys and hunters came once again, but Zorro still refused to return to civilization. That winter was mild, but after the snows came and the wildlife descended to lower country, we worried about him up there, shaggy and lonely without even the elk to keep him company.

In late spring, we got a call from folks about 15 miles up the road who had seen a big roan horse grazing by the fast-flowing Conejos River.

We figured it had to be Zorro down from the backcountry to get water, which had become scarce at the higher elevations.

Three of us—Marc, David and I—gathered our best roping horses, our ropes and all the gear we could think of and prepared ourselves for the ride of our lives.

We figured this was it—after 2 years, it was time to bring Zorro home no matter what we had to ride through. Thus determined, we set off.

The horse the neighbors had seen was indeed Zorro. He looked fat and sleek, and was grazing peacefully by the river when we spotted him.

Made Our Plans

Zorro had conveniently chosen to be near some old corrals used to bring the summer cattle in and out of the backcountry. So from a cautious distance, we made plans to get him to the pens…with about 10 backup and just-in-case plans besides.

STANDING PROUD. Mounted on Zorro, Jane Van Berkum carries the American flag at the start of the weekly rodeo held at the guest ranch.

Well, the whole thing took about 10 minutes. There was no crazy riding through rough country, no spectacular roping or magnificent capture under impossible circumstances.

Instead, Zorro calmly trotted along behind Marc toward the corrals, while David and I posted ourselves in strategic places to dissuade Zorro from making a break.

But he never even thought about it. He merely entered the corrals and waited for us. He was very nervous and did a lot of snorting, but he let me catch him. Later that night, back at the ranch, I saddled and rode him, and he behaved like a perfect gentleman.

And he still is. He's surefooted as a mountain goat and savvy as they come. I've ridden many horses, and hope to ride many more, but there'll never be another like Zorro.

I've ridden him exclusively for 7 years now, often in the backcountry. When I lead guests on overnight rides, I picket him to a stout pine tree, but he never even tightens the rope. On our morning and afternoon riding breaks, he grazes quietly nearby, reins dragging gently in the grass.

But once in a while, he just stands, still as stone, and gazes off into the distant backcountry.

When "AJ" came into our lives about 10 years ago, he was dirty, neglected and missing one eye.

It was easy to read his thoughts that day as we peered through the bars of the stall. If the pinned-back ears on this 12-year-old gelding didn't convey the message, then turning his backside to us did.

"Just go away and leave me alone," he seemed to say.

Despite the attitude, we sensed an even deeper emotion…despair. It's no wonder. His former owner rarely came to visit or check on him, and he was never allowed to frolic in the pasture with the rest of the horses.

The poor thing had no muscle tone, and he was so filthy that we could hardly tell the difference between his white body and occasional brown markings.

But, one eye and all, he was still a horse—and that's all our 10-year-old daughter, Shauna, cared about.

We were told that AJ was a Medicine Hat, a breed of horses recognized for their distinct coloration. Most of them are all white or white with a few patches of dark coloring around the eyes, chest, flanks or tail.

The history of the breed can be traced back to several Native American tribes, who thought these white horses were special because of their intelligence and rare markings. Medicine Hats were the most valuable and respected of all their horses.

Unfortunately, AJ had not been valued like his ancestors. He lost his right eye as a yearling, when he was either kicked or gored by a bull. Left untreated, the wound became cancerous, and the eye eventually had to be removed.

Grueling Process

No one bothered telling us that this scrawny, scrappy-looking horse was about the orneriest critter at the stable. Had we known, we never would have let Shauna on his back.

Day after day, AJ fought us every step of the way—from

Love Helped a One-Eyed Gelding See His Potential

Neglected horse triumphed over a life of hardships to become a champion …and a 4-H girl's best friend.

By Carole Ann Lee, Portland, Oregon

things as simple as putting on a halter to the big stuff, like tightening the cinch. The first year was a grueling process of teaching Shauna the importance of a firm but gentle hand and showing AJ that he could trust us.

Finally, after nearly 18 months of gentle care and Shauna's calm, quiet nature, we were rewarded one day when AJ perked his ears and gave a soft nicker of recognition when he saw us.

Up until then, he had been emotionally dead. It made no difference that we brought him carrots, cleaned his stall each day and gave him a quality diet of hay, grain, vitamins, exercise and, most of all, love.

Friendship Develops

The trust between Shauna and AJ grew into a bond that was clearly visible. No longer was it a soft nicker that greeted us, but a full-blown, roof-raising whinny!

As time passed, AJ gradually turned from one of the homeliest, most cantankerous horses in the barn to a solid, well-muscled animal that loved life and his family.

When Shauna was old enough, she became involved in 4-H. Between AJ's eagerness to please and the expertise of Shauna's riding coach, they were soon winning ribbons at the county fair and horse shows.

With each new ribbon they won, we watched with amazement as AJ's self-esteem returned to him. His fluid gait and confidence made him a joy to watch in the showring.

This bliss, however, did not last long as cancer again raised its ugly head. AJ underwent surgery, and the prognosis was not good. The veterinarian said he had "one good year left and one bad one".

The news was devastating, but as we prepared for the worst, AJ prepared for the best. In record time, he recovered both physically and emotionally from his surgery. Just 2 months later, Shauna took him to the county fair.

Not only did they earn high marks from the judges, but they also qualified for state competition. Out of love and consideration for AJ's health, Shauna withdrew her name from the state team. Just knowing they'd earned the position was reward enough.

More Than Luck

At that point, we didn't know much about Medicine Hat horses and didn't understand the strong spirit AJ had.

Instead of watching his gradual decline like the vet had predicted, AJ proved he was both willing and able to keep going. Shauna continued working and showing him.

Although we felt lucky that AJ continued to remain in good health, a little voice in my head kept saying, "Luck has nothing to do with it. He's a Medicine Hat."

I found out that some Native Americans considered Medicine Hats sacred, ceremonial horses that were only ridden during battles or hunting trips. Riders often believed they were invincible when riding a Medicine Hat.

After 3 good years and still no signs of ill health, we began to wonder if there was an unseen force protecting AJ. "Maybe he's beaten the odds," we thought.

About that time, Shauna was entering her eighth and final year of 4-H. Who would have thought that her 20-year-old, one-eyed gelding would earn one of 4-H's highest county awards? Even up against three professionally trained horses, AJ and Shauna won the 1999 Senior Grand Champion trophies in both Western and English equitation.

AJ may not have understood all the pomp and ceremony, nor the significance of Shauna's final year in 4-H. But there's no doubt in my mind that he sensed the importance of that last 4-H show.

Without Warning

For another year, AJ's cancer showed no signs of returning, and he continued to clean up at open competitions. He gave his heart to Shauna—the little girl who loved him from the moment she first laid eyes on him.

Without warning, however, AJ's health took a sudden nosedive. On June 19, 2000, our beloved friend quietly died in a peaceful field of daisies, with his head resting in Shauna's lap and his family gathered around him for love and support.

Although our hearts still ache with the void he has left, AJ is at last out of pain. He died knowing he was loved.

Indian legend has it that when a Medicine Hat horse dies, its spirit returns to Earth to help guide a newborn Medicine Hat colt or filly. If that's true, there's a foal somewhere out there that couldn't have a better role model. After all, it takes a truly special horse to rise above the loss of an eye and become a champion like AJ.

Editor's Note: *AJ's inspiring story earned him a place in the Medicine Hat Horse Registry Hall of Fame. For more information about this breed, visit the Web site at www.themhhr.com.*

BLIND FAITH. After earning his trust, Shauna taught "AJ" how to turn on his blind side (above). As a team, they competed in horse shows (below) and were even together for Shauna's senior class photo (left).

A Country Boy's Senses Aren't So Common

He sees, smells, hears, tastes and touches nature in a special way.

By Dareld Satern, Vancouver, Washington

I JUST figured it out. I know why the country keeps calling those of us who were raised there. It's because our five senses are more acutely attuned to nature than those of our city neighbors.

There's been a lot written about the scent of newly mown hay or freshly plowed ground, but it's more than that. A farmer's economic survival depends on having well-developed senses.

For instance, your eyes and sense of touch tell you when the hay is ready to be cut. But you dare not cut it until you get up one morning and feel the lightness of the air and a slight breeze from the north, indicating dry weather is on the way. If the air is heavy, you know you must wait, particularly if you detect a fresh breeze from the southwest.

It's the same with combining grain. Threshing a few heads of wheat in your hands tells you when it's ready to harvest, but first you must look, feel and smell to determine the weather.

Virtual Paradise

For me, growing up on a farm was a virtual paradise. But I took it all for granted because I didn't know any differently. I figured everyone was surrounded by the same sense-stimulating beauty as I was.

There was a window at the foot of my bed, and on warm summer nights, I'd lie there with my nose pressed up against the screen, listening for the night sounds of the farm.

As I lay in the stillness, I'd hear the nighthawks diving for bugs to feed their young. They had a particular call as they climbed for altitude, then all of a sudden, they would fold back their wings and dive straight down, making a "swoosh" sound as they pulled out of their dive.

I could also hear the owls down by the river and the pigeons settling down to roost in the barn during those balmy nights. After a day's work was done, it was a pleasure just to listen to these quiet sounds of the night.

Vine-Ripened Berries

There was a river that ran along the west side of our farm, and gradually meandered past the north end before reaching the neighbor's place. I had a half mile of stream to swim, boat, fish and explore without ever seeing another person.

As a boy, it was my job to go down to the woods and get the cows for milking. There was a deep ditch that crossed the pasture where the wild berries really thrived. As I passed through there, the aroma of the dampness, the coolness of the shade and the taste of the berries usually made me a little late in getting the cows back to the barn.

Each season on the farm had its own sights, sounds, scents and feel. The dry grass of winter had a scent much different from the wet new grass of spring. The dry leaves of fall created an atmosphere entirely apart from summer.

Sensational Sunsets

We had a wooden fence that ran between the barn and the machine shed, and from there, we could look down over our bottomland and the river. On the hill beyond, there were tall fir trees on our neighbor's farm, and the summer sun set right between those trees. Every evening, we were treated to a picture-perfect sunset while sitting on the fence.

Photography is something I enjoy and have more time for now. It's a hobby that requires a person to see things in a more analytical way. Farming develops that eye for seeing detail, whether you're looking at crops or animals or a spectacular country scene. I think I'm a better photographer because of my early training on the farm.

So it's with developed senses that I remember the farm. If I'm out taking photos, fishing or just going for a drive, I feel more attuned to the country because I grew up a farm boy.

Photo taken in northwest Missouri by Eric Berndt/The Image Finders

When Mom Fixed Sunday Dinner for the Preacher...

He had a mighty hearty appetite, especially for fried chicken.

By Terry Keeling, Richmond, Texas

WHEN I was growing up in the 1940s and early '50s, it was customary for folks from the congregation to take turns inviting the preacher and his family over for Sunday dinner.

Country preachers didn't get paid much, and this was one of the perks of the job. They knew this and expected it.

There was speculation that a few preachers even fasted all day on Saturday in preparation for the free meal coming up on Sunday. I don't know if this was true or not, but I can remember seeing some preachers put away an unbelievable amount of food at our dinner table.

By the way, when I talk about Sunday dinner, I'm referring to the noon meal. The word "lunch" wasn't in our vocabulary at that time. Also, back in those days, we never referred to a man of the cloth as a minister or pastor—he was a preacher.

When it was our turn to bring the preacher home for dinner, my mother would fix most of the meal early in the morning, before we went to church. She'd cook the peas, make potato salad and bake pecan pie.

She would also have the fixin's for the corn bread mixed up and the chicken ready for the frying pan. That way, when we got back from church, all she had to do was warm up the peas, pop the corn bread in the oven and fry the chicken.

World's Eating Record

Fried chicken was the traditional fare for these Sunday dinners, probably because, like everyone else, we always had lots of chickens available. Early Sunday morning, Mother would send me out in the yard to chase down a couple of our finest fryers, pluck and clean them and bring them in the house.

This abundance of chickens may be the reason for the almost legendary affinity that country preachers had for fried chicken in those days. I'm told that with regards to the world's record for the most fried chicken consumed at one sitting, the first 100 spots on the list are held by preachers. I haven't been able to confirm this, but based on my childhood observations, I don't doubt it for a minute.

I can remember one preacher in particular, who came for Sunday dinner. I'll call him Brother Smith to protect his identity. He was a tall, lanky man, who always looked hungry. Mother would set the heaping platter of chicken in front of Brother Smith, because she knew that's where it would wind up anyway.

Brother Smith would first say the blessing. Normally, he was pretty long-winded when he prayed, but with that platter of chicken right in front of his face, he usually cut it pretty short.

Once he dug into his food, Brother Smith didn't talk much. He was an ambidextrous eater, and I still recall him with two drumsticks—one in each hand. After about 20 minutes, he'd loosen his belt a couple of notches, which was Mother's cue to bring out the second platter of chicken.

We always wound up with one piece of chicken left on

Joe Sibilski

sides, I guess he had to save room for the pecan pie.

About 40 minutes later, most of the food would be gone, and we would all get up from the table, go out on the front porch and sit for a while.

Times have changed in the past 50 years, and it seems like nobody invites the preacher home for Sunday dinner anymore. It makes me wonder if country preachers still have an appetite for fried chicken, or whether they've learned to acquire other tastes in divinity school nowadays.

the platter. Brother Smith had manners—either that, or it was the stern warning look Sister Smith gave him. Whatever the reason, he wouldn't take the last piece of chicken from the platter. He'd look at it—a lot—but he wouldn't take it. Be-

SEND-OFF. Issues roll off the mail line in the order your mailman delivers them.

Roll the Presses!

Here's a behind-the-scenes look at how Country is printed.

THE PROCESS of taking your photo and printing it in the pages of *Country* is a computer geek's delight, because nowadays, so much of it is done electronically.

But it still must start with a sharp high-quality photo. Today's printing technology is amazing, but it can't create a silk purse out of a sow's ear as we say in the country. In other words, it can't turn a fuzzy dull photo into the vivid, almost lifelike pictures readers have come to expect in *Country*.

Once we've selected a photo and our artist incorporates it into a layout, all done by computer, this layout is sent electronically to our prepress department at Reiman Publications. There, the photo is run through a special scanner that analyzes the different hues and separates them into four basic printing colors: black, yellow, magenta (red) and cyan (blue).

Combinations of these four colors create the entire palette of colors you see printed in the magazine. For example, green is basically a combination of cyan and yellow. If it's the tender green of an early spring leaf, it'll contain more yellow and less cyan. If it's a deep summer green of a lush cornfield, the combination will be heavier on the cyan and probably include some black, too.

The beautiful fall foliage of another picture is typically a combination of magenta, yellow and a dash of black. A brilliant multicolored sunset contains a mixture of all four colors.

Press Costs $15,000,000

These combinations of colors for each photo, along with the type, are then transmitted digitally to the printer. For many years, *Country* has been printed at Quad Graphics (which is headquartered in Pewaukee, Wisconsin, down the road from our offices), one of the largest printing companies in the industry.

The printer then uses these color combinations to create printing plates—one for each of the four basic colors.

These plates are then attached to large cylinders on the press to transfer the exact amount of each of the four ink colors to the paper.

The paper comes on large rolls, which is threaded through the press in such a way that the ink is applied to both sides of the paper at the same time. A typical issue of *Country* requires about 450,000 pounds of paper. That's enough to fill 10 semitrucks!

After all of this makeready is done, it's time to crank up the presses. *Country* is now being printed on a press so huge that all 64 pages of the body of the magazine are printed on one pass through the press. (The four-page cover section is printed separately on heavier paper on a different press.)

Once the press starts rolling, it's nothing but a blur of color. That's because this new press operates at a speed of about 70,000 impressions per hour. Figuring 64 pages printed at a time, that means this press is actually printing about 4,480,000 pages per hour!

By the way, this press costs over $15 million. Ouch!

The press also automatically folds the paper in such a way that when it's run through the bindery, the magazine is bound and stapled with all of the pages in the proper order.

Pinch Pennies on Postage

The next step is the mail line, and here's where another miracle of computer technology occurs. You see, the names and addresses of subscribers are ink-jetted onto the magazines in a specific order so that every post office across the country receives a bundle of magazines consisting of subscribers in that zip code. If there are three rural routes within a certain post office, we provide three bundles—one for each mail carrier.

Thanks to computerized mail programs, we even know the order in which your mailman delivers the mail on your rural route, and we address the magazines in that sequence! That saves your mailman from having to sort them before heading out on the route.

We do all of this to save the post office work…which saves on our postage cost…and enables us to print and send your magazine for the lowest subscription price possible.

Bartering Is One of the Joys of Country Living

By Inge Perreault, Oxford, New Jersey

SOME FOLKS may think bartering is a lost art in this age of high finance and credit cards. But it's alive and well here in the country.

I have a small flock of chickens, and the other day I asked my neighbor down the road if he needed some eggs. My hens are the type that lay those colossal brown eggs, and he gratefully accepted a carton held shut by a rubber band, since the eggs were so large that the lid wouldn't close.

In exchange, my neighbor offered me three heads of lettuce, three cucumbers, three eggplants and three peppers from his garden. What a treasure!

But after I returned home, I realized there was no way my husband and I could enjoy all of this bounty now that we're "empty nesters." So I called the neighbors up the road.

They're a retired couple in their 80s, and I offered them some of the fresh veggies. I gave them a head of lettuce, one cucumber, an eggplant and two peppers.

As luck would have it, they had just received a carton of peaches from a visiting relative and were all too happy to load me up with some. Now, my carton of eggs had provided me with two heads of lettuce, one pepper, two cucumbers, two eggplants and a whole bunch of fresh juicy peaches.

The entire matter came full circle when I took the outer lettuce leaves and the peelings from the cucumbers, eggplants and peaches out to the chicken yard, where they were a welcome addition to the hens' regular chicken feed. Soon I'll be blessed with more of their huge brown eggs…and so will my neighbors.

Photo: Steven J. Korba

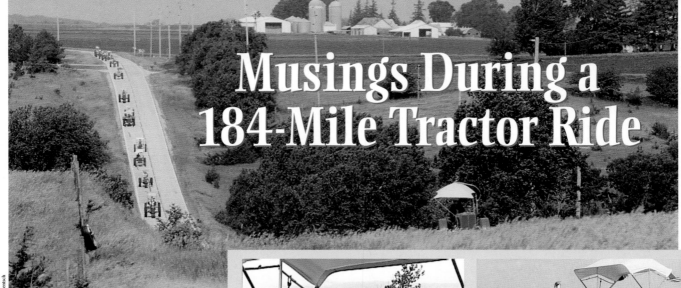

Musings During a 184-Mile Tractor Ride

You have a lot of time to think while purring along on a tractor.

By Roy Reiman

THIS SUMMER I joined the "Great Iowa Tractor Ride." And I can't wait to do it again next year.

During the sixth year of this annual event, *450* old-time tractors hummed single file, about 10 mph, along a rural route from northwest Iowa to central Iowa.

The parade stretched out for nearly *5 miles*, and over the 3-day span, we covered *184 miles* with tractors of every make and size.

Mine was a 1953 M Farmall, just like the one we had on the Iowa farm where I grew up. It was loaned to me by an old classmate who collects and renovates vintage tractors as a hobby.

Purring along on that sturdy old M brought back all sorts of youthful memories. Plus, you see things at 10 mph from the seat of a slow-moving tractor you never see from a speeding car.

Thoughts Along the Way

Here are a few of my observations during that 3-day trek along that winding rural route:

• Everybody waves in Iowa. Whether they're in a car, a pickup or on a tractor, these friendly folks wave at almost every stranger. And even if a guy is carrying a bale of hay, he'll jerk his chin up at you as a greeting as you pass.

• Why do they bother to mow the grass along roads? If the grass isn't blocking views and it isn't weed-invested, isn't that an unnecessary cost?

HUMMING ALONG. Here's me on my 1953 M, just like the one we had on our farm. Top photos show part of the 450 tractors stretched out for more than 5 miles along the winding rural route.

• Speaking of weeds, there really aren't any weeds these days in Iowa's corn and bean fields. The fields are clean and beautiful. Modern herbicides obviously really work!

• There aren't many fences anymore, either, dividing fields. On today's large farms, a single crop can stretch for a half mile or more undeterred by fences. One huge, waving field of blue-green oats reminded me of an ocean right in rural Iowa.

• Seems like it's always windy across the level plains of Iowa. A joke I heard: One day the wind stopped blowing, and everybody fell over!

• Folks sure eat well in this state. When I got home, I told my wife it was the first time I'd had a meal without mashed potatoes and gravy in 3 days!

• At 10 mph you see things like yellow butterflies chasing each other...large gardens that are obviously more than a hobby...personal landscaping touches that make a farm unique. One farmer had carved an old stump into a really artistic piece.

• Gosh, the rows of corn and beans are *straight*. That doesn't make the crop any better, but it sure exhibits a lot of pride in "doing it right."

• As a whole, I noticed grain farmers

Bill Gentsch

keep their places neater than livestock farmers. I concluded most people with livestock are just too busy to find time to mow, weed, paint, etc.

● Do you know that you can actually *smell* corn as you pass by slowly? It's a refreshing, satisfying aroma.

● Every now and then I noticed a tall, lone tree standing in the middle of a large field. I once heard that farmers use trees like that to ward off lightning; it usually strikes the highest point.

● "Urban farmers," as Iowans are prone to call city folks who live on a few acres in the country, don't have the same disdain for weeds as "real farmers." They tend to let thistles grow around their mailboxes, apparently not aware how fast those things will spread.

● I noticed some gardeners have found a good use for old tires. They put them around their tomatoes to support the plants, draw in heat and hold in moisture. Good idea!

● While I've always been partial to Farmalls, I have to admit that some of those early model Olivers were surely the *prettiest* tractors ever made, with their tasteful combination of green, gold and red. They stood out in the crowd.

● I noticed that each section of a concrete highway is numbered about every 100 yards or so. I'm sure this is done

so that maintenance crews can say, "There's a problem between sections 173 and 174…," or something like that. Anyway, I never knew that before.

● It was nice to see and hear meadowlarks again. I liked hearing them sing as a kid in Iowa, but we don't have as many in Wisconsin. Speaking of birds, I repeatedly saw red-winged blackbirds dive from power lines down to nests in deep grass of roadside ditches, and wondered how they can find those nests back amidst the sameness of all that grass stretching for miles.

● Whatever happened to corncribs? I know farmers don't use them to store ear corn anymore, so I guess they must have taken all those cribs down. I saw only *two* corncribs along this entire 184-mile route!

● They knew a lot about making seats on tractors way back when. The seat on my 1953 Farmall, though not thickly padded, had just the right

amount of spring below it; I found it just as comfortable as our family car I'd driven to Iowa.

● I found we were going *exactly* 10 mph. I timed 5 separate miles back-to-back, and we reached the mile crossroad right at 6 minutes each time, which would be 10 mph. (You get time to figure out things like this when you're purring along for hours.)

● It was nice that the event organizers routed us off main streets in small towns and had us drive past local senior centers, where dozens of old farmers were eagerly waiting to see all these tractors from yesteryear. I'm sure that gave them plenty to talk about at dinner that night.

● Every acre is *working* in Iowa. There just doesn't seem to be any "wasteland" here. It seems every fertile piece of land is being used to produce something.

● Every person seems to be *working* in Iowa as well. They don't just dislike laziness in Iowa, they *loathe* it. You don't see people just sitting around …unless there's a good reason for it …like when our 5-mile-long parade passed.

I was glad to see that many farm families—right in the midst of their busiest season—decided to take the day off with their kids, sit under a shade tree near the road and watch and wave at this unusual sight of 450 smiling tractor drivers, who were waving back.

I threw candy to a lot of the kids (and to the senior center folks as well).

As I did so, I often thought those kids had no way of knowing that I was enjoying this drive far more than they were going to enjoy those treats.

With the memories this drive revived…the comraderie I experienced with other folks…the fresh air, the food, the sights…I can't wait to do this again. ※

Jean Schell

Bill Gentsch

GOOD CONVERSATIONS were easy to come by at each stop, with the tractors lined up in orderly fashion. The 184-mile route took us right through the heart of many small towns, where church groups and 4-H clubs served up some incredible farm food.

C'mon, Let's Head For the Country…

Summer is upon us, and the backroads are beckoning. It's time for this issue's "armchair tour" of rural America.

DON'T FENCE 'EM IN. These horses on a ranch in Montana seem mighty interested in something on the other side of the fence. Could it be the grass is greener over there?

TREE-MENDOUS. A giant sequoia towers over the landscape (left) in Kings Canyon National Park in California. The sequoias growing there are over 2,000 years old.

ALL AGLOW. A patch of flowers in a barnyard in Wyoming County, New York (below) dazzles and delights amid the lengthening shadows at the close of another day.

LIFE'S A BOWL OF CHERRIES. Country kids, cats and summer just naturally go together. This happy-go-lucky farm girl from Iowa is certainly proof of that.

SIGN OF THINGS TO COME. A traffic sign in Antrim, Ohio advises motorists of Amish buggy traffic—another way of saying there's a scenic road ahead.

Terry Wild

Roger Kingsley

COLOR THEM PATRIOTIC. A family displays Old Glory from the porch of their country home.

HAY FEVER. Hay harvest is at a feverish pitch on this Pennsylvania farm. Like they say, "You gotta make hay while the sun shines."

TASTE TREAT. There's nothing like the taste of tomatoes picked fresh from the garden—especially the first ones of the season.

Jack Westhead

The Best of COUNTRY

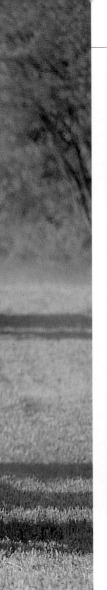

IN THE SWIM OF THINGS. These Iowa youngsters are doing swimmingly as they cool off with a dip in the Mississippi River.

A TOUCH OF VELVET. In the soft light of the late-afternoon sun, a deer grazes peacefully in Olympic National Park in Washington.

PRISTINE STREAM. Clear water reveals the boulder-strewn bottom of the East Branch of the Ausable River flowing through New York's Adirondack Mountains.

MERRY MEADOW. Wildflowers color a sun-splashed meadow in the Bighorn Mountains of Wyoming.

Jennifer Bartow Waters

HOWDY, NEIGHBOR. You're sure to meet friendly folks at every turn when you head for the country.

COUNTRY SKYSCRAPER. A whirling windmill is silhouetted (left) as the summer sun sets in South Dakota.

IN TALL COTTON. Cotton-candy clouds billowing on the horizon add to the sky-high feeling of roaming the wide-open spaces of eastern Washington.

PEACEFUL VALLEY. Stacks of baled hay (below) frame the snowcapped mountains in the distance on a ranch in Oregon's lovely Wallowa Valley.

Bonnie Nance

PAWS FOR A PICTURE. This cat appears to have stopped to smell the roses on a summer's day on farm in Kentucky.

SIGN OF THE SEASON. Looking almost as bright as the sun, black-eyed Susans in bloom are a surefire sign of summer.

Mike Briner

TURN THE PAGE for a gorgeous view of dusk settling over fields of dry green peas (used to make split pea soup) in Washington's Palouse region.

BRING BACK THE OLD 'COUNTRY' PHONE COMPANY!

IF YOU grew up in the country like I did, you have to be frustrated as I am these days when you place a long-distance call.

AT&T *supposedly* tried to make it easier when they changed things so you could make a credit card call without the help of the operator. But correctly pushing 25 digits (including the long-distance number you're dialing, plus all the digits of your credit card) is *not* necessarily easier than it was in the old days, when we just dealt with a friendly hometown operator.

That fact brings back vivid memories of the day in 1950 when I was a novice sea hand aboard a U.S. Navy cruiser. We were based in Philadelphia, a *big* city to me, considering I was just 6 months out of high school and fresh from the plains of South Dakota.

One Friday night in November, we were granted shore leave at the conclusion of a 2-week training cruise. Homesick and seasick, I immediately headed for the row of pay phones that lined every navy dock in those days.

I deposited a carefully preserved nickel (remember?) and dialed "O". Here is a roughly verbatim account of what transpired after the Philadelphia operator answered:

"I'd like to place a station-to-station collect call to the Bob Pence residence in Columbia, South Dakota, please," I said in my best telephone voice.

She was sure she had heard wrong. "You mean Columbia, South Carolina, don't you?"

"No, I mean Columbia, South Dakota." I had tried to call home once before, and I was ready for *that* one.

"Certainly. What's the number, please?" I could tell she still didn't believe me.

"They don't have a number," I mumbled.

The Philadelphia operator was incredulous. "They don't have a *number*?"

"No, ma'am."

"I can't complete the call without a number. Do you have it?" she demanded.

I didn't relish my role as a country bumpkin, but I knew authority when I heard it. "Well...the only thing I know is...two longs and a short."

I think that was the first time she *snorted*. "I'll get the number for you," she said with an admirable amount of tolerance. "One moment, please."

In deliberate succession, she dialed an operator in Cleveland, who was asked to call one in Chicago, who dialed one in Minneapolis. Then Minneapolis was asked to dial a Sioux City operator, who was asked to ring Sioux Falls, who rang Aberdeen and then—*finally*—Aberdeen rang the operator at my hometown of Columbia.

By this time, Philadelphia's patience was wearing thin. But when Columbia answered, she knew what had to be done.

"The number for the Bob Pence residence, please," Philadelphia said, back in control.

Columbia didn't hesitate an instant. "That's two longs and a short," she responded matter-of-factly.

Philadelphia was obviously stunned, but she plowed on. "I have a collect call from Philadelphia, Pennsylvania for anyone at that number. Will you ring, please?"

Again, Columbia didn't miss a beat. "They are not home."

Philadelphia paused to digest this. She didn't want to set herself up again, so she relayed the message to me that I'd already heard. "There is no one at that number. Would you like to try again later?" no doubt hoping her shift would soon end.

Columbia quickly interrupted: "Is that you, Dick?"

"Yeah, Margaret. Where are the folks?"

Philadelphia was baffled, but she knew she had to look out for the company. "Sir...madam...you can't talk..."

Columbia paid no mind. "They're up at the schoolhouse at the basketball game. Want me to ring?"

I knew I was on real thin ice with Philadelphia, so I said, "It's probably too much trouble."

Philadelphia was still trying to protect the company. By this time, though, she was out of words. "But...but..." she stammered.

Columbia was oblivious. "No trouble at all, Dick. It's halftime." My nickel was still in the phone, and I didn't want to start over, so I caved in. "All right."

Mustering her most official tone, Philadelphia made one last effort: "This is a *station-to-station* collect call!"

"That's all right, honey," Columbia said. "I'll just put it on Bob's bill."

Philadelphia was still protesting when the phone rang and was answered at the schoolhouse.

"I have a station-to-station call for Bob Pence," Philadelphia said, by now realizing that Ma Bell may have been bested.

"This is he," said the answering voice.

Philadelphia gave up. "Go ahead."

I'm glad I couldn't see her face when I began my end of the conversation the way all country folks do. "Hi, Dad. How's the weather?"

"Humph!" Philadelphia said, then clicked off the line.

I don't like to think about it, but AT&T no doubt began to automate its long-distance service the next Monday morning. And now look where we are.

—*Richard Pence*
Fairfax, Virginia

Country's Favorite Alaskan

In 1979, a stressed-out Boise, Idaho nurse packed up her two young sons and moved to a remote windswept ranch in Alaska's Aleutian Islands.

Ten years later, Cora Holmes took *Country* readers by storm with the first of her heartfelt and inspiring stories about raising a family and making a living on America's last frontier.

Reader response was so overwhelming, she followed up with eight more articles and two books: *Good-Bye, Boise...Hello, Alaska* and *"Dear Cora..."*.

Thanks to Cora's talent for storytelling and willingness to share heart and home, we almost feel like part of her family— and that she's a part of ours. You'll feel the same way after reading her story in the next few pages. ♂

Photo: Julie Habel

Welcome to Chernofski Sheep Ranch

A few of our favorite stories about life on the far fringes of civilization.

By Cora Holmes, Unalaska, Alaska

CHUCK'S HORSE "Grey" stumbled to his front knees on the steep narrow trail in front of me.

"Jump off!" I shouted, startling my own mount so that he skittered sideways on the loose rock. As I held on to my saddle horn with both hands, Chuck pulled Grey's head up firmly and got him back on his feet.

"What happened?" I asked as Chuck made a slow turn on the hillside and came abreast above me, his good-natured face already ruddy-cheeked from the cold.

"I don't know, Mom. Grey does that all the time." He grinned and patted his horse's neck. "I guess he feels the sudden need for a word of prayer and down he goes, to his knees."

What a difference, I thought as I watched Chuck guide his horse carefully across the rocky frozen terrain studded with tussocks of brown grass, lichen clumps and moss. Just 2 years before, this confident 16-year-old was a skinny white-faced boy who had gotten airsick just before the floatplane landed here.

My son Randall, meanwhile, was another matter entirely! He'd bounded off the plane with his older brother's new fishing pole and broke it in four pieces before Chuck's feet ever touched the ground.

A distant "Whoop!" alerted me my 12-year-old son was approaching. Bullheaded, determined, incorrigible and precious, he was Milton's shadow from the moment they met. At 10, Randall was ready for a hero, and Milton Holmes was sure enough hero material.

A New Life

Fifty-eight years old, slim, wiry, ginger-haired, with a nose too big for his thin face, Milton walked into our lives with a slight limp and the kindest green eyes I'd ever seen. His kindness drew us like a magnet—even his dogs loved him.

While I waited for cattle and horsemen to appear on the skyline of Anderson Butte, I wondered again at the fate that prompted me to answer a "help wanted" ad in a Boise, Idaho newspaper in August 1979.

THEY'RE NEVER ALONE. Milt has his faithful sheep dogs. Cora has her little orphan lambs. And they always have each other.

At 33, I was ready for a change from working the night shift in Boise's neonatal intensive care unit. Chronically tired, always irritable from a high-pressure job, I was a miserable mother, and I knew it.

The position of housekeeper and secretary for a remote ranch on an island I'd never heard of sounded perfect. The minute I stepped off the plane, I knew I was home. After 16 months, Milton and I were married.

A stiff breeze lifted the hair on my cheek. I thought about where we were on Earth's surface. Closer to Siberia than the continental United States, enclosed by the Bering Sea to the north and the Pacific Ocean to the south, our ranch is buffeted by gales, hidden by fog and jarred by earthquakes.

Yet, it's the most peaceful spot I've ever found.

We're Isolated But Not Lonely

OUR HOME, Chernofski Sheep Ranch, is located on the northwestern end of Unalaska Island. We are only one of three big ranches in the Aleutian Island chain. Ours encompasses 152,000 leased and deeded acres.

My husband, Milt, came here from Idaho in 1949 to work as a foreman and then bought the ranch in 1964. We raise Columbia sheep, Hereford and black baldy cattle and Morgan saddle horses to work the ranch. There are wild horse herds on the island, too, and we sometimes catch and train them.

It's very isolated here, since our island is accessible only by floatplane or boat. We receive mail only four or five times a year, and communicate with the nearest town, 80 miles away, by marine band radio. Sometimes we don't see another person for months at a time.

We order supplies once every 2 years, and have them shipped from Seattle by freight boat. This includes flour, sugar, coffee and other staples, plus oats and barley for the horses. We always order milk replacer, too, for all the orphan lambs I somehow latch onto against my better instincts!

We are mostly self-sufficient. Our home is heated with coal left here by the military in 1945. For lighting, we use kerosene lamps and electricity in the evening from a diesel generator. We also use the generator for shearing our sheep and for charging our batteries.

We raise all our own meat—beef, lamb and chickens—and we fish in the bay for cod and halibut and in the streams for salmon and trout. We try to time our calving so that we have a cow milking most of the time, and we keep some layer hens for eggs.

We make our living from the ranch, marketing wool, beef and lamb, woolen blankets and tanned pelts from winter trapping and hunting. During the summer months, we lease our bunkhouse facilities to a tourist company, and provide meals and guides for their guests.

175 mph Winds

Our oldest son, Chuck, 23, is a commercial fisherman based in the village of Unalaska on the other end of the island. His brother, Randall, 19, is still a big help on the ranch. He loves horses and is presently breaking three colts and two 2-year-olds.

His horse "Monty" is a vicious mustang that he caught from the wild herd on the island. He's now Randall's best saddle horse, but he still has to be watched because he'll bite or kick.

For fun, Randall fishes in the bay and beachcombs our miles and miles of shoreline. He also likes a trip to town when he can get it, but that isn't often due to the distance and the infrequency of floatplanes and boats.

Reading is important to him, too, especially in the winter when we have only a few hours of daylight. He likes to read Westerns and science fiction.

Milt oversees everything and fixes about anything. He's the plumber, electrician, carpenter, veterinarian, etc. It's a big responsibility in a place where an error in judgment could get us all killed.

For enjoyment, he reads and listens to the radio on stormy days when it's too tough to even make it to the barn. And we have a lot of days like that—our winds often reach 175 mph, covering us with rain, snow and salt-filled sea spray!

Milt also enjoys ancient Aleut culture—there are numerous village sites dotted around the island, some dating back more than 4,000 years.

No Hamburger Joints

Daily living takes up most of my time. Cooking everything from bread to ice cream 365 days a year takes real staying power. But I enjoy it and try to provide attractive, nourishing meals.

There are no hamburger joints out here, where you can just grab a milk shake if you don't like what's being served at home!

When I want to relax, I enjoy reading. We all enjoy *Country* magazine with its beautiful photography and articles about rural people we can relate ↵

to. I also enjoy spinning and weaving. There is a never-ending supply of wool in the barn, and the hills are full of exciting natural dyes.

I also love to hike. Our ranch's rugged terrain, with its high cliffy ridges and short mossy tundra, offers views that I often wish I could share with others.

And the Aleutian wildflowers and grasses get so lush in our damp, temperate summers that they look like bright-colored tropical foliage.

There's lots of wildlife to see, too, from sea otter families napping on the reef to Aleutian red foxes and eagles, both of which are predators and take their share of new lambs each spring.

There is a butte 2 miles from our ranch headquarters, rising 900 feet above sea level. From the top, I can sit on a boulder and look down at our ranch in miniature, with its green pastures and blue water.

Life out here doesn't change much from year to year. I guess we enjoy that, along with living in the slow lane and doing for ourselves, pretty much like country people everywhere.

Two Hands Are Nice, but...

WE'VE RECEIVED more than 700 letters from *Country* subscribers since the last article. Every time the mail comes—which is still only four or five times a year here—there's another bundle of letters from our *Country* friends. Probably the most common questions from letter-writers are why we want to live here on this isolated island, and how we handle medical emergencies.

We came to Alaska for the adventure and challenge, and to get away from the crunch of civilization. I'd rather be going down a steep hill on a runaway horse with a broken bridle than driving a car in the lower 48!

When we moved here, we took responsibility for our own lives. In a medical emergency, we have only ourselves to turn to. Between here and Unalaska village are 110 miles of mountainous unsurveyed country.

After reaching the village, the nearest hospital is still 800 miles away in Anchorage. So we practice a lot of preventive medicine, eat well, dress for the climate, respect the elements and take our chances.

Quick and Deadly

I had waited 5 months before coming out from Chernofski because I thought the lump beside my thumb came from breaking a blood vessel while helping Milt and Chuck butcher steers.

But I had a rare sarcoma, quick to spread and deadly. The minute the surgeon told me, I knew I was dead. I could see it in his eyes. Even with amputation and industrial doses of chemotherapy, my chances of surviving longer than a year were less than 25%.

In a strange numb state, sort of like I had forgotten how to breathe, I consented to surgery only if the cancer hadn't spread to my lymph system.

When I woke up in the recovery room without my right hand, I knew I had a chance to live, and everyone I loved made sure I had a lot of reasons.

Two hands are nice, of course, but one does most of the work, and the other acts as one side of a "vise." I learned that 2

ONCE A RANCHER... Randall (above) was a longshoreman and Chuck (below) had his own commercial fishing boat when these photos were taken. But when they visited the ranch to help illustrate their mom's first book, they fell into the daily routine as if they'd never left.

Photos: Julie Habel

MEALTIME PUZZLE. Milt and Cora get food delivered by ship every 2 years. This shipment of cans was caught in a storm and lost its labels, leading to some creative meal planning.

weeks after my amputation, when I attempted a counted cross-stitch picture and realized I couldn't thread a needle.

After handing the needle to Milt several times, I said, "I wish I could do this myself."

"I don't mind," he answered. "But when I'm not here, just do this:" He jabbed the needle into my denim jeans just above the knee. "Try that."

My Big Breakthrough

It worked! My first vise. In the months that followed, I discovered a great many vises. Teeth, for instance, or under my arm. Knees work, too.

Milton modified my kitchen and spinning tools to fit my hook so I could use my right arm as the primary worker. This accomplishment encouraged me so much that after I mastered sweeping, mopping and washing dishes, I went on to bigger and better things.

But I'm embarrassed to admit I still can't write with my left hand so anyone can read it. Whenever I write Chuck a check, he just shakes his head and teases, "I bet I'm the only guy at the bank whose check looks like it was written by a second grader."

We Find Time For Fun, Too

THIS MORNING Milt punched holes in a can of creamed corn and tried to pour it on his cereal. Let me explain why:

Our 2-year supply of groceries had made it safely by boat all the way from Seattle—getting transferred, stored and reloaded several times—until it got to within 20 miles of our island when it got caught in a terrific storm.

Everything was soaked, and the salt water disintegrated the labels from most of the canned food. I love puzzles and rather enjoyed grouping the cans by their code numbers. Now that I know the corn code, we won't mistake it for canned milk again.

However, the look on Milt's face was priceless and well worth all those hours we spent sorting in the storeroom. Before he realized what had happened, he held the can out at arm's length and said, "Whew! This cow needs some penicillin!"

We work hard to survive here. But we also take time out for fun. We beachcomb, sightsee in the boat, and fish for halibut, cod, salmon, Dolly Varden and pogies. We dig clams and pick mussels off the reefs. We pick flowers and dye wool.

We also play horseshoes and enjoy games of Scrabble. Whether working or playing, we have a lot of fun.

Old Man and The Sheep

ONCE UPON A TIME, a little old man and his crippled wife lived on a sheep ranch in the Aleutian Islands. Their children had grown up and gone. All they had left were the sheep.

Every day the little old man looked at them through his field glasses. They got shaggier and shaggier. One day he turned to his crippled wife. "We must shear the sheep," he said.

"Old man, you are crazy," she answered. The little old man shrugged and limped out to the barn on crutches from his fourth hip replacement.

The next morning, he started his track machine, put his crutches in the back and called his dogs. At the last minute, his crippled wife climbed on the back and held on with one hand.

They bounced over the tundra all day, but the sheep were too fast for them. The little old man did not stop.

He drove to the farthest point of his sheep range and turned around. The engine scared his sheep. They ran to- ♂

SWEATERS ON THE HOOF. Wool is the ranch's main cash crop. They sell it raw, or spin it into yarn and weave the yarn into rugs and clothes. "Milt and I like sheep," Cora says.

ward the barns. But it was a long way, and his machine sputtered and ran out of gas. He had to walk 2 miles home on crutches. All the sheep escaped.

His crippled wife screamed and wept. The little old man only shrugged and limped on.

Try, Try Again

The next morning, the little old man started his grown son's three-wheeler and put a can of gasoline on the handlebars. He called his dogs.

At the last minute, his crippled wife climbed on the back and held on with one hand. The little old man drove to his track machine and filled the gas tank, then off they went to find the scattered sheep.

They were everywhere. The little old man and his crippled wife could not gather them. All they had to show for 2 days of hard work was one injured ewe and a lamb that couldn't run.

His wife screamed and wept. "You are insane," she said.

The next morning, the little old man started his track machine and called his dogs. At the last minute, his crippled wife said, "Catch my horse." She got in the saddle and held the reins with one hand.

Again they went to the farthest point and turned around with the sheep in front of them. They gathered 200 sheep and put them in the barn.

The next day, the little old man sheared 40 sheep. His crippled wife said, "You're killing yourself."

The next day, the little old man sheared 45 sheep...and the next day and the next. His crippled wife helped hold them down with one hand.

On the fifth day, a man from the next island called on the radio and said, "If you will come get me, I will shear your sheep."

The little old man said, "Yes." He got his boat into the water. His crippled wife screamed and wept. "It's 12 miles of open sea."

The little old man said, "I'll be careful." And he was.

After all 500 sheep were sheared, the little old man took the young man back across the 12 miles of open water. On the opposite shore, they shook hands.

"You are amazing," the young man said. The little old man shrugged.

At breakfast the next morning, the little old man said, "Our coal shed is almost empty…"

SHARING THE LOAD. Working together on everything from washing dishes to shearing sheep is the key to survival on the ranch, and the wellspring of Cora and Milt's happy life.

ONE-ARMED WEAVER. After Cora lost her hand, Milt modified her tools and she kept right on weaving beautiful rugs and sweaters decorated with dyes from native plants.

Photos: Julie Habel

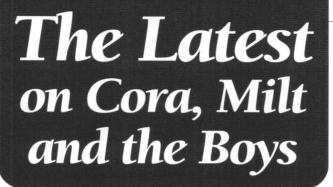

The Latest on Cora, Milt and the Boys

They're all together again, enjoying three grandkids and Cora's new novel.

CORA AND MILT finally sold the ranch in 1997 and joined Chuck, Randall and Randall's family in the village of Unalaska on the far end of the island.

"Milt and I are heavy into grandparenting," Cora says. "Killian is 11; Monty is 8; and Dakota is 16 months. I work at the public library in the afternoons 5 days a week, which leaves mornings free to babysit.

"Killian and Monty were just in their annual school play. And they're in Boy Scouts, so Milt helped them build their pinewood derby cars.

"We miss the ranch, but we're really grateful that we can be so involved with their lives. We're very happy with the way things turned out."

So are their sons. Randall now runs the shipyard at Horizon Lines. "It's a lot of responsibility, but he's been doing it for 2 years now and seems to like it," Cora notes.

"And Chuck is still fishing. He has a little boat he lives on and a little boat he fishes on. He never has cared much about money. As long as he keeps body and soul together, he's happy."

Camp Tender

Recently recovered from his sixth hip replacement—four on one side and two on the other—Milt can once again get around without crutches, Cora says. Always her husband's biggest fan, she adds, "People like Milt force us to be better than we are.

"He's almost 84, and it's just amazing how much stamina he has. Milt says he started out being a camp tender, and now he's come full circle. He does most of the cooking, and bakes brownies and bread several times a week.

"He's also very good with wood. He just finished a shoe rack to accommodate the shoe fetish I've developed now that I'm earning a wage again. And he recently refinished an old pioneer desk for the library.

"He also loves watching all those old television shows he missed—like *All in the Family*. Remember, this is the first television he's ever had."

Budding Novelist

Meanwhile, Legend Books (*www.coraholmes.com*) recently published Cora's first novel, *Outside Man*. Based on an ancient Aleutian legend, the story follows a grieving mother, recently returned to a remote Alaskan island, as she struggles to unwrap the mystery of the stranger from a mummy's cave.

"I wrote this book because I wanted to say something about the unique and difficult emotions that arise between adopted children and their parents," Cora says.

"But I wanted it to be exciting and entertaining, too. For example, I got much of the story's exotic setting from notes Chuck wrote during his 2-week, 110-mile hike across the mountains from the village to our ranch.

"I still get an incredible amount of mail from *Country* readers," she notes. "I think it's because I was able to write things people could identify with—all the joys and heartaches. And I think a lot of people could imagine themselves doing what we were.

"They'd write and say, 'I laughed and cried, and I was right there with you on that boat.' I've been touched and humbled by all the people who seemed to get some good out of what I wrote."

PROUD GRANDPARENTS. After selling the ranch, Milt and Cora moved to the village of Unalaska, where Chuck and Randall live. Cora writes and works at the library while Milt "tends camp." They also dote on their grandkids, Killian, Monty and Dakota (above).

They Learned to Enjoy the Simple Things

We asked 4,000 readers who've subscribed since the very first issue: "How has love of the country shaped your life?"

I WAS BORN in a small Quaker town in central Pennsylvania during the Great Depression. I had a happy childhood, even though I had four older brothers who wouldn't ever let me play ball with them.

(So I'd wait on the sidelines until the ball came my way, throw it into a huge rosebush and run to Mom for protection.)

In our community, we knew everyone in town. And whenever anyone needed help, others were always there to comfort and support them.

After getting married and living in a city for many years, it was good to get back to the country after retirement. My husband, Gene, recently had a minor heart scare, though, so we decided to move a little closer to medical care and our roots in Pennsylvania. But I'm never far from the country in my mind and heart.
—*Janet Albright*
Lewisburg, Pennsylvania

IN THE COUNTRY, our neighbors—both human and animal—teach us that love given is returned. You're never lost in the country. A knock on a door brings help, unlike in the city, where you're just as likely to get it slammed in your face.

In the country, caring for others is a way of life, and I'm certainly a better person for it. —*Susan Brown*
Clarion, Pennsylvania

LIFE ON THE FARM has made us appreciate the small things. It was very difficult in the early years, with wood cookstoves, outhouses, kerosene lamps, iceboxes and plow horses. Today, we are grateful for all the modern conveniences many people take for granted.

Our farm also allowed us to instill Christian values of hard work, responsibility, honesty, generosity, community and church involvement in our children. Our hope is that those same ideals will be passed on to our grandchildren as well.

That is the life of a good farmer—to plant the seed, watch it grow, enjoy the bountiful harvest and know that you left the land a little better than when you began.
—*Mary Louise and Bill Sheets, Sunbury, Ohio*

I'VE LIVED all my life on a farm that's been in my family since 1895. We've been lucky to do a good bit of traveling, but to me, there's no place like this farm.

My wife, Harriet, and I started farming right after I

Country Inspired Us to Find a Better Life

I CAN'T BELIEVE it's been 20 years since that first gorgeous issue of *Country* landed in my mailbox! I'll never forget that day, especially since your magazine eventually convinced us to move to the country.

I grew up in Tampa, Florida. Just about the time I thought we would never really take the plunge and move away from the area where I'd always lived, we received an issue of *Country* with a story about Cora and Milt Holmes, who lived in the Aleutian Islands, far away from everyone. I was so intrigued with this story that it gave me the courage.

So pushing my fears of the unknown aside, we began searching for land, which eventually led us to an acreage 40 minutes north of town. As soon as I saw the honeysuckle blooming along the fence and the porch on the back of the house, I was sold.

We've lived here 16 years, raised our children here and watched them blossom from carefree kids into responsible hardworking adults. I credit a solid foundation of faith in God and family roots. But some of their success surely comes from fresh country air, homegrown food and a lifetime of caring for everything from pigs, cows and an ornery old goat, to geese and chickens.

The country has been very good to us, and I want to thank *Country* magazine for helping my family find a better and richer life.
—*Diane Clark, Lutz, Florida*

returned home from a hitch in the military. We always did it the old way—milking cows and raising hogs, cattle and chickens to make ends meet.

Sometimes it was a struggle, but we stuck with it and are glad we did. We raised three daughters here. It was hard work, but a good life.

—*Wayne Mackeprang*
Sabula, Iowa

LOVE OF the country is going into your backyard—whether its 200 acres or 200 square feet—and seeing the possibilities for gardens and green places for children to play. Country isn't just a place. It's a state of mind.

—*Elaine Smith, Tooele, Utah*

Magazines Made Learning More Fun

FOR 42 YEARS, I taught fifth and sixth grade in the little South Dakota town where I was born. We only had 250 students in 12 grades, but we're very proud of the job we did. And *Country* helped.

I used *Country* and *Country EXTRA* to supplement our textbooks in geography, social studies and English. "Now *This* Is God's Country" brought geography lessons to life. And in English, one of the kids' favorite assignments featured *Country* postcards.

I'd cut photos from the magazine and paste them on tagboard. (I've kept every issue since the premiere; a friend gave me her copies to cut up for class.) Then each student would write two postcards and "mail" them to other students. We had lots of fun reading them aloud and pretending we were visiting faraway locations in other states.

So, thank you for helping me share my love of the country and make learning fun.

—*Rosalee Sternhagen, Avon, South Dakota*

ly turned earth, new mown hay and even cow manure. But as long as I have my wits about me, I still have beautiful memories I'll treasure forever. All the progress in the world won't take that away. —*Stephan Pappas*
Wantagh, New York

I LEARNED all my values while growing up on 5 acres above the Grass River near Canton, New York. We grew corn and vegetables, and raised pigs and cows. When we weren't working hard on the farm, we were working even harder in school.

But we played hard, too. One winter we built a bobsled that crashed on the ice and buried me in a snowbank. Mom rescued me, and we turned around and built a toboggan. We ended up with the same result.

The values I learned in the country have stood me in good stead all my life. And you can't beat the memories.

—*Lauren Clough*
Fernandina Beach, Florida

I WAS THE LAST farm manager at The State University of New York at Farmingdale. I never got tired of watching students from the city who had probably never even seen a cow learn to wash udders and hook up a milking machine. Or the look of fright on their faces the first time they reached under a laying hen for the eggs.

But they usually learned fast, and they learned good. Within a few days, they were almost pros.

The ag department is long gone now. Houses and strip malls have replaced the potato and vegetable farms.

I miss the smell of fresh-

I GREW UP on a farm, where I drove a Farmall H, milked cows and picked wild blackberries.

My husband of 40 years was a farmer, too, and we raised two children to love the land and all the creations of God. Our children have chosen to raise their families in the country, too.

Living in the country lets you see God in all His glory. We're blessed by the stars at night, rainbows after a rain, the new beginnings of spring and the colors of fall—all the things city folks drive to the country to see.

—*Ann Newton Jackson*
Lester, Alabama

MY HUSBAND was a fish farmer who really enjoyed his work. The fish were interesting little creatures to him. When I wasn't helping out on the farm, I taught school full-time for 46 years.

After I retired in 1981 and my husband passed away, I moved to town and devoted myself to church activities. But I kept the fish ponds, which I rent to two brothers.

I still like to drive out to the ponds and watch the fish. I'll always have a soft spot for my life in the country.

—*Frieda Elcan*
Lonoke, Arkansas

AS A YOUNGSTER on the farm, I grew up nursing animals back to health. As an adult, I nursed people back to health. The deep compassion instilled in me by my parents and grandparents often helped me comfort grieving families.

Country life teaches you to care for animals, people and their feelings.

—*Mrs. Alvin Dominey*
Huntington, Texas

Julie Habel

Grandpa's Handshake

By Barry Blackstone, Ellsworth, Maine

FIRM GRIP ON LIFE. Like the author's grandfather, this farmer exhibits character from a lifetime of hard work. Count on him being true to his word.

I can still see him carrying a bale of hay in each hand the full length of the barn to a stall where the yearlings were kept.

Those hands helped me with my chores more times than I can remember. But there's one thing I'll never forget—the assurance of Grandpa Blackstone's handshake.

I was just a boy the first time we shook hands. I'd agreed to help Grandpa pick up rocks for a dollar a day. He removed his glove, extended that huge right paw and said, "We've got a deal!"

When his grip swallowed mine and I felt its power, I began to understand that a handshake was no trivial thing. To Grandpa, it signified a sacred oath.

He not only expected you to keep your end of the deal, he was determined he would keep his.

As Good as His Word

We made many other deals during my boyhood, including the $1,500 I borrowed from him to buy a trailer. Each one was sealed with a handshake—never a pen. His handshake was as good as his word, and his word stood for honor and integrity. So there was no need for fancy written agreements.

I went to visit my grandmother recently. She and Grandpa had been married for over 50 years. Even though he passed away more than 20 years ago, hardly a visit goes by that she doesn't speak of him.

Last time I saw her, she reminded me of the day when Grandpa thought I'd gotten old enough to mow his lawn. He took great pride in the appearance of his yard, and I didn't realize until years later just how much of an honor it was to be given that responsibility.

I was given $3 for the 3-hour job—quite a raise from a dollar a day picking up rocks. Plus, there were other perks. Halfway through each mowing, Grandma would invite me into the house for cookies and a bottle of Orange Crush soda, my favorite as a child.

Once again, the deal was sealed with a handshake. My hands had grown by that time, but Grandpa's hand still swallowed mine.

Today, all transactions must be in black and white, witnessed and notarized. Even then, many aren't binding as folks wiggle their way out through legal loopholes.

Now that I've reached adulthood and the deals I make have grown, too, I have more appreciation than ever for Grandpa's handshake. It was Carroll Blackstone's pledge that what was agreed to was as solid as the hand that shook on it.

Oh, to feel that big hand in mine one more time! ✧

WHEN I think about my Grandfather Blackstone, the first thing that comes to mind are his hands.

Grandpa had the hands of a dairyman—big and powerful from a lifetime of milking cows. Even after he switched to modern milking equipment, those hands remained sure and fast as he changed the milking machine from one cow to another.

country kids

LINDSEY PEEBLE'S smile says it all—you just can't beat growing up in the country. The next 12 pages give you a glimpse of rural life from the perspective of country kids just like her.

This heartwarming photo was taken by Lindsey's mom, Susan Peebles, of Francois Lake, British Columbia.

GOD'S GOTTA BE SMILING on these little cherubs. "I took this photo at our church's vacation Bible school," says Angela Donnelson of Stanwood, Wash. "It's so cute the different ways the little ones prayed."

ONE DAY our 6-year-old grandson, Joey, was over at our farm, spending time tagging along with his grandpa. Out of the blue, he asked, "Grandpa, do you farm for money or for fun?"
—*Sandra Dame, Oldcastle, Ontario*

EMILY, our 5-year-old niece, often follows her dad around the farm asking a lot of questions.

One day in kindergarten, the teacher was talking about the importance of good manners. "What do you do when you break something?" she asked.

Emily quickly responded, "Go to town to get parts!"
—*Elizabeth Weber, Dimock, South Dakota*

I DIDN'T realize how much my 3-year-old son, Christopher, loved farming until his first day of preschool.

When the teacher held up a flash card for the color red, Christopher shouted, "International!" And when she held up a green card, he yelled, "John Deere!" —*Wendi Harrell, Carthage, Illinois*

ARE YOU SURE this is where milk comes from? "My 3-year-old niece, Leann, seems to be wondering this as she tries her hand at it," says Kathy Dawson, Ewing, Mo.

IT'D BE EASIER if one of you pushed! "My boys were gleaning corn the combine missed," explains Cindy Ferree of Jonesboro, Indiana. "Wyatt and Colt were husking the corn while Case tried to pull them to a new spot."

102

The Best of COUNTRY

COWMOUFLAGE. "Our grandsons blended in with the Holsteins at their uncle's wedding," notes Agnes Kraemer, St. Jacobs, Ont.

YEAH! NO MORE SCHOOL! "Our son Ryan enjoys being outdoors every chance he gets," says Mary Fosnow of Mundelein, Illinois.

OUR SON, Kyle, celebrated a birthday recently by having several friends sleep over, including one boy, Colin, who lives in the city.

We decided to let Colin gather eggs. He was very excited and couldn't wait to cook one for breakfast.

"I've never had homemade eggs before!" he said.

—*Anna Lizanna*
Pass Christian, Mississippi

MY 3-year-old grandson gave me a big hug and kiss and said, "Oh, Grandma, I love you."

Since he is a bit partial to me, I said, "Now go tell Grandpa that; he likes to hear it, too."

So he ran over to his grandfather, put his arms around him and said, "Oh, Grandpa, I love your wife."

—*Leona Swisher, Mulkeytown, Illinois*

MANE SQUEEZE. "My 13-year-old granddaughter, Hope, took this picture of her horse 'Sally' and little sister, Hannah," explains Elaine Aurand of Stockton, Ill. "It seems Hannah's taken after her sister and become a horse lover, too."

LOVE AT FIRST SIGHT. "Our granddaughter Brittany always gives a hug to the big goose statue on our patio," relates Pamela Mauer from Camby, Indiana.

"You been farming long?"

The most famous "Country Kids" of all are these "Little Farmers." California twins Chris and Matt Jacobs had just discovered the pockets in their new overalls when mom Denise snapped their picture.

In 1982, founder Roy Reiman was visiting his daughter Juli at Iowa State University, and she dragged him across the cold campus to see a copy of the photo, which was hanging outside a professor's office in the Agronomy building. Juli knew he'd love it, and she was right—Roy worked out an agreement with Denise for exclusive rights to the picture. Turning it into a 14- by 18-inch poster, he added a little humor with the caption, "You been farming long?"

Since then, more than *2 million* copies of the poster have been sold, and the Little Farmers have found their way into country homes throughout North America, not to mention Europe and Asia.

Copies of the large, full-color poster are still available at $4.99 each plus $1 shipping and handling from Country Store, Suite 8279, P.O. Box 990, Greendale WI 53129.

AT DINNER, my husband told our 3-year-old granddaughter, Alexis, "Clean your plate and you'll get bigger."

"No, I'll get dessert." Alexis replied.
—*Marjorie Bushey*
Middlebury, Vermont

WHEN our son Bob was in first grade, the students were having difficulty reading in front of the class one day. The teacher, Mrs. Webster, got up and said, "Now this is the way I expect you to read."

She opened the book and started to read slowly and evenly. Bob stood up and said, "No wonder Mrs. Webster can read so good—look how long she has been in the first grade."
—*Eleanor Olek*
Wayne New Jersey

I HAD just returned home with a crafts project I was working on, and our 4-year-old grandson asked me why I was making it. I explained that it kept my hands busy, as idle hands were the devil's workshop.

A few weeks later, he saw the finished product and said, "Grandma, did you make that at the devil's workshop?"
—*Betty Hemminger*
Riverside, California

FINE DINING. "During harvesting, I often take meals to the field," says Eleanor Uhlman, Morton, Ill. "That's my granddaughter Hannah sitting on her dad's knee and sharing a few bites."

TASTE-TESTER. "Sarah was supposed to bring the tomato in from the garden," recounts Grandma Mary Szymanski of Warren, Michigan.

PUMPED ABOUT SUMMERTIME. "We were at my grandparents' place in Mink Creek, Idaho, which is a favorite family gathering spot," says Sheri Scott of Toquerville, Utah. "That's my niece Lexie cooling off her feet at the old water pump in front of the cellar."

'So That's Where My Good Scissors Went!'

The melting snow reveals all sorts of treasures her kids carted outside to play with.

By Valerie Van Kooten, Pella, Iowa

COOKIN' UP GOOD TIMES. Like the author's kids, Danielle Hunter had fun fixing "supper" in the sandpile, says Grandma Cynthia Thornton of Coker, Alabama.

AS SPRING gradually crept in last year, my yard became a treasure trove of items the snow had been hiding.

Over there, in the sandpile, was a set of plastic measuring cups I'd been looking for. In my flower bed was an antique serving spoon I'd picked up at a garage sale, and under the deck was the bath towel I'd long since given up hope of finding.

No, I'm not usually this unorganized…it's my kids. Although my 17-year-old is past the stage of dragging half the house into the yard, my 13- and 11-year-old sons are not immune to it. When they've got a project in mind, nothing in the house is sacred.

Starting a fort behind dad's shop? No problem…it will take a lot of nails, hammers, pieces of sheet metal and snacks, lots of snacks. That's why I found so many cups and plastic glasses out there.

A go-cart race track? Okay…it's going to take lots of poster board to make signs and some scrap fabric for flags. That explains why my good scissors were lying abandoned on the track.

A new puppy? Of course, it will need food and water bowls, and my mixing bowls will do the trick. They were old anyway, weren't they, Mom?

Mom Fesses Up

I have a confession to make. My sons come by it honestly. My younger sister, brother and I grew up on a farm and had endless creative projects and ideas that had to have driven our mom crazy.

I well remember the perfume project, where we were going to bottle and market a scent that would make millions. We gathered every container in the house and proceeded to mix together talcum powder, bubble bath, perfume—whatever we could find. The result was a sticky congealed mess.

Another time we set out to create the perfect cake recipe. We stirred together flour, eggs, sugar, all in vastly uneven proportions, and baked it. It was thin and hard and resembled pancakes. We threw it over the fence to the hogs.

Then there was the haunted house in the barn. As high school students, we had planned a slumber party for our friends, and a haunted house in the barn would be the perfect frightening way to end the evening. We spent weeks in the haymow stringing extension cords, hauling up old pieces of furniture and hammering together signs.

When I was last up there a year or so ago, there were still traces of that haunted house. And I complain that my kids don't put things away!

Although we were constantly making messes, I don't remember my parents ever complaining. We were farm kids and were encouraged to get outside, try things, be adventurous.

I'm trying hard to be that way, too. I won't even groan the next time the boys ask to use the spaghetti strainer to catch minnows in the creek. ✦

HAMMOCK TIME. Cradled in Grandma's quilt, this girl doesn't have a care as she shares ice cream with her kittens. Photo by Bonnie Nance of Owensboro, Ky.

SHHH! "Our son Justin was shushing the neighbor's cows because he thought they were mooing a bit too loudly," says Susan Hayward of North Kingstown, Rhode Island.

OUR three-year-old grandson, Jordan, had been helping get the nursery ready for his expected baby sister. That evening Jordan put his head on his mom's stomach and said, "You can come out now. Your room's ready."
—*Elaine Stone, Roy, Utah*

JUST A HUNCH, but little Brian Armstrong may have been set up for this cute photo taken by Aunt Janet Strayer, Flagstaff, Az.

AW, MOM...PLEASE? "Justin was hoping to keep this frog, and wasn't happy when his mom told him to set it free," explains Aunt Annette Polson from Burton, Ohio.

Back in the 1950's, my two brothers and I spent our summer vacations at our grandparents' home in the country. Our days were filled with fun and laughter, tempered with daily doses of good old-fashioned religion.

Grandfather was a gentle man with warm blue eyes. But he also had a strong voice and was as stern as he was lovable. Grandmother, a mere 5 feet tall and pleasantly plump, was well-known for her cooking. Both were devout Seventh-day Adventists.

One of Grandfather's admonitions to us each summer was the importance of observing the Sabbath Day. From sundown on Friday until sundown on Saturday, we were compelled to forgo all recreation. Sabbath was a time to spend communing with the Lord.

During the remainder of the week, Grandfather gave us free rein to enjoy ourselves. All he asked was that we find time each day to memorize a verse from the Bible.

We were expected to recite this verse in the evening when our grandparents came together in the family room for an hour of devotions.

My brothers and I thought this was a fair deal. Our grandparents had waterfront property, and we loved to spend our days fishing. But we figured we could find a few moments to memorize a Bible passage. After all, Grandfather never specified how long it had to be. A verse was a verse, we reasoned.

Evening devotions always began with Grandfather leading us in song. I can still remember singing beautiful hymns like *The Old Rugged Cross* and *Abide with Me*.

Then Grandfather called on my brothers and me to stand, one at a time, and recite our Bible verses. We'd respond with passages like, "And God said, 'Let there be light,' and there was light." or "In the beginning, God created the heavens and the earth."

I'm sure our grandfather was on to us—knowing full well that we picked

Grandfather's Rule: Thou Shalt Not Fish on the Sabbath

By Kathryn Phillips
Norwalk, Connecticut

the shortest verses to memorize. But he never let on. He only smiled and said, "Amen."

One Friday morning after breakfast, as we gathered our fishing gear, Grandfather gave us a gentle reminder of the Sabbath. All morning we tried in vain to catch some fish. Since we were not allowed to fish on the Sabbath, we were determined to make up for lost time by catching an impressive stringer before sundown.

No one noticed that lunchtime had come and gone. We didn't feel hunger pangs—our only concern was a tug on our lines. After what seemed like hours, my younger brother let out a shout. He had a nibble! My older brother and I dropped our lines, ran to his rescue...

and helped him haul in a snapping turtle! After that, we forgot about fish. It was open season on snappers—with each of us intent on catching the biggest one.

Suddenly, my older brother shrieked, "The sun has set!"

With the speed of lightning, we grabbed our gear and bolted for home. But as we sneaked through the kitchen, we could already hear our grandparents singing *Sweet Hour of Prayer*.

There was no time to clean up. Worse yet, we had not memorized a Bible verse. But my older brother's face lit up as he grabbed his Bible and flipped the pages to a two-word verse—"Jesus wept."

Hurriedly and with heads bowed, we snuck into the family room. We sat as close as we could to each other and tried not to make eye contact with our grandfather.

Grandfather cleared his throat as a warning sign of the big trouble we were in. He was a force to be reckoned with when defied.

Finally, my older brother was called upon to stand and recite his Bible verse. Fidgeting, he said, "Jesus wept." As he sat down, there was not the usual "Amen" from Grandfather.

It was my turn. Not having memorized a new verse, I copied my brother and said, "Jesus wept." No "Amen" there either.

Then my younger brother stood and nervously repeated, "Jesus wept."

Just loud enough for us to hear, Grandfather said, "And so shall you all, right after Sabbath."

The next evening after the sun went down and Sabbath was over, the Bible verse most appropriate for the occasion would have been "There shall be weeping and gnashing of teeth." It was a lesson I never forgot from those wonderful summers spent at my grandparents' house in the country.

A Helping Hand

A teenage boy and his friends learned an important lesson about being good neighbors.

By Brad Johnson, Englewood, Tennessee

YEARS AGO, my friends and I often went camping on Friday nights in the woods or fields behind our houses. Sometimes we'd even go to the Great Smoky Mountains or Watts Bar Lake.

I was usually pooped by the time I got home Saturday morning. So my normal routine was to rest for a while, help Dad with some chores and then catch a nap before playing softball on our church's team. Afterward, we'd usual-ly play basketball at the church until midnight.

My friends were important to me. So after I finished mowing the lawn, haul-ing hay, cutting firewood or working in the garden, I tried to spend as much time as possible with them.

I remember one of these weekends with my friends in particular. It was the summer I was 15, and vacation was al-most over.

I'd just returned from our Friday night camping trip. I tossed my sleeping bag on my bed and flopped down beside it, hoping to make up for the sleep I didn't get the night before.

I had no more than collapsed on my bed when I heard Dad's old Dodge pick-up rumbling up our steep gravel drive-way. As usual, he was whistling when he came through the front door and tossed the newspaper into his recliner. "Braaaad! You home?" he called.

I reluctantly answered, rolling over and peering down the hallway through my open bedroom door. Dad walked hurriedly into my sight. There was a spring in his step, which I recognized as his "he-has-a-task-for-me" walk.

Loved to Work

Dad loved to work…and he enjoyed having me work with him. When I saw him open the closet door to grab his work gloves, my suspicions were con-firmed. I slowly crawled off the bed and trudged down the hall to see what he wanted…but on this morning, my steps didn't have the same spring as his.

"Did y' see Gene Copeland hauling hay on your way home?" he asked. "He's tryin' to do it by himself, bum leg and all. I thought maybe we might go help him."

Dad assumed I shared his excite-ment, which was definitely not the case.

Aside from being tired, I knew that job would probably take all day. I might not finish in time for the softball game—and even if I did, I probably wouldn't have enough energy to play well.

Besides, I'd been hauling hay all summer. Hadn't I hoisted my share of bales? In a matter of seconds, one excuse after another popped into my mind.

Dad Was Waiting

But what about Mr. Copeland? I did feel sorry for the old guy. And I certainly didn't want to disappoint Dad, who was already lacing up his boots.

By the time I had changed into my jeans and work boots, Dad was outside waiting for me. We drove up the road to the field where he had seen Mr. Copeland working, but he was nowhere in sight.

"I guess he's on the other side of the hill," Dad announced.

I looked over at him. His weathered face held no expression of concern about the summer heat, as I'm sure mine did. No, Dad was exactly where he wanted to be. His eyes were sparkling, and he gave me a slight grin as his callused hand gripped the parking brake and yanked it into place.

We set out across the field on foot, headed toward the hilltop. The distinct aroma of hay hovered pleasantly in the air as we walked past bales scattered about. The summer sun, glowing brightly from its noonish perch, bore down on us, and the humidity reinforced its heat. But God's grace could be felt in a slight breeze.

We topped the crest of the hill and saw Mr. Copeland below. I'll never forget that image: The tired old rancher squirmed off of his tractor and hobbled over to a bale. After each step with his left leg, he'd jerk his body weight to swing his right leg forward.

Somehow, he'd hoist the bale onto the trailer, then limp back up to the tractor to drive to the next bale and do it all over again.

I felt ashamed for my earlier reluctance to help. But I was glad to be able to make up for it.

Glowed with Compassion

I looked over at Dad. Not always the warmest man, his face, often hardened and stubborn, glowed with compassion. He was glad to be there, too.

We both waved and ambled down the hill while Mr. Copeland watched us curiously. "Howdy, Gene," Dad said with a smile. "Thought y' might like a hand."

Mr. Copeland, his eyes shaded by the brim of his cowboy hat, grinned gratefully. "That'd be fine," he replied. At first, he wanted me to drive the tractor so he could "pull his own weight" bucking bales. But Dad tactfully managed to talk him into driving.

We worked our way to the top of the hill, where I saw a young man jogging toward us. Even from the distance, I could tell it was my good friend Mike.

Then a bright-red Mustang turned off the road and parked behind our truck. A red-headed kid stepped out and also began to come our way. It was Chris, another of the bunch that had camped out the night before.

I knew they were both as tired as I was…and they, too, had the all-important softball game later. Both started loading bales, explaining that they had called me at home and Mom had told them where I was.

Shortly, three more neighborhood boys spotted us out in the field and joined us. Chris, the clown of the group, kept us all in stitches while we worked.

Hay and dust clung to our sweat-drenched bodies, and the sharp stems that protruded from the bales clawed our skin. Yet, the smiles and laughter amidst the hard work bore witness that everyone was glad to help out.

Appreciated the Help

After we stacked the last of the hay in the barn, Mr. Copeland thanked us. I know he appreciated the help—I could see it in his eyes, once he slid his hat back far enough to reveal them.

He pulled out his wallet and offered to pay us. But we simultaneously chorused "No, thanks" and "Just glad to help out".

Dad didn't say a word. He just smiled at us and beamed with pride.

That was 12 summers ago. The funny thing is, I don't remember who won the softball tournament I was worried about missing. Afterward, I'm sure we played our usual game of basketball, though I don't recall that, either.

What I do remember is Dad's compassion and his pride in my friends and me. I recall the camaraderie and the fun of working together to help someone in need.

Most importantly, I'll never forget the expression of thankfulness written on Mr. Copeland's face. I'm glad I was there to help out.

GETTING DOWN TO EYE LEVEL. "Fascinated by the baby goat, our granddaughter Karli got what you might call a kid's perspective," says Jane Taylor of Connelly Springs, N.C.

GOING OUT ON A LIMB. "My son Caleb decided to get a different perspective on a beautiful fall day by hanging upside down from a tree in our yard," notes Jane Knisely, Imler, Pa.

GIMME A BREAK! "I don't know if Robert was exhausted or just fed up with the trials and tribulations of being 4 years old," says his great-aunt Erin Timmons of Mt. Pleasant, Mich.

I WAS helping a group of preschoolers make valentine hearts and asked the children the names of family members to write on their hearts.

When I asked one little girl the name of her dad, she told me she would have to think a bit.

After a while, she came back and said very seriously, "I got it! My daddy's name is Honey." —*AbbaGail Hills*
Eden Prairie, Minnesota

MY great-grandson John, 4, was at the day care center when a tornado warning was issued. The teacher ushered everyone into the basement.

When John's mother arrived to pick him up, she asked him why he was in the basement.

"We're down here because there's a vicious tomato coming," he answered matter-of-factly.
—*Mrs. Robert Bremer, Carlinville, Illinois*

I WAS helping my son Christopher brush his teeth when he started to talk. "Wait until I am done brushing your teeth," I told him.

As I resumed brushing, he again tried to talk. In a firmer tone, I said, "Chris, wait until I'm done brushing your teeth."

When I finished brushing, I asked, "Now, what did you want to tell me?"

Chris replied, "That's not my toothbrush."
—*Rebecca Cordova, Vancouver, Washington*

LOOK AT THAT! "My great-nephews Cody and Brady were peering into the chicken coop at a petting zoo," relates Lisa Mallmann of Hortonville, Wis.

WE GOT DAD TO SLEEP...can we go play now? Ruth Gilman of Stuart, Iowa snapped this photo of her son Gary and his children, Eathen and Leah.

REARIN' TO RODEO is 3-year-old Wade Rogers. Joan Berger of Nevada City, California snapped the photograph.

WHILE VISITING us at our mountain home in Arkansas, our granddaughter tried to imitate the birds she heard each evening.

We kept hearing one particular bird, but could never see it. Our granddaughter continued to return its call, until one night when she asked, "What's it going to do when it finds out I'm not a bird?" —*Inez Conner, Riverview, Florida*

WE MOVED to an old farmhouse in December, just after an early snow had melted and soaked into the manure in the barnyard. We knew our 4-year-old son was excited about moving to the country, but we didn't know how excited until he burst through the door with a big grin on his face and shouted, "Mom, it smells just like a rodeo out there!" —*Shirley Thomas, East Helena, Montana*

LOVE YA, MOM. "My son Warren flashed this sign during roundup," says Sherri Johnson of Adin, Calif.

CAN'T RESIST. Larry Javorsky of Hamilton, Mont. says this youngster reminds him of his own son, Joey, whom he calls the "Master of Disaster."

Some Warm, Fuzzy Memories Of Ugly, Itchy Long Johns

IF YOU grew up north of the Mason-Dixon Line, odds are your mother made you wear long johns during the winter—especially in the days before school buses, when children walked to class.

It didn't matter whether you were a boy or a girl. From the time the wild geese flew south in the fall until they returned north in spring, all youngsters trudged off to school wearing their itchy, baggy union suits.

Here's how two subscribers remember those "good old days."

The Long and Short of It

THANKSGIVING usually marked the first snow flurries in the area where I grew up, and by early December, winter had set in.

We children loved the cold weather almost as much as we enjoyed summer—there were snowball fights, ice-skating parties and church sleigh rides.

It was exciting to bundle up and pile into a straw-filled sleigh, singing familiar songs and calling out greetings to passersby as a team of horses pulled us through the snow.

On cold and snowy nights, we had just as much fun indoors —popping popcorn, making fudge, playing games with the family and drinking hot chocolate.

Only one thing prevented us from really enjoying winter during the 1920s—the dreaded long underwear that Mother made us wear during those cold months.

We wore traditional union suits with long legs, long sleeves, buttons up the front and, of course, a drop seat. They kept us warm and comfortable on our 2-mile walk to and from school…and for that we were grateful. But they were *so* ugly and itchy—and not very flattering for a girl.

That wasn't the worst part, however. There were no automatic washers back then—doing laundry was an exhausting day-long chore of heating water, scrubbing, bluing, wringing and hanging the wash on a clothesline in the basement.

To keep laundry to a minimum, we were allotted just one pair of long johns, which we had to wear the whole week, from one Saturday bath night to the next.

After 2 or 3 days, the legs and arms of my underwear were stretched out of shape and just hanging on my skinny adolescent limbs.

I tried to remedy the situation by folding the stretched-out fabric snugly around my legs. But the fold resulted in a big wadded-up lump under my cotton stockings that was almost as bad as the saggy, baggy look.

It's said all good things must come to an end—and the same is true of all bad things. Come early spring, when the snow had melted and the danger of blizzards had passed, we were allowed to cut off the long sleeves of our union suits and the legs just above the knee.

What a great day that was! Even if the walk to school was still a bit chilly, pride kept us warm. So did the excitement of saying good-bye to lumpy, bumpy legs until next winter!

—Christine Sentiff
Brockport, New York

Coping with Life's Ups and Downs

GETTING ready to travel from our home in California to visit family in Utah last Christmas, I decided to purchase some thermal underwear so I could play in the snow with the grandchildren. This brought back childhood memories of wearing long underwear to school.

Winter could be harsh in Iowa, where I grew up. The temperature

Julie Habel

would drop well below freezing and stay there for months. And when we had snow, it was always accompanied by winds, which blew the flakes into mountainous drifts.

Long johns were a necessity to keep out the cold as we waited for the school bus—or so Mother insisted. There was no need to bother protesting when she dug them out at Thanksgiving every year. (This was a reason to give thanks?)

It wouldn't have been so bad if it weren't for the fact that some of the girls had more "modern" mothers. They didn't require their daughters to wear long johns—even if their knees got cold as they waited for the bus. (Girls were not allowed to wear slacks to school back then.)

We took a lot of teasing from these liberated girls—and from the boys—about our long-legged underwear. Finally, when we were 9, we'd run into school each morning and head straight to the restroom, where we rolled up the legs of those horrible undergarments to above the hemlines of our dresses.

Unfortunately, our scheme had a few snags. For starters, our rolled-up underwear made huge bulges above the knee and were tight enough to cut off

"*It became a race to finish my recitation before they fell...*"

circulation—at least early in the morning. As the day progressed, they began to stretch and slide down—first one leg and then the other. The more we rolled them up again, the more stretched-out they became.

The most embarrassing moment of my young life was the day I was standing in front of the class reading *The Wreck of the Hesperus*. I felt so proud reciting Longfellow's poem—until I became aware of my rolled-up long johns slowly slipping down over my knees.

It became a race to finish my recitation before my long johns fell all the way down. I rushed through the rest of

WASHDAY. Union suits hanging on the clothesline (above) were a sure sign Mom was doing the weekly laundry. Remember how they'd freeze stiff on a wintry day (at right)?

the poem and gingerly started to walk back to my seat. Halfway to my desk, both rolls of underwear fell down at the same time.

I immediately dropped to the floor and covered my legs with my skirt so no one would notice. "I can't move," I whispered to the teacher as she came to help me. (She must have thought I'd broken all my bones.)

Just then the recess bell sounded, and all my classmates headed out to play—not caring about my predicament. After they left, I confided in the teacher and tearfully told her the whole story.

Not long after that, the rules were changed so girls could wear slacks under their dresses in cold weather, provided they removed them before classes started. We didn't mind that stipulation—it was much easier to rush to the restroom every morning to remove our slacks than to roll up those infernal long johns.

—*Mary Frohnen*
Vacaville, California

South Dakota...Now *This* Is God's Country!

In each issue, we invite readers to tell us why they think a particular area is the best place to live. This time, Greg Latza shares his love of South Dakota.

I was raised on a farm in South Dakota, and while my photography career has carried me to a handful of other states, there was never a question that I would someday return to God's Country and make my home here.

To realize the true beauty of our state, you must appreciate its diversity, starting with the weather. Nearly every weather phenomenon, except hurricanes, has been known to occur at one time or another. When windchill is factored in, 200 degrees separate the hottest summer days and coldest winter nights.

THE BEST SPOT. Map shows the highlighted area author says is the country's *best* location.

These weather extremes have tempered our land and people and helped make us who we are.

Diversity exists among wildlife as well. From noble bald eagles to ♂

116

"FARMERS grow vast fields of sunflowers. In summer when they're in bloom, they brighten the landscape and offer spectacular scenery."

"NOTHING says country quite like a windmill, and I can't think of a better way to view the countryside than from the top of one (at left)."

"I SPOTTED this youngster 'driving' an antique tractor at an auction."

"RETIRED farmer Dean Robinson has cut hair as a sideline business for 40 years and still does 2 evenings a week in his Frankfort shop."

"A COWBOY checks a ewe on the 40,000-acre Hickman Ranch near Ottumwa. The spread's so vast you can go miles without seeing anyone."

pronghorn antelope to paddlefish, the range of species is endless.

The Missouri River divides the state into two halves. Native South Dakotans refer to these halves as "East River" and "West River."

The landscape in the eastern half is flat to slightly rolling after being leveled and swept clean by glaciers. The western half was left untouched, and the land is rugged.

Early homesteaders sunk their roots in the rich topsoil of East River, and today the area is home to thousands of family farms. On a summer evening, you can drive down any gravel road past these institutions of family unity and see kids swaying on tire swings and families doing chores together.

West River is primarily ranch country, with vast herds of cattle and isolated pockets of people. It's the true West, with cowboys still herding cattle and communities that seem untouched by time.

Across the entire state, rural business is still mostly done on a handshake. A person's promise is as good as his signature.

In this country, the words neighbor and family have nearly the ♂

"I SNAPPED a view of eastern South Dakota farmland (left) while in a second hot-air balloon flying high above this one. What a thrill!"

"THIS lone horseman is gazing over a ridge near Custer. There are places so rugged that driving is impossible and walking isn't much easier. A horse is the only alternative."

"CHILDREN learn to ride about as soon as they learn to walk in ranch country. This youngster's getting a boost from his father."

"I'M ALWAYS on the lookout for scenes, like this trio of cats in a barn door, that bring back memories of my childhood on the farm."

The First 20 Years

119

"EAST RIVER is dotted with hundreds of glacial lakes, where the fishing is fantastic. I watched as these canoeists paddled their way across pretty Lake Herman near Madison."

"NEIGHBORS catch up on the news while waiting at the grain elevator. Corn harvest brings lines of tractors, wagons and trucks—the only traffic jams you'll find in small towns."

same meaning. You're just as likely to sit down to supper with your closest neighbor as you are with your brother or sister.

That neighbor probably knows your family history as well as you do, and he enjoys sharing stories about your parents and what farming was like years ago.

Like family, these neighbors lend their hands and hearts in times of need. When a tragedy strikes, it isn't unusual for a fleet of combines to descend upon the farm and help with the harvest.

Over the years, some families have grown to create their own communities.

The phenomenon began when four or five future farmers or ranchers were born to one family. Because a lot of land was needed ↪

"**SOUTH DAKOTANS** are proud of their rural heritage and strive to preserve it for future generations. Antique tractor pulls and old-time threshing bees (above) are popular events."

"**THESE** well-worn chore gloves hanging on the clothesline symbolize the hard work that goes hand in hand with a successful farm. Of all of the photos I've taken, this is a favorite."

"**SYLVAN LAKE** is one of the highest and most picturesque lakes in the Black Hills. It's special to me because I proposed to my wife, Jodi, on one of those big rocks as the sun was setting."

"**A COWBOY** holds Old Glory (right) as the festivities get under way at a rodeo in West River."

"**DAYTON HYDE** closes a gate behind him as he heads out to check on wild Mustangs that roam his wild horse sanctuary near Edgemont. It's one of the few remaining Mustang herds."

"**AFTER** a long day harvesting watermelons near Huron, youngsters enjoy the fruits of their labors (above). The area is known for its big juicy melons sold at roadside stands."

"**THIS** farmhouse withstood prairie winds for 100 years, but fell shortly after I got a photo."

to sustain so many youngsters intent on carrying on the family tradition, the original spread expanded, creating huge tracts owned under the same name.

As a result, most of the students in some western schools share the same last name. (Sometimes it's the teacher's last name, too!) The starters for the basketball team might all be cousins.

With neighbors acting like family and having family for neighbors, it's no wonder that the entire state of South Dakota feels like one community, one family.

That's the way it ought to be in God's Country.

"**HIGH SCHOOL** football is a big event in small towns. On this particular Friday night (right), the team from Menno (pop. 768) took the field against rival Bridgewater (pop. 533)."

"**TURN THE PAGE** and you'll see a roundup. It's a West River ritual that brings ranch families and neighbors together for hard work, hearty meals and good-natured joshing."

Rural Life's Heavenly for Pickup-Driving Priest

Meet a down-to-earth pastor as Father Berns keeps a weeklong diary of life at four country parishes.

Photos: RJ & Linda Miller

PROFILE: Father Eric Berns is pastor at St. Mary's Ridge Catholic Church and three other country churches in Monroe County, Wisconsin. He keeps his horse across the road from the rectory, and for a hobby, photographs rattlesnakes out in the wild.

Sunday, July 25—Good Sunday morning from St. Mary's Ridge Catholic Church near Cashton, Wisconsin. I'm pastor here as well as at three other rural churches: Sacred Heart in Cashton, St. Augustine in Norwalk and St. John the Baptist on nearby Summit Ridge.

I'm always charmed by the way people around here refer to ridges and valleys, rather than road names. A person doesn't live on Highway D—he lives "over on Irish Ridge"…or "down on Brush Creek," instead of on Highway 33.

As for me, I live at the rectory atop St. Mary's Ridge. The cornerstone of our church is dated 1897, and in 2006, we'll celebrate the 150th anniversary of the founding of the parish.

I keep my Quarter Horse, "Rocky," in the pasture across the road. Beyond his pasture lies Hall's Valley, which

leads to my friend Ormie's place, the Schmitz farm where I hunt, and Joe's place where I get my truck repaired. Stan's house is in between.

Ormie takes care of our church grounds. The Schmitzes are dairy farmers, and Joe is a fine mechanic. Stan works for the phone company. They all work hard and fish when they can.

I've been a priest for 8 years now, and of the three assignments I've had, this is the most peaceful and beautiful location. A friend once told me, "When you grow up around here, these hills wrap their arms around you and make it hard for you to leave."

Today was a typical Sunday. I was up early and had a cowboy breakfast of black coffee and nothing else. I should change that habit.

I was off to Mass at St. John's and then to St. Augustine's. Afterward, I visited Emily, a teenage girl who would make any parent or pastor proud. She's recovering from having her appendix out.

I returned to the rectory at noon, and Bill showed up. He's a parishioner at St. Augustine's and runs a farm implement dealership. He showed me his

motorcycle, which he let me take for a spin down the ridge. I sold my bike a year ago. As I tell people, "That's how come I'm still here."

In the early afternoon, I accepted an invitation from Fr. John to join him for lunch at his rectory in Cashton. Father John recently arrived from Ghana, and with his humor and good cooking, he helps keep the mood light as we serve the four parishes together. Today, he made peanut butter soup, a popular recipe in Ghana and one that is quickly becoming my favorite.

I came back out to St. Mary's and took a nap before the 4 p.m. Spanish Mass in Norwalk. We are blessed with a Mexican community in the Norwalk area. I hope my Spanish improves with time, and I'm sure these parishioners pray for the same!

Kirk, a farmer who lives nearby, called, and we arranged for a day in August to search for timber rattlesnakes on his farm. Photographing rattlesnakes is a hobby of mine, and I've got some nice close-up shots in my collection.

Timber rattlesnakes are a protected species, and Kirk is working hard to maintain their population. I'm excited to spend a day with him once again. Last year, he led me to one that measured 55 inches long. He assures me that snake has a big brother in the neighborhood, too!

As the sun started to drop behind the oak and maple trees in the yard across the road, I went to spend some time with Rocky.

There is a large settlement of Amish in this area, and the shocks of grain in the Amish neighbor's field were casting long shadows. Amish buggies were starting to run down the ridge in good numbers, many of them carrying young couples. Sunday night is courting night in the Amish community.

Later, I headed into the church for my night prayers and then practiced the piano for a while. My pride and joy is a beautiful Yamaha baby grand that I keep in St. Mary's Church, and I take lessons in La Crosse, 35 miles away.

This Friday night, we'll put the piano to good use at our second annual outdoor concert in the yard behind the rectory. The view is spectacular, and we have

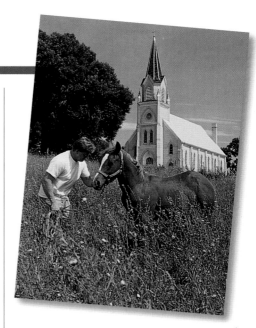

STEEPLECHASE. Father frolics with Rocky in the pasture next to St. Mary's Church.

some good talent from the parish lined up.

Then, on Saturday, we have our first annual archery tournament and bow raffle. This event was Ormie's idea and will be topped off with a pig roast and two-man country band from Iowa called The New Buckaroos. They played at Sacred Heart's summer picnic in June, and everyone thought they were great. So it'll be a busy week.

Monday, July 26—A knock on the door awoke me sometime around dawn. It was my neighbor Jimmy Schmitz. His mother, Sandy, is the organist at St. Mary's, and Jimmy's dad, Melvin, has a trucking business as well as the farm.

Melvin had attended the Monroe County Fair on Sunday and brought back a prize hog for our upcoming pig roast. "I got your pig," Jimmy said. He then let me know I'd need to give it food and water for few days. Hope I don't get attached to it.

I finished my usual breakfast of coffee and prayed my morning prayers in the backyard with its magnificent view. It was a glorious morning, and our place was already busy. Ormie had ordered blacktop for the rectory driveway and the parochial school driveway next door.

Monday is usually my day off, so my parish workload was light. I enjoyed lunch in Norwalk with some parishioners. They served a lunch of smoked meats from Lehner's Market. Theresa Lehner runs the only grocery store in Norwalk, and she's a saint. Her butcher, Greg, still uses the recipes of Theresa's late husband to stuff sausages and smoke meats.

In a few weeks, Norwalk will host its town festival, Norwalk Black Squirrel Days. If there are squirrels of any other color in Norwalk, I haven't seen them. A tractor pull is one of the main events, along with a parade and fierce competition for the coveted title of Black Squirrel Queen—or something close to it. Last year we were proud that one of our own parishioners—a big burly man named Mike—won the competition.

Norwalk also livens up the slow win-

THE OL' HEAVE-HO. Father Berns pitches hay out of the haymow for his horse, Rocky.

ter months with a festival in February. The highlight is the outhouse race, in which competitors start in one outhouse and race to another while wearing only a union suit in Wisconsin's frigid winter weather. They wanted me to compete last year. Though I possess a red union suit, I declined the invitation.

After lunch, I stopped by Pete Schmitz's house. For the record, there are more Schmitz families in this area than there are black squirrels in Norwalk. Pete's the uncle of the dairy farming Schmitzes near the rectory, and he'd just bought a beautiful new truck that he let me take for a spin.

Back at the rectory, I wanted to relax outside for a while before an important church meeting in Cashton tonight, so I tried to work with Rocky.

When I got Rocky last December, about the only things I knew about horses were that I wanted one, and I love the way they smell. I don't have much experience when it comes to training them, and it shows. Halfway through today's session, Rocky jumped over the corral, leaving me in the center of the pen feeling foolish.

After tonight's meeting, we had another rehearsal for our outdoor concert. I was amazed to listen to the performers. This concert will be a class act! One of the singers had the lead role in a Chicago performance of *Phantom of the Opera*, and he'll be singing *The Music of the Night*. It'll be awesome. To round out the program, Brody, a young dairy farmer, will sing some Garth Brooks country songs. ♂

I considered getting some of my priest buddies on the stage to sing Garth's song *Friends in Low Places*... but on second thought. The rehearsal ended after 11 p.m.

I stayed behind in the church to practice some of the piano pieces that I'll be playing at the concert. Then I said my prayers and headed to bed well after midnight.

Tuesday, July 27—It was another glorious morning here on the Ridge. I had a more balanced breakfast of a tall glass of water, Gordy Geier's homemade venison ring bologna and black coffee.

After the 8 a.m. Mass in Norwalk, I returned to the office for some time at my desk. Before I knew it, the day was half gone.

I worked outside for a bit in the afternoon. Then I cleaned up—got "back in black"—and drove to La Crosse to visit Al Malin in the hospital.

Al had undergone back surgery. The poor man had taken a nasty fall when a rafter gave way during a roofing project in May. Al's one who is accustomed to hard work, having farmed all his life on the farm that his son's family now operates. It has been sad to see such a strong man immobilized from pain, but the surgery went well, and he was all smiles and full of hope. We thanked God for that.

I stopped back at the rectory for 15 minutes—just enough time to eat a roast that I had thrown in the Crock-Pot earlier. The meat was delicious. Parishioners are too kind to me, always filling my freezer with meat from animals they raised.

Then I was off to St. Augustine's in Norwalk for a meeting. I was pleasantly surprised to see 16 parishioners in attendance to help plan their summer picnic.

It was getting late when I returned to the rectory. Across the road, I saw the lights on in the Schmitz farm shop. I couldn't think of anything more relaxing than ending a day chewing the fat with neighbors around a tractor under repair. So I turned around and pulled into the Schmitz driveway.

"Hey Father! You want a glass of cold lemonade?" asked Jimmy, who was busy working on a beautifully restored 1952 Super H Farmall tractor his grandfather owned.

PIG IN A JOKE. A little porker is the center of attention as Father Berns and Dennis Kelbel share a few laughs.

Photos: RJ & Linda Miller

Keeping him company were two other young men I know well. Chris is a diesel mechanic, which probably explains why everyone on the Ridge calls him "Diesel." With Diesel was Chuck Mlsna, a recent high school graduate I taught the catechism in preparation for his Confirmation. Chuck is heading to technical college this fall to study diesel repair. We joked about Jimmy's misadventures working on the tractor, and I laughed until my sides hurt.

Wednesday, July 28—I got up a little after sunrise this morning, had my coffee and spent some time in the church. After my prayers, I practiced the piano for Friday night's concert. My piano teacher will be at the concert, so the pressure will be on to play well. I worked the rest of the morning in the office.

In the afternoon, I played with Rocky for a while. Then I drove over to say hello to my neighbor Jim Schroeder. Jim is someone I could listen to all day. He has a deep melodic voice and a way of smiling and rocking his head that delights a listener. He's an interesting man, full of stories about life on the Ridge in the old days. He taught me how to roast a pig and loans me his grandmother's antique sausage stuffer.

After I left Jim's, I went to Dennis Kelbel's farm. Dennis raises hogs, and I wanted to talk with him about several pigs I'll be needing for upcoming parish events. "Take your pick," he said.

Just for kicks, I asked if I could catch one. Dennis laughed and said, "Good luck."

I tried several times in a pen full of 120-pounders, and when I finally grabbed one by the hind legs, it was like holding a jackhammer in my hands. I let go of the hog and raised my hands in the air like a champion. Dennis was doubled over laughing.

I had the 8 p.m. Mass at St. Mary's, a longstanding tradition here on the Ridge on Wednesday nights. I love to greet parishioners after church and talk with them about country things.

Mike Schmitz confessed that he'd accidentally sprayed his lawn with Roundup and killed it. His good wife, Darlene, made him reseed it. "Without rain lately, I've gotta water that grass every day," Mike complained.

Thursday, July 29—After coffee and leftover roast for breakfast, I had 8 a.m. Mass over at St. John's on Summit Ridge. St. John the Baptist is the picture of a small country church. The 135-year-old building is a simple red brick German structure that has seen very few changes in all those years. Behind the church is the cemetery filled with headstones bearing German names of families still living on Summit Ridge.

I grew up in Richland County, and tonight I had to drive an hour back to my hometown for a funeral vigil. I called my friend Dan, who also happens to be my dentist, and he loaned me his beautiful motorcycle for the trip. The sun was shining warmly as I left on his bike. After the vigil, I visited friends in the neighborhood of my childhood.

I returned late to St. Mary's Ridge, just as the dress rehearsal for tomorrow night's concert was wrapping up. People were excited and seemed to be ready, so I excused myself to my office for a bit of desk work before hitting the hay.

Friday, July 30—The big day! I woke up early and looked out my back window to see Melvin's gooseneck trailer decorated and transformed into a beautiful concert stage. The backdrop would be Mother Nature, with our impressive view of the long winding valley to the south accented by silos and Amish windmills on the horizon.

About noon, Bill arrived with his

flatbed implement truck. With the help of five strong men, we carried my baby grand down the aisle of the church, out the front door and onto Bill's truck. Bill then eased the truck around to the back of the house, where we set the piano in place on the stage. As he worked, we all watched the sky, nervous about the forecast of rain.

Come evening, I started off the concert with a prelude jazz number. On cue, the singers and musicians arrived across the lawn in Carl Bargabos's reproduction 1920s convertible Mercedes roadster. It was an elegant beginning to an evening that was classy to the last moment.

Lightning was visible almost 360 degrees on the horizon, but we stayed dry. Then, almost miraculously, the full moon came out from behind a cloud halfway through the show. After the last song, the piano was safely returned to the church. It was well after midnight by the time the last guests left, and I was exhausted.

Saturday, July 31—Morning came early. I woke up at 5:30 a.m. to a beautiful sunrise and stumbled to the coffeepot. I had to get busy, because we had promised fresh roast pork by 1 p.m. at the archery tournament.

I dumped two bags of charcoal into the roaster my brother Paul and I had made from an old fuel barrel and the gearbox from Dad's manure spreader. Once the charcoal was ready, I went to the walk-in cooler in the basement and fetched the first pig. The second one would be roasted in the afternoon.

By 7:30, the place was hopping, even though the competition wasn't scheduled to begin until 11 a.m. A representative from Mathews, Inc. arrived and set up an impressive display of bows. Mathews bows are made in the town of Sparta, only 20 minutes away, and they're acknowledged by most bow hunters to be the Cadillac of bows.

This was a fund-raising event for the parish, and judging by the crowd, it looked like a success. We had 114 competitors in the archery tournament, which took place in the rolling meadows below the church.

I removed my pig from the roaster and served it promptly at 1 p.m. Then The New Buckaroos arrived with their pedal steel guitar and two-man band. They kicked off their performance with *That Old Time Rock 'n' Roll*, and the mirth continued into the evening.

It turned out the winner of the tournament was someone with whom I had grown up in Richland County. At the trophy presentation, he held up the tro-phy, and then peeled off the $100 prize money taped to it and handed it back to me. "Use this for the church," he said as everyone applauded.

After we raffled off four Mathews bows, my parishioners gave me a large box filled with odds and ends. I pulled the items out one at a time for the amusement of the crowd: a shoebox filled with horse manure, a mock bow made from a willow branch and kite string, and stuffed animals.

After a good laugh, I was told to dig a little deeper in the box. Hidden in the bottom was a new Mathews Outback bow, a gift from my parishioners. I almost cried as I said, "I guess I'll have no more excuses in the woods this fall."

"My people"—that's how I like to refer to the families and farmers I serve in these parishes on and around St. Mary's Ridge. They are people who grew up in these hills and who wrap their arms around you and don't let you leave. From their fields, they see the steeple of St. Mary's Church watching over them and reminding them that God indeed dwells on the Ridge.　　　⌖

SERMONS ON THE MOUNT? Atop St. Mary's Ridge overlooking the farming valley is a tranquil place for prayer and meditation.

Country Folks Are the Salt of the Earth

*They're seasoned with life's simple pleasures…
like a stroll down a shady lane.*

By Barry Blackstone, Ellsworth, Maine

YOU CAN TAKE the boy of out the country, but you can't take the country out of the boy. That reality came shining through recently when the congregation I pastor gave me a salt lick for my birthday. After a recent sermon on salt, they wanted me to always have a memory of a salt lick on the Blackstone Homestead where I grew up.

If you're from the city, you're probably wondering, *What in the world is a salt lick?* It's a big block of salt—roughly a cubic foot in size—that farmers set out in the pasture so the cattle can get their proper intake of salt. And if you were raised on a farm, you've probably got a big smile on your face, because you know that cattle weren't the only ones who licked 'em!

Among the memories of growing up on a farm that I've shared with my congregation is that of peeling a potato and rubbing it on a salt lick before eating it.

Never Too Busy

There was always lots of work to do on my family's dairy farm, but we seemed to have enough time to stop and peel an apple or potato we'd just harvested.

It's been ages since I've seen anyone peel an apple before eating it. Today's hurried and harried generation doesn't have time to peel apples…let alone walk down to a cow pasture and rub a potato on a salt lick.

I recall my dad stopping in the middle of the busy potato harvest to peel one of the Katahdins he'd just dug up. He would jump off the tractor, find a nice one, peel it with his pocketknife and take a bite out of it.

If dinner was still an hour off and we were digging potatoes in a field near the cow pasture, I'd stop and do the same thing. After a quick trip to the cows' salt lick for seasoning for my raw potato, I had a meal fit for a king.

Simpler Times

My salt lick sits proudly on a shelf in my study. I am thankful I pastor a people who, though they've taken me out of the country, want me to stay a country boy.

It's also a symbol of an unhurried time when a person could enjoy the simpler pleasures of life.

Perhaps the act of eating a potato that you've just dug from the field and salted on the salt lick in the pasture belongs to a bygone era. If so, I feel sorry for those who were born too late to enjoy such an experience. It falls in the same category as enjoying the song of a sparrow, the serenity of a sunset or the solitude of a stroll.

Yet, if by chance we could revive those days, we might realize that in all our progress, we've lost the real seasoning that makes life worth living—peace and tranquility.

As for me, the city might have my body, but my country homestead still has my heart and soul…salt lick and all.

SPLASHED WITH SUNLIGHT and shadows, this country road near Peacham, Vermont offers wonderful sights during an autumn stroll.

YOU'VE HEARD of country folks giving you the shirt off their backs. Well, one *Country* reader went so far as to give a precious Christmas ornament off her own tree.

That's how helpful *Country* and *Country EXTRA* readers are—and one of the many heartwarming stories we've heard over the years in response to the "Can You Help Me?" section.

This is the feature in which readers ask fellow readers for help answering a question, sharing a long-lost recipe, locating an operator's manual for an old tractor, etc. The outpouring of help is often amazing and sometimes very touching.

For instance, back in 1995, Louise Capracotta of Webster, New Hampshire asked for help locating a 1974 Norman Rockwell collector's Christmas ornament. The following Christmas, Louise says, "A box with an unfamiliar return address arrived in the mail. When I opened the box, I found a Norman Rockwell card with a message that read, 'I took this off my tree so you could have it. I'm a big fan of Norman Rockwell, too.'

"Then it clicked—my request must have made it into *Country*. Shaking like a leaf, I reached inside the box and pulled out the ornament I'd sought for so long. Tears ran down my face.

"I called the New Jersey woman named Bettina who sent me the ornament, and we visited for 15 minutes.

"Talk about the Christmas spirit being alive and well! I never thought I'd get that ornament." After that, I received two more letters from women who offered to send one.

"I may never meet Bettina, but I think of her as my angel—and am so grateful for her kindness and thoughtfulness."

Dog's Best Friend

Audrey Bath of San Rafael, California discovered that *Country* readers were her dog's best friend when she asked for dog treat recipes for "Jake." "Would you believe I received *13,000 replies* to my tiny request for homemade biscuit recipes for Jake?" she reported incredulously.

"Along with recipes and personal letters, I've received hundreds of bone-shaped biscuit cutters, cookbooks and photographs galore. My request generated an outpouring of generosity from readers in every state, plus Canada, Switzerland, China and Africa."

Here's one of Jake's favorite biscuit recipes:

WHOLE WHEAT DOG BISCUITS

- 2-1/2 cups whole wheat flour
- 1/4 cup wheat germ
- 1 garlic clove, crushed
- 4 tablespoons margarine
- 1 egg, beaten
- 1/4 cup milk
- 1 tablespoon molasses
- Water

Combine flour, wheat germ and garlic in a large bowl. Cut in margarine. Stir in egg, milk and molasses. Add enough water so mixture can be shaped into a ball. Roll dough onto a floured board to a thickness of 1/2 inch. Cut into desired shapes and place on a greased baking sheet. Bake at 375° for 20 minutes. Cool. **Yield:** about 2-1/2 dozen.

A High Note

"Back in the Oct/Nov 1999 issue of *Country*, I wrote asking my fellow readers for advice on starting a kitchen band at the senior citizens center where I was activity director," writes Anita Harned from Bardwell, Kentucky.

"I got letters from 37 states, including audio tapes, pictures and diagrams showing how to make different instruments. It sounded fun, so we forged ahead and created the Carlisle Golden Oldies Kitchen Band.

"In 2000, we decided we were ready for the big time, so we entered a talent contest and won a first-place ribbon! We've been going strong ever since. We picked up our second blue ribbon at the Jackson Oakes Assisted Living Battle of the Bands.

"Anytime anyone will have us, we hop aboard our tour bus (the senior citizens center van) and head to area nursing homes, banquets, festivals and Christmas parties. Our audiences always seem to enjoy us, and I'm sure we have even more fun than they do.

"It all started when *Country* readers answered our call. So I want to thank everyone who helped and encouraged us from the bottom of my heart."

Turn to the next two pages for more examples of how readers lent a helping hand.

BLUE-RIBBON BAND. After *Country* readers helped get them started, this award-winning kitchen band has had a ball playing at festivals, parties and assisted living centers.

We receive some pretty amazing stories for this "I Can't Believe It!" feature in *Country EXTRA*, but one submitted recently by Dale Gardner of Colton, California really put a lump in our throats.

By way of background, Dale wrote to our "Can You Help Me?" column, asking for the words to an old cowboy song entitled *Little Joe the Wrangler*. In about 3 months, he received more than *1,400 answers*!

"People sent letters with the words, sheet music, photocopies and tapes of the song," Dale reports. "Some even recorded themselves singing the song and sent me the tape! It was wonderful.

"At least half the people thanked me for requesting the song, saying it brought back memories that had been buried for years.

"Many included heartwarming accounts of how a father, brother, cousin, uncle, friend or someone else had sung that song and how much it meant to them.

Heartfelt Letter

"But the most touching letter was one I received several weeks ago," Dale goes on. "It moved me so much that I called the writer, Elmer Anderson from Safford, Arizona, and got his permission to send it to you; I really felt it would touch the hearts of your readers."

Here's what Elmer wrote:

"I'd like to thank you for asking about *Little Joe the Wrangler*. That was one of my favorite songs back in the early 1930s. The only person I ever heard sing it was my brother Joe, so it fit us well.

"We were both orphaned when we were young. Our father was killed in an accident, and our mother, Rosa Smith, who was trying to raise six children by herself, got sick and had to give us boys up for adoption. We were living in Pawnee, Oklahoma at the time, and I was adopted by a farm family in Kansas. But then sickness hit the

I Can't Believe It!

Overwhelming response to "Can You Help Me?" proves country folks are always glad to lend a hand.

family, and I was on my own again—no home and no family.

"I became a transient, working wherever I could get a meal and a place to sleep. One day, I got a job working for a dairyman who had a lot of hay to put up. He also hired another drifter named Joe, who needed work, too.

"We were putting bales of hay in the barn one day when he told me he was born in Pawnee, Oklahoma. I told

MAIL MOUND. Dale Gardner (left) got answers from readers in every state, plus Canada, Australia, Germany and South Africa.

him I was, too. He asked me my mother's name, and when I told him it was Rosa G. Smith, we were stunned to realize that we long-lost brothers had been reunited by fate.

"That happened in Kansas in 1932. Joe and I rented a farm for $5 a month and worked all over for farmers for $1 a day and dinner. We lived in the old farmhouse for several months and learned a lot about each other. Joe sang the song often; that's where I learned it. You can imagine how special it is to me.

More Good News

"One day I wrote to the postmaster in Pawnee and asked if anyone still lived there by the name of Rosa G. Smith. About a week later, we got a letter from our mother; she was living there with our youngest sister.

"Shortly after that, I fell in love with a wonderful little orphaned girl and got married. Then a man who owned a 40-acre farm got transferred to another town; he didn't want to sell his family farm, so he asked us to move in and take care of the home and livestock.

"The family had a nice home, four milk cows and some chickens, so it was a great boost for us.

"There's an old saying that if someone shuts a door, the Good Lord will open a window, and it sure has worked for us many times. It took a long time and a lot of hard work, but we eventually owned our own farm—still do. We're retired, though, and live in Arizona near our kids and grandchildren."

Dale concludes, "Thank you for letting me share this letter with you from a man who commands the respect of us all. I know there are thousands of readers out there who will applaud my friend and yours, Elmer Anderson."

Thank you, too, Dale, for sharing this wonderful story.

Sister's Squeaky Shoes Are Silenced

Friendly Country readers come to the aid of a nun with noisy footwear.

By Sister Mary Richard Boo, Duluth, Minnesota

SQUEAKY SHOES are an annoyance, but in the peaceful silence of a monastery, they can be a disaster! Moreover, new shoes are hard to come by in most convents, so Sister Rebecca Burggraff (pictured below), a Benedictine Sister from Saint Scholastica Monastery in Duluth, Minnesota, turned to *Country* readers for advice on ridding her shoes of their squeak.

"I know the old saying that if your shoes squeak, it means you haven't paid the shoemaker for them yet. But these shoes are paid for, and they still squeak. Does anyone know a remedy?" Sister Rebecca wrote in her letter, which appeared in the "Can You Help Me?" section of a recent issue.

Soon, letters and more letters from readers all across the country began arriving at the monastery for Sister Rebecca. But what Sister found more interesting than the advice the letters contained were the people who wrote them.

Along with offering cures for Sister's squeaky shoes, the readers who wrote were reaching out, willing and eager to share a little of their own lives and past experiences.

Several writers were in their 90s. At least three were prison inmates eager for mail and asking for friendship. One correspondent explained that he had been in the shoe business for over 40 years, and another was a current manager of a shoe repair shop.

Some Sole-lutions

Topping the list of suggestions for curing Sister's squeaky shoes was to sprinkle some talcum powder inside them, shake them well and then dump out the excess powder.

Other remedies writers shared with Sister to rid her shoes of their squeak included using Vaseline, PAM Cooking Spray and Neats Foot Oil.

However, a 77-year-old Pennsylvania man who worked in his grandfather's shoe repair shop as a boy advises against applying any oil to shoes, telling Sister it destroys leather and "could possibly make you slip and fall."

He explained that when shoes are properly constructed, a thin piece of paper is inserted between the inner and outer soles.

"When the time comes to resole your shoes, make certain the cobbler knows how to put a paper between the leathers. I remember as a boy cutting paper inserts from the local newspaper for my grandfather," he wrote.

A retired shoe repairman told Sister that the shank inside her shoe may have worked loose and that a few correctly placed nails should take care of the problem.

One writer recommended Sister Rebecca return her shoes to the manufacturer for replacement, while a gentleman from Texas suggested she trade her squeaky shoes for a good pair of cowboy boots.

Laced with Kindness

While the suggestions may have varied, the unifying feature of all the replies was the fact that these individuals took the time to try to help. It takes time and effort—and 37¢—to write a letter, and they expended all three.

These are folks who would stop to give directions to a stranger, to find the owner of a lost dog or invite a neighbor in for a cup of coffee. They're people who are, in fact, a lot like Sister Rebecca herself.

Today, the letters Sister received are neatly alphabetized in a homemade file box, and she's busy answering as many of them as she possibly can. Certainly, she says, she will continue to write to the prison inmates "because they're lonesome and looking for mail."

And what of the shoes?

Well, Sister Rebecca shook some talcum powder in her shoes, and now she no longer squeaks when she walks up the chapel aisle.

But something even more valuable than a usable pair of shoes came out of this question-and-answer experience. Sister Rebecca—and the rest of us—were reminded that the spirit of kindness isn't just alive among country folks… it's flourishing.

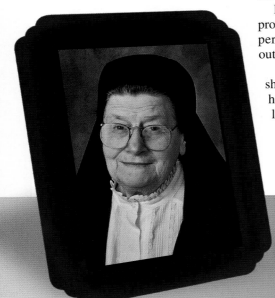

Julie Habel

POUND FOR POUND, you can't beat a country get-together for fun. Here, pumpkins are weighed in at a festival in Elkader, Iowa.

C'mon, Let's Head For the Country...

There's a rustling in the trees, a whisper that fall will soon arrive with all its glory. Join us as we take a sneak peak.

Alan L. Graham

TINGES IN THE TREETOPS. Hints of autumn are just beginning to show up in the trees surrounding a barn near Peacham, Vermont.

SUMMER'S SWAN SONG. A pair of graceful swans swim among a few fallen leaves in the Finger Lakes region of western New York.

Bill Banaszewski/Finger Lakes Images

AN ASPEN-LINED TRAIL leads into the John Muir Wilderness in California's Sierra Nevada. It's a hike, but, oh, the scenery's worth it.

STRAIGHT AND STATELY. Like the changing of the guard, aspens stand soldier-like, awaiting another changing of the seasons at Owl Creek Pass in southwest Colorado.

FEAST YOUR EYES on Mooselookmeguntic Lake (below) in the mountains of western Maine. The Native American name means "portage to the moose feeding place."

The First 20 Years

Allen Karsh

CROSSING THAT BRIDGE WHEN YOU COME TO IT isn't an adage to worry about when it is a covered bridge along the scenic backroads near Tunbridge, Vermont.

RIPE FOR THE PICKIN'. Amish farmers harvest a pumpkin patch in Lancaster County, Pennsylvania. That wagonload sure will make a lot of jack-o'-lanterns and pies.

EASY DOES IT. A sign in the Coronado National Forest in Arizona warns of a bumpy road ahead. That's okay—you'll want to slow down and enjoy the sights anyway.

Don Shenk

Morey K. Milbradt

Pat & Chuck Blackley

Don Shenk

MADE IN THE SHADE. A neat-as-a-pin farmstead (left) is nestled below a glowing maple tree on a farm near Barton, West Virginia.

CLINGING TO THE PAST. Vines sporting their fall colors climb a weathered old barn that's seen many an autumn come and go.

OFF THE BEATEN PATH. A canoeist quietly picks her way through the dense vegetation of the High Tor Marsh in Ontario County, New York.

Bill Banaszewski/Finger Lakes Images

THE IDYLLIC VILLAGE of West Barnet lies peace-fully in the Vermont countryside. You can almost hear neighbors calling out to one another.

AWASH WITH BEAUTY. Letchworth State Park (left) in western New York never looked more spectacular than on this bright autumn day.

Julie Habel

GOOD EATIN'. All across the country, as you head down the backroads, you'll find road-side farm stands displaying a cornucopia of nature's bounty this time of year.

FALL FIX-UP TIME. An Iowa farmer takes advantage of a sunny day to paint the barn. Bet his wife's going to be mad—he's wearing a good pair of overalls to paint in!

TURN THE PAGE and you'll see a stand of aspens just starting to turn color below snow-capped mountain peaks in the high country. This heavenly scene was photographed up where the air is rare in the Uncompahgre National Forest in southwestern Colorado.

A TASTE OF THE COUNTRY

EDITORS' POTLUCK

JOIN THE *COUNTRY* STAFF for a good old-fashioned potluck. From left to right: Jerry Wiebel, editor; Sandy Ploy, art director; Robin Hoffman, our meat-and-potatoes managing editor; and Maxine Burak, editorial assistant.

Some of our favorite recipes from 20 years of "A Taste of the Country" appear on the next several pages. So dig in...and be sure to save room for dessert!

GOLDEN MASHED POTATO BAKE

- 8 medium potatoes, peeled and cubed
- 1 package (8 ounces) cream cheese, cubed
- 2 eggs
- 2 tablespoons all-purpose flour
- 2 tablespoons minced fresh parsley *or* 2 teaspoons dried parsley flakes
- 2 tablespoons minced chives
- 2 teaspoons salt
- 1/4 teaspoon pepper
- 1 can (2.8 ounces) french-fried onions

Place potatoes in a saucepan and cover with water; cover and bring to a boil over medium-high heat. Cook for 20-25 minutes or until very tender; drain well. In a mixing bowl, beat the potatoes and cream cheese until smooth. Add the

SUNSHINE COCONUT PINEAPPLE CAKE

- 2 cups all-purpose flour
- 1-1/2 cups packed brown sugar
- 2 teaspoons baking soda
- 1 teaspoon salt
- 2 cups grated carrots
- 1 cup flaked coconut
- 1 cup chopped pecans
- 3/4 cup vegetable oil
- 2 tablespoons lemon juice
- 1 teaspoon vanilla extract
- 1 can (20 ounces) crushed pineapple

FROSTING:
- 1 package (8 ounces) cream cheese, softened
- 3 tablespoons confectioners' sugar
- 1 carton (12 ounces) frozen whipped topping, thawed
- Flaked coconut, optional

TERIYAKI SALMON

- 1/2 cup vegetable oil
- 1/4 cup lemon juice
- 1/4 cup soy sauce
- 1 teaspoon ground mustard
- 1 teaspoon ground ginger
- 1/4 teaspoon garlic powder
- 4 salmon steaks (6 ounces each)

In a large resealable plastic bag or shallow glass container, combine the first six ingredients; mix well. Set aside 1/2 cup for basting and refrigerate. Add salmon to remaining marinade; cover and refrigerate for 1-1/2 hours, turning once.

Drain and discard marinade. Place the salmon on a broiler pan. Broil 3-4 in. from the heat for 5 minutes. Brush with

DILLY CUCUMBER SALAD

- 1 cup sugar
- 1 cup white vinegar
- 1/2 cup water
- 1 tablespoon snipped fresh dill *or* 1 teaspoon dill weed
- 2 teaspoons salt
- 4 medium cucumbers, thinly sliced
- 1/3 cup sour cream

In a saucepan, combine the sugar, vinegar, water, dill and salt. Bring to a boil over medium heat. Remove from the heat. Place cucumbers in a large bowl. Pour vinegar mixture over and toss to coat. Cover and refrigerate overnight.

Drain and discard vinegar mixture. Stir sour cream into cucumbers. Cover and refrigerate until serving. **Yield:** 6-8 servings.

In a large bowl, combine the first seven ingredients. Combine the oil, lemon juice and vanilla. Drain pineapple, reserving juice. If necessary, add enough water to juice to measure 3/4 cup. Add oil mixture and pineapple juice mixture to dry ingredients; stir just until moistened. Fold in pineapple.

Place in a greased 13-in. x 9-in. x 2-in. baking dish. Bake at 350° for 40-45 minutes or until toothpick inserted near the center comes out clean. Cool on a wire rack.

For the frosting, in a large mixing bowl, beat cream cheese and sugar until smooth. Fold in whipped topping. Spread over cake; sprinkle with coconut if desired. Store in the refrigerator. **Yield:** 12-16 servings.

Meet the Cook

Danella McCall, Paradise, California
SUNSHINE COCONUT PINEAPPLE CAKE

This recipe is an old family favorite. My mother made it for us all the time, and now, I make it for my family. It tastes like a piece of sunshine.

eggs, flour, parsley, chives, salt and pepper; mix well.

Transfer to a greased 3-qt. baking dish. Bake, uncovered, at 325° for 45 minutes or until a thermometer reads 160°. Sprinkle with onions; bake 5-10 minutes longer or until golden brown. **Yield:** 12 servings.

Meet the Cook

Cathy Hanehan, Saratoga Springs, New York
GOLDEN MASHED POTATO BAKE

My husband and his brother are partners in a dairy farm, so I use lots of dairy products in cooking. The comforting creamy potatoes complement many main dishes.

Meet the Cook

June Stinson, Cedar Bluff, Alabama
DILLY CUCUMBER SALAD

In England, where I was born and raised, friends get together twice a year for English tea. We'd serve an assortment of dishes, and this cucumber salad was always a favorite.

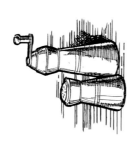

reserved marinade; turn and broil for 5 minutes or until fish flakes easily with a fork. Brush with marinade. **Yield:** 4 servings.

Meet the Cook

Jeannette Henderson, Stayton, Oregon
TERIYAKI SALMON

Salmon is special here in the Northwest, and we've often had the privilege of catching some in the Columbia River. This recipe never fails to be a hit, whether we broil the salmon in the oven or grill it outdoors.

CORN PUDDING STUFFED TOMATOES

8 medium tomatoes
1 teaspoon salt, *divided*
1/2 teaspoon pepper, *divided*
2 tablespoons all-purpose flour
2 tablespoons sugar
1/2 teaspoon baking powder
2 eggs, lightly beaten
1 cup half-and-half cream
1 cup whole kernel corn
2 tablespoons butter *or* margarine, melted
Minced fresh parsley

Cut a thin slice off the top of each tomato; scoop out and discard pulp. Sprinkle inside of tomatoes with half of the salt and pepper. Invert on paper towels to drain.

In a large bowl, combine the flour, sugar, baking powder and remaining salt and pepper. Combine the eggs, cream,

---

CARIBBEAN ROAST PORK LOIN

2 teaspoons olive oil
1 teaspoon pepper
3/4 teaspoon ground cinnamon
3/4 teaspoon ground nutmeg
1 boneless rolled pork loin roast (3-1/2 pounds)

Combine the oil, pepper, cinnamon and nutmeg; rub over roast. Place on a rack in a shallow roasting pan. Bake at 350° for 1-1/2 to 2 hours or until a meat thermometer reads 160°. Let stand for 10 minutes before slicing. **Yield:** 10-12 servings.

BLUEBERRY BUCKLE

1/4 cup shortening
3/4 cup sugar
1 egg
2 cups all-purpose flour
2 teaspoons baking powder
1/2 teaspoon salt
1/2 cup milk
2 cups fresh *or* frozen blueberries*
TOPPING:
1/2 cup sugar
1/3 cup all-purpose flour
1/2 teaspoon ground cinnamon
1/4 cup cold butter *or* margarine

In a mixing bowl, cream the shortening and sugar. Beat in egg; mix well. Combine the flour, baking powder and salt; add alternately to creamed mixture with

---

BACON POTATO CHOWDER

12 bacon strips, diced
2 medium onions, chopped
6 celery ribs, sliced
12 medium potatoes, peeled and cubed
2/3 cup butter *or* margarine
1 cup all-purpose flour
2 quarts milk
2 medium carrots, shredded
1 tablespoon salt
1 teaspoon pepper

In a large skillet, cook bacon over medium heat until crisp. Remove with a slotted spoon to paper towels. Saute onions and celery in the drippings until tender; drain.

Place potatoes in a Dutch oven and cover with water. Bring to a boil. Reduce heat; cover and cook for 20 min-

---

Meet the Cook

Denise Albers, Freeburg, Illinois
CARIBBEAN ROAST PORK LOIN

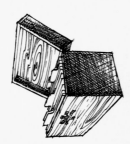

Here's an easy and different treatment for a boneless pork loin roast. Simply combine the oil and seasonings, rub it over the roast and bake. The meat turns out tender and serves a big group.

corn and butter; stir into dry ingredients. Spoon into tomatoes. Place in a shallow baking dish. Bake, uncovered, at 350° for 38-40 minutes or until a knife inserted near the center of corn pudding comes out clean. Sprinkle with parsley. **Yield:** 8 servings.

Meet the Cook

Jean Smalls, Cooper City, Florida
CORN PUDDING STUFFED TOMATOES

I use tomatoes and sweet corn harvested fresh from my garden to make this tasty—and attractive—side dish.

utes or until tender. Drain; set potatoes aside. In the same pan, melt butter. Stir in flour until smooth; gradually stir in milk. Bring to a boil over medium heat; cook and stir for 2 minutes or until thickened.

Reduce heat; add onion mixture, potatoes, carrots, salt and pepper. Cook for 10 minutes or until heated through. Sprinkle with bacon. **Yield:** 12-14 servings.

Meet the Cook

Bob Wedemeyer, Lynnwood, Washington
BACON POTATO CHOWDER

This is a hearty, stick-to-your-ribs potato soup. In place of the bacon, you can substitute cubed cooked ham.

milk. Fold in blueberries. Pour into a greased 9-in. square baking dish.

For topping, combine the sugar, flour and cinnamon; cut in butter until mixture resembles coarse crumbs. Sprinkle over batter. Bake at 350° for 40-45 minutes or until a toothpick inserted near the center comes clean. Cool for 10 minutes before cutting. Serve warm or cooled. **Yield:** 9 servings.

*Editor's Note: If using frozen blueberries, do not thaw before adding to batter.

Meet the Cook

Helen Dodge, Meriden, Connecticut
BLUEBERRY BUCKLE

I used to buy baskets of delicious blueberries from a man who had numerous bushes. One of my coworkers gave me this recipe, and it's become a favorite.

Meet Our Amish Friend Elsa...

WHEN Elsa Kline first wrote us and offered to keep "A Week in the Country" diary, she was a shy 19-year-old Amish girl baking cookies and canning produce for sale at a nearby farm.

She was also a dreamer with 5,000 copies of a self-published cookbook stacked in her parents' house, and a hunch that people might buy one if they got to know her. She was right.

In a series of warm funny stories, Elsa went on to share her life with us as she got married and started a family of her own. Amish adults aren't allowed to be photographed, so we couldn't show a picture of her. But through her writings, Elsa gave us a glimpse of real Amish life—not the Hollywood version. And she showed us that we're all far more alike than different.

As for those 5,000 cookbooks—they were barely the beginning for a girl with dreams as big as Elsa's. You'll enjoy getting to know her in the next 10 pages.

Photo taken in Holmes County, Ohio, where Elsa lives, by Steven J. Korba

Amish Woman Journeys Down Country Road

PROFILE: Elsa Miller is a 21-year-old Amish woman who lives with her family in Holmes County, Ohio. In addition to helping out at home, Elsa works in an Amish kitchen and is planning her upcoming wedding.

Sunday, Oct. 1—Greetings from Holmes County, Ohio. There are over 18,000 Amish living here, making this the largest Amish settlement in the world.

I live with my parents, Mose and Edna, in a small town called Trail. We have a barn and pasture for our horses, but my father doesn't farm. He makes and installs kitchen cabinets for a living.

I have two older sisters, Esta and Mary, both married, and two younger brothers, Mike, 19, and Andy, 17, who live at home. I'm 21 and engaged to be married next spring.

My 83-year-old grandmother, Orpha Hershberger, lives beside us in the little house—or "mommy haus" as we say in German. It's our Amish custom to have our elders live with or near us so

Come along for a "visit" as Elsa Miller keeps a weeklong diary of life in the heart of Ohio's Amish Country.

we can care for them.

Grandma was brought up without running water or indoor plumbing. When I catch myself complaining about not having a phone, television or a car, I think back to Grandma's stories about life when she was growing up. She was happy with what she had back then, and I should be, too.

We're Old Order Amish and rely on horses and a buggy for transportation. We don't have electricity in our home, but unlike Grandma at my age, we do have a gas refrigerator, gas stove and a gas-powered wringer washer.

I got up at 6 a.m. to make eggs and toast for the family breakfast. Then I put on my white cape, apron and Sunday dress to get ready for church.

In the Amish tradition, we have church every other Sunday. The service is held in a member's home because we don't have church buildings like other religions do.

We take turns, so every family only hosts church a couple of times a year. About 100 people usually attend—good motivation to do spring housecleaning!

My fiance, Allen, came over and together we walked to a neighbor's house where the services were being held this morning.

Allen and I were baptized last spring.

PENNY FOR THEIR THOUGHTS. Wonder what these Amish teenagers are pondering?

SCHOOL DAYS. On a good day to play hooky, these Amish children (left) walk under a canopy of brilliant fall colors on their way to class.

In the Amish church, it's customary to be baptized in your late teens or early 20s—when you're ready to make a commitment on your own. It's a decision that's brought me peace and joy.

Church started at 8:30. First, we sang songs out of our German hymnal for an hour. Then two preachers spoke on Matthew 18 and Corinthians 5 for about 2 hours.

After the service, I helped serve the lunch—homemade bread with peanut butter spread, lunch meat, cheese and pickles, with pie and cookies for dessert. We got home at about 1 p.m.

Allen spent the rest of the day at our house, and in the evening, we were all invited to a carry-in supper back at the house where church was held. After eating, we sang German songs and had a great fellowship.

It was a nice cool walk back to our house. Allen left soon after we got home.

Allen is a furniture maker, and I met him about 4 years ago at a softball game. Softball is a popular summer pastime among Amish teenagers—there are leagues and the teams usually play once during the week and on weekends, too. Allen and my brother-in-law played on the same team, and it was at one of their games that my brother-in-law introduced us.

Since he lives 8 miles away, I won't see Allen again until the weekend. Like a number of other Amish teens, he used to have a car, and I saw him more often then. But as part of his baptism commitment, he had to give up "his wheels."

Monday, Oct. 2—I got up at 5:30 a.m.—my usual time—and saw Dad and Mom off on a vacation. They're taking a 2-week bus tour to New England.

Then, before I went to work, I hand-washed a couple of my head coverings and cleaned and brushed our church clothing, including Allen's mutza (church suit).

I work 5 days a week at Yoder's Amish Home, which is a farm open to tourists near where I live. I've been working there for 7 years. (Amish children only go to school through the eighth grade, or about age 14.)

My job is baking and canning food to sell to the tourists who visit. We normally don't open for tours until 10 a.m., but this morning we had an early bus scheduled for 8:30. I had 20 loaves of fresh-baked bread, 10 pans of cinnamon rolls and three pans of brownies ready for them.

Visitors kept asking me to write out the recipes that my grandmother and mother taught me as a girl. So about a year ago, I published my own cookbook called *Amish Home Cooking with Elsa*.

In addition to the baking and canning recipes I use at work, the cookbook includes breakfasts, main dishes, desserts—even an Amish wedding menu, which I'll be using very soon.

Yoder's closes at 5 p.m. By 5:30, I had the kitchen cleaned up and was ready to go home.

Mom always has supper ready when the family gets home from work, but since she's gone, it'll be my responsibility to feed my two brothers for a couple weeks. Tonight I made mashed potatoes, dressing and gravy and fried some canned steaks. For dessert we had fresh peaches.

I cleaned the supper dishes, then folded the fresh-scented laundry Mom had washed and hung out to dry before leaving this morning. By then it was 10 p.m., and I was ready for bed.

Tuesday, Oct. 3—I awoke to a nice, warm fall day. Mike and Andy got up when I did and left for work about 6 a.m. They do construction work for our brother-in-law.

I like to see how Grandma is doing each day before going to my job. She is a sweet little "mommy" and still able to do her own housework. She also does a lot of quilting.

We have a kitten that Grandma likes to feed. We also have two horses, a buggy horse named "Lucky" and a riding horse we call "Buddy." I feed them morning and night. I give Buddy an apple from our tree every night, so he's spoiled rotten.

It was another busy day at work. I baked my usual bread, cinnamon rolls and brownies—plus some pumpkin chocolate chip cookies.

After my evening chores and supper, I started a grocery list—and I couldn't help but think about the wedding. It's scheduled for May 3, 2001…on a Thursday, which is the day we typically hold our weddings.

It'll be an all-day celebration. Like our church services, the ceremony will be held in a member's house. Afterward about 300 people will come to our place for the reception, with about 25 friends and family helping to prepare the meal. In the evening, we'll cut the wedding cake and open gifts.

Yoder's closes for the season at the end of October. I'll have time then to plan the wedding details, but it's fun to daydream in the meantime.

Wednesday, Oct. 4—My 5:30 wake-up time sure seemed to come quickly this morning. I packed the boys' lunch buckets, and they headed off to work.

COUNTRY FRESH. A breezy autumn day is perfect for drying the family laundry Elsa washed.

A Week in the Country...

HORSIN' AROUND. Youngsters amuse themselves with their toys in the back of a buggy.

The horses were out in the field overnight, so I brought them up to the barn and fed them. Then I washed our laundry and hung it outside on the clothesline to dry. About that time, the sun peeked through the clouds—I hoped it would stay out so the clothes would be dry when I got home.

We had four busloads of visitors scheduled for today, including 130 first graders. I baked a chocolate chip cookie for each of them, plus 30 loaves of bread...and I lost count of how many pans of cinnamon rolls. By the end of the day, we'd sold out of baked goods, but we sure had plenty of dirty dishes!

I was tired by the time I finished washing those dishes and got home. So I was happy to see Grandma had made chicken potpies for our supper. It's one of my favorite meals.

After supper I went grocery shopping. I figured it would give me some practice for when I have a home of my own...although I had to admit that I was getting eager for Mom to return. I felt like I'd become a mother overnight!

Thursday, Oct. 5—It was raining when I woke up, and I wasn't sure whether the boys could work in it. But they headed out anyway. Before I left for my job, I made a Rice Krispie ice cream dessert for supper tonight.

We only had a couple busloads of visitors, but I was still hopping all day. After my normal baking, Esther, who helps me a couple times a week, and I made 30 gallons of applesauce. We'll need that to make apple butter on Saturday. Then I diced tomatoes, onions and peppers and cooked a batch of spaghetti sauce for canning.

While making our own supper tonight, I wondered where Dad and Mom were. We hadn't received a postcard from them yet! I sure hoped they were enjoying themselves, because this vacation was very special and a long time in coming.

I finished my chores for the evening, and, with a prayer for our parents, went to bed at 10.

Friday, Oct. 6—Today's my day off work. So after the morning chores, I did the weekly housecleaning plus some laundry.

About 9:30 a.m., my cousin dropped off her 7-month-old son, Justin, for me to look after for the day. I love children, and babysitting is one of my favorite things to do.

In my spare time, I also enjoy making handcrafted cards, reading the Bible, visiting with my family and friends—and, of course, going to softball games.

The boys came home from work early this afternoon. They spent the rest of the day setting their crossbows to get ready for the bow and arrow deer hunting season, which starts tomorrow. The guys have been looking forward to it, now that softball is over.

Tonight Eli and Gloria Yoder, the people I work for, picked Allen and me up and took us out to eat at our favorite restaurant in Mt. Hope. What a treat!

After supper, we visited Allen's sister and her family before going home.

Saturday, Oct. 7—There was frost on the grass and rooftops when I woke Mike and Andy at 5:30 to go deer hunting. They saw several deer, but didn't have any luck.

Saturdays are usually busy days at Yoder's Amish

Home, especially in October when apple butter is cooked in an iron kettle over a fire.

Another girl and I baked 50 loaves of bread, 25 pans of cinnamon rolls plus cookies. We also canned some pepper and tomato relish.

We had five busloads stop by. As always, I met some interesting people, which makes my job enjoyable. So the time went fast.

But all day long, I wondered what to make for our supper, and I still did not have a clue on the way home.

When I walked in the house, there was Allen. He'd made supper for me! What a blessing after a busy day.

After supper, we relaxed by playing a game of Phase 10.

I have enjoyed sharing my week with you, and I hope that through this diary, I've given you a glimpse into the lifestyle of Amish young people.

I would love to visit with you in person. So if any of you ever get to Holmes County, stop at Yoder's Amish Home. I will be in the kitchen!

Who's Next? Would you like to share your country lifestyle with the rest of our readers by keeping a weeklong diary of your activities? If so, we'd like to consider you for a future issue.

Drop us a note telling a little about yourself, the best time of year to keep a diary at your place and what goes on during a typical week. Send it to "A Week in the Country," *Country*, 5925 Country Lane, Greendale WI 53129.

SUNDAY STROLL. A family heads down the road to a neighbor's house for church.

MAUDIE RABER ANSWERS YOUR QUESTIONS ABOUT THE AMISH

IN today's fast-paced world, there's a lot of interest in the Amish, and a curiosity about their simple way of life. So, to promote understanding of your country neighbors, we invited readers to submit questions they had about the Amish.

Then we asked *Country Field Editor* Maudie Raber, who is Old Order Amish, to answer these questions. Maudie and her husband, Andy, live on a farm near Millersburg, Ohio. In addition to farming, Andy operates a sawmill with seven employees.

Here are Maudie's answers to some questions from readers:

Q: Who founded the Amish religion and why?
—Mary Dacolias Wrightwood, California
A: The Amish are a Protestant religious group descended from the 16th-century Anabaptists. They believed baptism should only be conferred on adults, and from that movement, the Mennonite, Hutterite and Amish religions emerged.

The Amish take their name from Jacob Ammon, a Swiss Mennonite bishop, who broke away from the Mennonites in 1693 to form a more conservative church.

Q: Why can't the Amish use electricity or own automobiles, but they are allowed to use gas-powered appliances and ride in cars? *—Phyllis Kelsey, Eddyville, Iowa*
A: The Amish don't feel electricity is wrong. It's things that are run by electricity that we don't want. If we stay away from electricity, we aren't tempted to have a TV and similar things that our church bans. Like anyone else, we're tempted to do what we shouldn't do.

We consider a car a worldly possession. But as far as accepting rides, Jesus never owned a boat; however, he rode in them.

Q: Are the Amish of German descent? Do Amish children speak German first and learn English later when they go to school? *—Mrs. Vernon Glanz, Scottsbluff, Arizona*
A: The Amish were originally from the region along the Ger-

Read what this Amish farm woman has to say about her religion and way of life.

Randall Pershing

AMISH BOYS, like this teenager, work alongside their fathers and learn how to handle the lines of a team of draft horses at an early age.

man-Swiss border and spoke German, although a different dialect than we use now.

German is still our main language. The children start learning English before they go to school…although they sometimes forget and mix in some German words. Even we old people do that sometimes!

Q: Farming is central to the Amish way of life, but does everyone farm?
—Cheryl Masters Commerce, Texas
A: Not all the Amish can farm. A lot of men work as carpenters, as furniture makers, in sawmills or in factories.

Farming is really a hard way to make a living nowadays, with milk prices so low. But it's the best place to raise a family. On the farm, Amish families work together, and the children learn how to take care of the farm animals and each other.

Q: Do all Amish girls learn to sew? Do you sew by hand or use a machine? *—Mary York, Woodland, Washington*
A: Yes, we teach all our girls to sew, but some learn more easily than others! One of my daughters prefers cleaning the barn to sewing, but she can sew when she needs to. Another daughter loves to sew and makes fine quilts.

We use treadle sewing machines. Some use battery-powered machines.

Q: What breed of horse do the Amish prefer for pulling their buggies? *—Carol Mulder, Elk Grove, California*
A: We use Standardbreds for buggy horses. They are lighter and have more speed than the Belgians or Percherons we use for farmwork. Many have Saddlebred horses for riding, too.

Q: I'm curious why the Amish hold their worship services in their homes instead of in a church. *—Caitlin Overton Lenoir, North Carolina*
A: When the Amish church started, the members faced persecution. They held church services in their homes so they would not be found out. Also, the early church members couldn't afford to build churches. Now, it's mainly tradition.

GETTING HITCHED AMISH STYLE

Blair Seitz

There's lots of food, fun and camaraderie at an Amish wedding.

By Elsa Kline, Millersburg, Ohio

EDITOR'S NOTE: *Last winter, Elsa Miller, a young Amish woman from Holmes County, Ohio, kept a diary of her country lifestyle for the "Week in the Country" section of the magazine. She mentioned that she was getting married in May, and we thought it would be interesting to follow up and learn about an Amish wedding. So we asked Elsa—now Mrs. Elsa Kline—to share her wedding day with us in this issue.*

ALLEN and I were married on Thursday, May 3. Amish weddings are usually on Thursdays. That's because the reception is held in the home of the bride's parents. Sunday is a holy day when we don't work. So holding the wedding on a Thursday gives us time to prepare the food in advance as well as a couple of days to clean up afterward.

You'll appreciate the importance of that when you learn how many potatoes we peeled for our 450 guests! But I'm getting ahead of myself.

Back in January, I started sewing my wedding dress. We're Old Order Amish, and the bride doesn't wear a white wedding gown. Instead, I wore a traditional navy dress with a white cape and apron and a black bonnet.

My two witnesses wore the same kind of dress that I did. Allen and his two witnesses wore a white shirt and black dress suit called a mutza.

Months before the wedding, we reserved the equipment we needed for the reception, including a gas-powered walk-in cooler to refrigerate food as well as a food warmer. The food warmer consists of a huge gas burner that heats a tank of wa-

ter for keeping big kettles of food warm until it's served.

We also rented a mobile kitchen that had five ovens, tables, 300 place settings and all of the cooking kettles, roasters, mixing bowls and utensils we needed for such a big gathering. It arrived the Thursday before the wedding.

Some families hold their reception in the house, moving the furniture out to make room for everyone. We held ours in the shed where we store our buggy, and we had it cleaned out and ready to go when the mobile kitchen arrived. So with the help of friends and family, we went right to work Thursday evening setting up tables.

It got really exciting on Friday night, when we fixed up the bridal table. Allen set out the dishes while my sister Mary and I put the finishing touches on the skirt for the bridal tablecloth I'd made.

Homemade Date Cake

I've collected family recipes and published a cookbook called *Amish Home Cooking with Elsa*. One of my favorite recipes in that cookbook is date pudding cake, and I wanted to serve it at the wedding reception. So on Saturday, several aunts and cousins came to help bake some.

We also hung baskets of flowers here and there and spruced up the landscaping around our house.

With all of the activity, I was ready for a nap after church on Sunday afternoon.

On Monday, it was back to work again. We cleaned house and washed windows. Dad and Allen set up benches around the big long tables where we'd be eating.

It got even busier on Tuesday, when 10 friends and neighbor ladies came to help prepare food. They made a caramel sauce for the date pudding cake and a strawberry glaze with fresh strawberries. They also chopped up carrots, parsley and cooked potatoes for homemade stuffing and cut up radishes, red cabbage, cucumbers and bacon for the tossed salad.

Getting Excited

After the helpers left, I had some quiet time to think and kept wondering—is this actually *my* wedding we're preparing for? Before when I'd helped with preparations, it was always for a sister or cousin. But this time it's for me!

With just 1 day to go, I woke up Wednesday morning concerned about getting everything done. It was a beautiful sunny day, and my sister Esta and I picked bouquets of lilacs and set them on the windowsills in the shed. (My colors were lavender, sage green and cream.)

Then Esta, Mary and I peeled 250 pounds of potatoes to mash. I thought we'd never finish! Mom and my aunts mixed the stuffing ingredients in big mixing bowls.

My wedding cake arrived at 5 p.m. After that, about all that was left to do was a little last-minute cleaning.

I got up a 3:30 a.m. on my wedding day. Allen kidded me and said it must have been because I was nervous. But I had things I needed to get done, including arranging the flowers on the bridal table, before the helpers arrived at 6 a.m.

Since we Amish don't have churches, it's tradition to hold the wedding ceremony at a neighbor's place. Ours was held two doors down in the second story of our neighbor's barn.

You may think it's unlucky for the groom to see the bride before the ceremony. But in an Amish wedding, it's customary for the bride and groom and their witnesses to walk to the ceremony together. The morning was warm and sunny when Allen and I and our witnesses headed out at 7:30.

Lasted All Morning

The service started at 8:30 and lasted until noon. That may seem long for some people, but it went really fast for me.

We started out singing hymns, and that was followed by two ministers preaching for a couple of hours. About 11 a.m., all of the helpers came over from my parents' house to watch the actual wedding ceremony. It was performed by the bishop, who is also my uncle.

Then, after some more singing, we all went to my parents' place for lunch. My cousin Gary drove Allen and me back with a horse hitched to an open buggy. There were balloons tied to the buggy, and the horse even had glitter on his back. It was great!

There were about 300 guests for lunch. To serve that many people, we had 23 cooks, 36 table servers, eight coffee and water servers and 11 young boys and girls to hand out mixed nuts and mints. It's an honor to be asked to help at a wedding. I always looked forward to serving at my cousins' weddings.

UP, UP AND AWAY. The children released balloons with the newlyweds' names on them. Two of the balloons were found 50 miles away.

After we ate, Allen and I gathered the children together, and they released 50 balloons with our name (my new name!) and address tied to them. The children got quite a kick out of it. It was fun for Allen and me, too, because we later heard from people clear up by Cleveland, who'd found two of the balloons and wrote to congratulate us.

We gave gifts to all of the people who helped cook and serve, then opened our wedding gifts so everyone could see what we got.

Friends Helped Celebrate

At 5 p.m., after our first group of guests left, we served a second meal—this time to about 150 of Allen's and my unmarried friends. It's customary to have a separate celebration with just the young people. It's a fun social event, and you never know when a get-together like this might lead to another wedding in the future!

After we finished eating, we sang songs. Then Allen and I cut our wedding cake. But the wedding cake wasn't served to the guests. It's tradition to give all of the helpers a piece to take home with them.

Our guests didn't go away hungry, though. In total for both meals, we served 250 pounds of grilled chicken breasts, 250 pounds of mashed potatoes plus stuffing, 40 heads of lettuce for salads, 40 quarts of corn…and I lost track of how many gallons of gravy.

Black Raspberry Pie

For dessert, we served date pudding cake, 30 black raspberry pies and 30 angel food cakes. And, oops, I almost forgot the 650 dishes of ice cream!

By 8 p.m., everyone had left, and Allen and I helped our families clean up. Like most couples, we didn't go on a honeymoon and finished helping with the cleanup on Friday.

Then, on Friday evening, my husband and I settled into our home in Mt. Hope. We're renting a place there until we can buy some land on which to build a house of our own.

Happy Anniversary to These Amish Newlyweds!

Although they live a slower-paced life, their first year of marriage flew by.

By Elsa Kline, Mt. Hope, Ohio

EDITOR'S NOTE: *Readers first got to know Elsa Kline about a year and a half ago when she kept "A Week in the Country" diary. Back then, she was known as Elsa Miller, a 21-year-old Amish woman engaged to be married.*

We did a follow-up story a few issues later, in which Elsa described her wedding day and the preparations that went into it—like peeling 250 pounds of potatoes for more than 450 wedding guests!

Elsa and her husband, Allen, have been married a little over a year now. We thought it would be interesting to learn how these Amish newlyweds are doing. So we asked Elsa to give us an update.

ALLEN AND I got married on May 3rd of last year, and we moved to Mt. Hope, which is a town of about 50 people in the heart of Amish country in Holmes County, Ohio.

We're renting a two-story house, a barn, shed and a small field for our horse "Anno." Like traditional Old Order Amish,

we don't have electricity, depending instead upon a gas-powered refrigerator, stove, wringer washer and well pump.

However, we do have a telephone—at least for the moment. We're renting from a newer order of Amish, who allow phones in their homes, and we were granted permission from our order to use it since it's here. But someday, we hope to build our own home, and then we'll have to give up the telephone.

Some people may think of a house without electricity, computers and other modern conveniences as a rather spartan existence. But we love our rented home, especially when we think of all of the people in the world with no place to call home.

Canned 200 Quarts

We have a large garden in the backyard where we grow sweet corn, potatoes, tomatoes, peppers and other vegetables. Last year, I canned about 200 quarts of applesauce, tomato juice, pizza sauce, spaghetti sauce, etc., and froze things like sweet corn, which we keep in a rented locker box. That's enough for the two of us, but as our family grows, we'll need to can even more.

That reminds me—Allen and I are expecting our first baby in August!

I really enjoy canning, cooking and baking. (Elsa has published a cookbook of family recipes called *Amish Home Cooking with Elsa*, which is available through our Country Store catalog.) But it was quite a change when I first got married and didn't have Mom next to me in the kitchen to offer helpful hints or answer my questions.

We eat a lot of spaghetti. But Allen's favorite meal is mashed potatoes, dressing, sweet corn and chicken—or better yet, steak.

Before we got married, I worked in the kitchen at a tourist attraction called Yoder's Amish Home. I continued working there several days a week for a while, but now I'm down to 1 day a week. I'm looking forward to staying home all the time to be a housewife and mother when the baby's born.

Day Starts at 4:30 a.m.

Allen works at a furniture factory, making kitchen hutches and tables. It's about a mile from our house, and he rides his bike to work.

A typical day for us starts at 4:30 a.m. I'll pack Allen's lunch, and he heads off to work at 5:30. Then I'll wash clothes and hang them out to dry, mow the yard, work in the garden or do some baking.

Allen gets home at 4:30 p.m., and we eat supper about an hour later. After supper, we may work in the yard or garden together, visit family or neighbors—or Allen may work with the new horse he bought. That's his hobby.

Since morning rolls around so early, we try to wind down our evening by about 9:00. But in the summer, it's often closer to 10.

My parents live 5 miles away, and about once a week, I'll drive Anno down to see my mother and 84-year-old grandma, Orpha, who lives in a little house next to them.

Anno is a good horse and easy for me to handle. But don't ask me how he came by his name—he was called that when we bought him.

Hosted Church Service

Shortly after our wedding anniversary, we hosted our first Sunday church service. The Amish hold church services in their homes rather than at a church, and each family within a district (consisting of a group of about 35 families) is expected to take a turn once or twice a year.

Newlyweds are given about a year to get their household set up before they're expected to host the service. Good thing, because we had more than 120 people at our house!

That meant some serious spring housecleaning—from top to bottom, inside the furniture drawers and out.

Several days before the service, the bench wagon arrived with all of the benches, songbooks and dishes we'd need to accommodate everyone. Since we have a storage shed, we set the benches up and held the worship service there.

In our district, the worship service starts at 8:30 a.m. and lasts until about noon. The children sit with their parents, and if they're well-behaved, they get treats of pretzels, crackers and cookies afterward.

After the service, the host family serves lunch, and the peo-

ple visit and have fellowship until late in the afternoon. That's most likely what's going on if you take a Sunday afternoon drive through Amish country and see lots of buggies parked by a barn, or people sitting on benches and visiting in the yard.

The lunch is a simple fare, including sandwiches of homemade bread, cold meat and cheese or a peanut butter spread we make out of peanut butter, marshmallow cream and pancake syrup. (Of course, there are no calories in it!) The menu also typically includes pickles, pickled red beets, cookies and pies.

I was a little nervous hosting so many people for the first time and lay awake the night before wondering if I had enough food. But everything went pretty well.

Enjoy Camping

Of course, we do more than work and go to church. We like to have fun, just like other newlyweds.

Allen and I enjoy fishing and camping. A couple of times during the summer, we'll go for a weekend camping trip to Tappen Lake, and occasionally just for a day of fishing. It's about 50 miles from our house, which is too far to take a horse and buggy. So we hire a van and driver to take us.

Winter offers a nice break from gardening and all of the other summer chores. I spend it stamping and creating enough homemade greeting cards and envelopes to last a year. Then I'm ready for spring again.

We also have fun spending time with our families, including Grandma Orpha. Moving away from her and my parents was my hardest adjustment to being married. But God brought Allen and me together for a reason, and I couldn't ask for a better husband.

We'd frozen the top of our wedding cake, and we celebrated our first anniversary by eating it for supper. If every year is as wonderful and passes as quickly as our first year did, we'll be married 10 years before we have our first argument! ✦

It's a Girl!

WE'VE BEEN FOLLOWING the life of a young Amish woman, Elsa Kline of Mt. Hope, Ohio, including her engagement to husband Allen and their wedding. So readers feel as though they know Elsa, and some even sent wedding well wishes.

In the Aug/Sep 2001 issue, Elsa wrote about their first year of marriage ("Happy Anniversary to These Amish Newlyweds!", page 16) and mentioned that she and Allen were expecting their first child. Many readers have asked about the baby, and we're happy to report that Elsa had a girl, Elizabeth Gail, on August 17. She weighed 7 lbs. 13 oz.

Both Mom and daughter are doing well. "She has dark hair, and Allen and I are both blond, so that was a surprise," says Elsa.

Amish for a Day

Join our intrepid editor as he visits his very first Amish family.

By Robin Hoffman, Managing Editor

BEFORE I even knock on Allen and Elsa Kline's door, the cheery flower beds, pumpkins and cornstalks in the front yard throw me a little off balance. I expected something more...serious, and probably should have known better.

Many of you may remember Elsa as the author of *Amish Home Cooking with Elsa* and three warm funny stories she wrote for *Country* before and after her Amish wedding in 2001.

Since then, she has become a mom and moved back to her hometown of Trail, Ohio, where she and Allen bought the house she lived in as a little girl.

To get a feel for everyday Amish life, I planned to spend a day doing what Elsa normally does. Turns out, though, they get up at 4:30, so I decide to do what she normally does after 8 or so.

When I arrive, she has already made breakfast, sent Allen off to work, baked a batch of buttermilk cookies, washed a load of laundry and hung it out by the light of a harvest moon.

Better late than never, I pitch in and eat cookies as Elsa frosts them. She is petite, blond and speaks with a soft German accent. In her traditional crisp blue Amish dress and white head covering, she looks exactly as I expected.

CAMERA SHY. The Amish prefer not to be in photos, so you have to settle for the author (above) driving "Betty" and an Amish buggy. It's a shame, because Allen, Elsa and Gail are *way* more photogenic. That's their surprisingly modern house and tidy barn at the top.

Just about everything else takes me by surprise. I always regarded the Amish as a people trapped in time, and couldn't have been more wrong.

Great Chatters

We spend the morning chatting, chopping peppers for a batch of relish and fixing lunch, which is delicious, by the way. Meanwhile, the cutest little pigtailed blond 2-year-old in the world barrels around on a John Deere pedal tractor, rummages through kitchen drawers, pulls the stuffing out of a doll and babbles happily away in German.

That's Gail, and "She's a handful," Elsa says. But she's so sweet and well-behaved, I'd peg her at barely half a handful. And I'm a tough grader.

As we talk about everything from the trials of being a first-time mom to the Amish religion, Elsa seems remarkably relaxed and open, as if chatting with reporters is the most normal thing in the world. In fact, all the Amish I meet on this trip are great chatters.

My biggest surprise, though, is the way Allen and Elsa live: If you toss in a television and a couple weeks' worth of dust bunnies, you basically couldn't tell their house from mine.

They aren't hooked up to the electrical grid. But they have running water, thanks to a gasoline-powered pump. The lights, furnace, range, refrigerator and water heater run on natural gas.

A compact Honda electric generator

powers her wringer washer. "We used to have a gas engine underneath the washer," she explains. "The noise and fumes were terrible. This is much better and safer."

I expected to find the subsistence farmers we see in movies and tourist magazines. But today, less than 10% of the 18,000 Amish in Holmes County farm full-time, notes Paul Miller with the Amish and Mennonite Heritage Center in nearby Berlin. They outgrew the supply of affordable farmland long ago.

Members of the Swartzentruber Amish order still farm and maintain much stricter rules about modern conveniences. But they're less than 3% of the county's Amish population, he says.

Most Amish have to shop at the grocery store, commute to work and compete with the "English" for jobs and housing. ("I'm sorry," Elsa apologizes. "I don't know what else to call you. There's Amish, Mennonite and English. But we're all one family in Christ.")

The Furniture Factory

At lunch, an employee with a car drops Allen off so he can guide me back to the Mennonite-owned furniture factory where he's the general manager.

Along the way, signs for Amish furniture makers line the roller-coaster roads like pickets in a fence. It's clearly the preferred livelihood replacement for agriculture.

Allen doesn't share Elsa's German accent, and has been out and about more than she has. As a teenager, he played on a competitive softball team that traveled to tournaments as far away as Colorado.

Like all Amish kids, Allen only had 8 years of formal schooling, but says, "This is the job I always dreamed of." He notes that he's 4 weeks into a 12-week Dale Carnegie management course alongside mainly college-educated businessmen.

"It's interesting," he says thoughtfully. "They're definitely pushing my comfort zone."

Things are no less incongruous at the factory, where Allen uses a computer and Amish craftsmen operate state-of-the-art computer-guided routers.

But they can build up to 20 beautiful dining room tables and 10 hutches a day, providing a good living for more than 20 employees. And he's excited about plans to expand in the near future.

End of the Day

Back in Trail, Elsa and I drop Gail off at her parents' house just across the road. My "Amish for a day" plan suffers another setback with all this driving around. I was looking forward to a buggy ride, but Elsa's beloved little buggy horse, "Anno," died last year, and she doesn't trust the new one yet.

We drive my car a few miles south to Yoder's Amish Home, where Elsa cooked full-time for 8 years. It's a pic-

"*They're definitely pushing my comfort zone...*"

turesque Amish farmstead that Eli and Gloria Yoder run as a tourist attraction.

"This is where I got the idea for my cookbook," Elsa says. "Everybody kept telling me I should write down my recipes, so one winter I did."

Then she hired a photographer, found a printer, ordered 5,000 copies and dove into the competitive world of cookbook marketing. She was 19.

Of the dozens of professional writers I know, only one has actually tried anything like Elsa. And I'd bet the ranch he hasn't sold 40,000 copies like she has. I'm in awe of what she has accomplished.

Emma, our guide, explains that everybody at Amish church services—from children on up—sits on backless wooden benches for 3 solid hours. I try to picture Gail holding still for that long.

"I can remember exactly what she's going through," Elsa smiles. "It's pretty hard." Then she adds more seriously, "But it's good training."

Emma notes that the average Amish family has seven children. I glance over at Elsa, who just rolls her eyes. Later she says, "Gail plays a lot with the kids who live up the hill from our place, and they've been a very good influence. Their mother is so calm, and they're such good kids. I don't know how she does it."

I don't tell her that's exactly how I'd describe her and Gail. She'll surely figure that out on her own someday.

I ask how many Amish kids join the church. She doesn't know the statistics, but so far six of Allen's seven siblings have joined. Of the five kids in Elsa's family, an older sister and a younger brother chose other churches.

"You'd like all your family to join the Amish church," Elsa says. "But we're all still together, and we're all happy." She seems more at peace with her life than any 25-year-old has a right to be.

At the end of the day, Elsa sends me home with a Cool Whip container full of buttermilk cookies and a far greater appreciation for Amish culture.

Like all of us, they're trying to balance the values they hold dear against the necessity of earning a living in a modern world. It's hard, hard work, but they truly seem to view the job as a blessing, not a burden.

COOKING LESSON. I helped Elsa make pepper relish from her cookbook recipe. She's mercifully patient with inept assistants.

COUNTRY has always been a little different from most other magazines—starting with the fact that it doesn't contain advertising.

This absence of advertising is all the more reason why we *have* to do things differently. You see, ad-based magazines cover 60% or more of their costs with these ads, whereas *Country* subscribers must pay for 100% of our costs with their subscriptions.

So Roy Reiman, founder of Reiman Publications, reasoned that there must be some *unique* things in *Country* to tickle readers' fancy—so much so that they'll want to pay all of the freight. "Make them different, then better," Roy's always said of *Country* and other Reiman Publications magazines.

That's led to some "crazy" ideas other publishers wouldn't dream of doing—like our marginal notes, even tucking hundred dollar bills alongside a rainbow picture in a handful of magazines, so one lucky reader in each state and Canadian province would find that proverbial "pot of gold" in his or her issue of *Country*.

Another Crazy Idea

It's that philosophy that also led to our "Needle in the Haystack Contest" that's been a part of *Country* since 1990.

In his "Country Comments" in the April/May issue of that year, Roy describes how this contest came about:

"I've always believed that no one ever really outgrows a Cracker Jack box. The "surprise" inside, that is.

"You always know it isn't going to amount to much—maybe just some little plastic gadget, but you still dig down inside that box to find *what kind* of plastic gadget it is.

"For a long time now, I've thought the same thing should be true of every issue of *Country*. There should be some sort of surprise inside each issue that makes readers search through it page by page, just for the fun of seeing if they can find it.

"Finally, I challenged our staff to

give some thought to this and then submit their best ideas. This resulted in several novel suggestions, but the out-and-out best one came from one of our youngest staffers, Sharon Selz. I think you'll agree it's a great one.

"I wanted the surprise element to be something truly *country*, that is, something that would fit in with our audience and content. And Sharon's suggestion surely is: 'Let's take our readers on the hunt in each issue for a needle in the haystack.'"

Out of that suggestion, *Country's* Needle in the Haystack Contest was born.

We hide a drawing of a needle in every issue of *Country* (two in *Country EXTRA* for *extra* fun). It could be under a headline, in the margin, a photo or illustration—just about anywhere, which is why it's like looking for a needle in a haystack

Readers who find the needle tell us the page on which it's located. We then

FOUND IT! Paul Ward, Covington, Georgia, jokingly sent us a photo of a tree on his property that resembles our needle. Well, almost anyway!

draw 50 names at random from among the correct entries, with the winners receiving a prize.

The prize for that first contest was an apple pie baked by Amish homemaker Maudie Raber of Holmes County, Ohio. Maudie's one of our Field Editors.

She baked the 50 pies in her farm kitchen, took them to town in her horse and buggy and had them shipped by Federal Express in a special container to arrive fresh at the winners' homes the next day.

Thousands of Entries

Response to the contest was amazing. *Thousands* of readers began hunting for the needle in the haystack after the contest was first announced. Roy even received a letter from actor Ernest Borgnine. (We didn't even know he was a subscriber.) "I have looked and looked, and cannot find that insufferable needle," Ernie wrote from Beverly Hills. A day later, he wrote, "I found it!"

Almost 20 years later, the Needle in the Haystack Contest is still a point (pardon the pun) of interest among subscribers. In fact, we typically get *6,000 to 8,000 entries per issue*!

And talk about tenacity! Early in 2005, we received this letter from Robin Bacon of Kingsport, Tennessee:

"My mother has the July 1997 issue of *Country EXTRA* and has been trying to find one of the needles hidden in it. She has found the needle on page 29, but she cannot locate the other one. Could you please let us know where the other needle is located?"

Now *that's* a serious needle searcher!

One more thing: Just for fun, we've hidden a needle somewhere in this book. There's no prize for this one—we just thought you'd enjoy searching for it. Good luck!

It Takes a Sharp Eye To Find the Needle

One reader has been searching the haystack for one for 8 years!

Hurrah for the January Thaw!

Julie Habel

WINTER on the Minnesota prairie seemed never ending, with deep snow and day after day of frigid temperatures. As is often the case, it hit with full force in mid-November, became even worse in December, and when I turned the calendar to January, it was a cold reminder that spring was still a long way off.

Then one mid-January morning, I awoke with a warm feeling. Sunshine flooded the bedroom, and I rushed to read the temperature on the indoor/outdoor thermometer by the window.

"Could it be?" I wondered. "Could this be the January thaw?"

On the way to the barn, I noticed the snow had lost its crunch as I walked on it. Instead, it had a soft feel under my boots.

The barn cats had been holed up out of the cold and wind. But today, some of them followed me out into the sunshine. *They, too, must feel it!* I thought to myself.

Around noon, I saw and heard little drops of moisture from the melting snow dripping from the eaves. Soon, it was running off the rooftops like a summer rain. No doubt about it, this was the long-awaited January thaw!

In the barnyard, ruts in the ice and snow made tiny dams in

This break in the weather arrives almost like clockwork…giving hope to folks weary of winter.

By Darwin Anthony, Trimont, Minnesota

the path of the snowmelt. Recalling the fun I used to have as a child, I broke those dams, giving the water its freedom to run downhill toward a large pond in the field.

Of course, after a lifetime on the Minnesota prairie, I knew that the January thaw was just toying with me—providing just enough warmth to let my guard down and even take my heavy coat off as I spent the whole day outdoors.

Late in the afternoon, the sun sank low in the sky. Its warm rays vanished, and I reached for my coat again. The puddles quickly froze over behind newly formed dams, and the crunch returned to the snow as I walked across the yard.

As dusk settled in, the gentle southerly breeze that brought the January thaw now felt raw and damp as it blew across the landscape. Dark clouds formed in the northern sky as I went back to the house, portending the return to the reality of winter.

Still, it was a beautiful day. As I reflected on it, it occurred to me that some folks may wonder why we live on the Northern prairie, where it's so cold for so long.

I'd answer by simply saying, "If we lived where it was warm all the time, how could we appreciate the January thaw?"

QUOTES FROM THE COUNTRY

Even My Barn Chores Bring Contentment

We asked 4,000 readers who've subscribed since the very first issue: "How has love of the country shaped your life?"

I REMEMBER the '29 Crash, and how the seven of us survived. In the spring, we picked wild poke greens and sassafras. Then came asparagus, gooseberries, cherries, strawberries, vegetables, blackberries, apples, grapes and peaches. We knew how to work.

I got married, moved across country and eventually worked in the fields alongside my three sons. They knew how to work, too.

In 1971, the nest emptied and I moved to Florida to try the life of a town woman. What a shock! There was rent to pay and no garden.

One day while visiting my son and his family in Tennessee, I knew it was time to get back to the country. He built me a nice house close to his garden, and welcomes my spare hands.

I turned 81 this year and found myself canning tomatoes and peaches on my birthday, just like I always have. And I wouldn't have it any other way.

—*Rebecca Wells Duncan*
Parson, Tennessee

I STILL LIVE in the little town where I grew up as a farmer's daughter. With no brothers, we girls became our father's helpers.

After my own kids grew up and left home, those early lessons came in handy when I sold my town business and became a full-time farm-her (as I call myself).

Dad had retired and happily became his daughter's helper (and teacher). He is no longer with us, but I'll always cherish the time we spent feeding cattle and working the land together.

I have learned to love the land and all God's creatures, great and small (although it's hard to love a green bug when you're trying to grow wheat). I am honored to call myself a farmer's daughter, farm wife and farm-her.

—*Becky Gilbreath*
Apache, Oklahoma

WHEN I ASKED my husband, Darrell, how his love of the country shaped his life, he replied, "The country made me. It's all I ever knew."

We live in the house on the farm where he was born 81 years ago. Darrell is retired, but still helps feed the cattle and makes sure he's here to drive the baler tractor at haying time.

For me, living in the country has been a learning experience, but mostly a joyous one. We raised three daughters and two sons here, and enjoyed lots of church and community activities.

Add in country sunrises, sunsets, bright starry nights and the fun of watching wildlife parade past our door, and I don't think he missed much by never living in the city.
—*Audrey Seyb*
Donnelson, Iowa

YOU COULD SEE for miles and miles on the prairies of western Saskatchewan where I grew up. I walked to school across pastures full of crocuses blooming in the spring and meadowlarks singing on fence posts.

Then we moved 300 miles north, where poplars, tama-

"Keepin' It Country" Sure Paid Off That Day
MY WIFE AND I grew up in small towns in central Texas. After long careers as schoolteachers, we retired to a remodeled two-room country schoolhouse outside a town of 540 people.

When traveling, we like to "keep it country" by driving mainly rural roads. In 1993, our love of the countryside worked out even better than usual when we crossed paths with *Country's Reminisce Hitch* (pages 55-61) on its way to California.

It was so exciting to ride in the wagon and get to know driver David Helmuth and his bride, Vikki. My wife, Joyce, and I are right behind David and Vikki in this photo (above).
—*Eldon Ball, Milano, Texas*

racks, willows and fruit trees cut down the view. But it was an area abundant in wild fruit. In winter, we played cards, went to school dances and tried to stay warm in temperatures down to -60°.

I married a farmer. We raised a family and took time out from work whenever we could to have some wonderful times fishing and camping with friends.

I have never once wanted to live anywhere else. My life begins and ends with a love of the country. —*Eva Campbell Lloydminster, Alberta*

AFTER STRUGGLING through the Depression years on my parents' farm, I was leery when my husband, Wilbert, wanted to buy 80 acres of overgrown yellow sand. But he was determined.

We quickly discovered that the sand wouldn't grow corn or beans. So we thought we'd plant a few evergreens. The trees grew so well we now have the largest choose-and-cut tree farm in the area.

Meanwhile, we raised five fine young people, and lived a good life in the country. Surroundings and people do shape our lives. And at this point, we enjoy the shape we're in. —*Peg Matthes, Ida, Michigan*

WE'VE NEVER had the opportunity to move to the country, but when we read *Country* magazine, we transcend to a peaceful, beautiful place. It reminds me of the Rudyard Kipling poem, *If*. You probably know the beginning: "If you can keep your head when all about you are losing theirs..."

And it concludes with, "Yours is the Earth and everything that's in it." —*Ruth Kortanek Indianapolis, Indiana*

LIKE MOST KIDS raised on farms during the Depression, I thought farming was just entirely too much work. When I grew up, I didn't want any part of country living.

Then I met my future husband, who told me that any girl he married had to like farming because that's what he intended to do. So back to the farm I went.

To my surprise, I learned to love everything about country life. I even learned to appreciate the satisfaction of a hard day's work.

I live in town now after more than 50 years of marriage. But I still love to drive out into the country and enjoy all the work today's farmers put into raising their crops and livestock. —*Mrs. George Leidal Wadsworth, Ohio*

WE LEARNED that for a better tomorrow, start working on it today. —*Mrs. Arnold Zimmerman Deary, Idaho*

AS EACH new day dawns, I wake to the sights, sounds and smells of the country and find myself spiritually renewed. My husband and I farm 40 acres with three Belgians named "Duke," "Thunder" and "Miss Molly." We don't own a television and we

Country Depicts The America I Love

I CAME to Utah from England in 1959 at the tender age of 21. I had planned to stay a year, then move on to Australia. Before the year was up, I met a local farmer, got married and I've been enjoying life in the country ever since.

We raised two sons and a daughter on our little farm. Our youngest son now helps run the place.

As you can see from this photo (above), we've enjoyed *Country* from the beginning, as well as several other Reiman magazines. I also send gift subscriptions to my brother and sister in England. In other countries, life in America isn't always depicted in a flattering way, but I think your magazine does much to show why I love it here. —*Janice Hansen, Tremonton, Utah*

heat our house with wood.

Living in the country has taught me that it's the little things that matter most. Even the morning barn chores can send a feeling of contentment washing over me, reminding me how lucky I am to gaze on the beauty God has provided. —*Sandy Augustine Lena, Wisconsin*

I HAVE LIVED in the country all my life. I have been a farmer's daughter and farmer's wife. The country has not only shaped my life, it has been my life. I can't imagine living in the city.

However, I think country is something you have in your heart, and cannot be taken from you, no matter where you live. —*Catherine Jenne Sherburne, New York*

MY LIFE in the country has taught me to enjoy every precious little moment. I treasure memories of holding fluffy kittens, being the first to discover a batch of newly hatched chicks, sharing our swimming hole with water snakes, carrying wood to the house each evening and pumping water by hand.

The country taught me to respect the animals around us and to enjoy our down-to-earth, genuinely caring neighbors. I learned to respect God and all his creations. And I learned to respect myself.

I appreciate life more deeply and completely because of my country roots. —*Peggy Childers Payette, Idaho*

Saskatchewan...*This* Is God's Country!

*In each issue,
we invite readers
to tell us why they
think a particular
area is the best
place to live.
This time,
Clarence Norris
shares his love
of Saskatchewan.*

I've been traveling and photographing Saskatchewan for over 15 years, and I never cease to marvel at the diversity of the geography, the incredible wildlife, the richness of our history and the warmth of the people. From vast prairie grasslands and pristine northern lakes, rivers and forests, to the historic tapestry of our pioneers and fur-trading roots and diverse ethnic cultures, surely, this is God's Country.

I live in the heart of the province in Saskatoon. It's a perfect location for fanning out in all directions to capture on film the beauty of

THE BEST SPOT. Map shows the highlighted area author says is the country's *best* location.

our great outdoors.

North of Saskatoon, in the Lac La Peche area, is where I like to go to photograph endless fields of wheat blowing in the wind and patterns of ♂

"**IN AUTUMN**, swathes of grain create a mosaic of colors and patterns (far left). This aerial view is of a large wheat farm near Wakaw."

"**SASKATCHEWAN** is known as Canada's Breadbasket, as symbolized by these ripe heads of barley silhouetted by the setting sun."

"**THESE** farm youngsters were having a ball exploring the fields near Lac La Peche."

"**AFTER** a field has been swathed and the windrows have dried, giant combines separate the grain from the straw. Farmers work into the night bringing in the harvest."

"**YELLOW** aspen leaves and sapphire blue lakes make Prince Albert National Park a wonderland of color in the fall. It's so tranquil."

"THE AREA around St. Denis, with its rolling hills, neat farmsteads and vast and varied field patterns, is one of my favorite places to go in autumn."

"THIS old toolshed surrounded by aspens caught my eye on one of my trips to the country. Someone took pride in keeping it nicely painted."

"I SPENT an hour photographing the reflection of this dock at Lac La Peche, then just sat to watch the shadows lengthen and twilight set in."

"ABANDONED pioneer homes near Dorintosh remind us that although this is God's Country, the land was sometimes unforgiving for settlers."

grain swathes drying in the autumn sun. Here you'll also find rolling hills, vast alkaline sloughs and the edges of our northern forest.

Toward evening on one trip to the area, I discovered Lac La Peche. The lake was calm, and the shoreline was gilded with gold from the fall leaf colors. There was a small dock perfectly reflected in the still waters, and I spent over an hour capturing it on film. Then I packed up my gear and just sat on the dock to enjoy the twilight. I have never forgotten the experience.

A number of years ago, our family traveled to the Pacific Ocean, where I was eager to photograph lighthouses. We had a great time, but I never saw one lighthouse on that trip. Later that fall, back in Saskatchewan, I spotted a lighthouse on the hills above Jackfish Lake near the town of

"THIS PRONGHORN antelope seems to blend into the prairie near Sceptre."

"I TOOK my daughter Jennie to see this old well near St. Denis. I wanted to show her how her grandparents and other pioneers obtained their water."

"SURPRISED to find a lighthouse in Saskatchewan? This one beckons fishermen at sunset and guards the shoreline of Jackfish Lake near Cochin."

"**SASKATCHEWAN** has a mixed forest of aspen, pine, spruce, maple and many other trees. These oak leaves in Saskatoon provided a nice frame to record the dazzling blue sky on a sunny fall day."

Cochin. I was thrilled to finally find a lighthouse—even though it was in the middle of a prairie province—and I've returned many times to photograph it.

Once, as I was taking pictures of the lighthouse at dusk, there was a young couple next to it, holding hands and looking out at the setting sun. Turns out they were getting married soon and would be starting a new life together. I was able to capture the magic of the moment forever for them.

South of Saskatoon lie two more of my favorite locations. The first is the Great Sandhills near Sceptre. It's where the soil has been eroded to such an extent that there are large expanses of permanent sand dunes, some up to

three stories tall. The patterns in the sand in the early-morning or late-afternoon light are incredible.

Here, too, I've been able to photograph mule deer, pronghorn antelope, porcupines, burrowing owls and many other species of wildlife. And the sunrises and sunsets are second to none—perhaps that's why Saskatchewan is called the "Land of Living Skies."

Farther south, near the Canadian-U.S. border, is Cypress Hills Interprovincial Park, where you can climb above the prairie to the highest point between the Rocky Mountains and Labrador. It's the only area of Saskatchewan that escaped the effects of the last ice age and offers forests of lodgepole pines, fescue grasslands and breathtaking ⌁

"**SOMETIMES**, blustery autumn winds whip across the open prairie, prematurely stripping the trees of their leaves and scattering them everywhere to create a yellow carpet around the barnyard."

"**AUTUMN** is harvesttime—when crops are gathered, loaded onto trucks and sent to market."

"**SHANNON LAKE** in Narrow Hills Provincial Park sparkles like a jewel. The northwoods is a land of pristine beauty, so much so that I can almost smell the crisp air looking at this photo."

167

"**EVERYONE** pitches in on the farm, including these youngsters, who were digging potatoes in the rich earth for the family's supper table."

"**AS HILLS** cloaked with pines and aspens provide a colorful backdrop, large bales of straw dot the beautiful Wapti Valley (below)."

"**THE NEEDLES** of the tamarack trees turn golden in fall, before being shed for the winter."

vistas of the prairies far below.

One fall, I left the prairies and rolling grasslands behind and traveled far north to capture the autumn colors up there. I passed through Prince Albert, our gateway city to the North, and then explored Prince Albert National Park.

It's home to a multitude of clean, clear lakes nestled in valleys of pine, spruce, golden tamarack and yellow aspen trees. I awoke to crisp, clear mornings, perfectly calm lakes and endless reflections along the lakeshore.

I hiked quietly along the shoreline in the early morning and was rewarded with sightings of elk, deer, moose, red foxes, downy woodpeckers and gray jays. All the while, I heard the distant call of a loon.

There was a peacefulness that made me momentarily forget the hustle and bustle of the everyday world. I just sat back and marveled at the wonders of creation and rejoiced in my discovery of yet another corner of God's Country.

A Dream For My Son

She hopes he can grow up in the country—just like she did.

By Heather Ray, Perry, Georgia

MY HUSBAND and I took our son Jeffrey to the fair recently. We live in Perry, Georgia, home of the Georgia National Fair, so it was a pretty big deal.

Jeffrey was 6 months old and was not impressed. He allowed himself to be posed, blinking and sweating, next to a big Jersey heifer, then promptly fell asleep. He slept through the exhibits of pygmy goats and rabbits, waking up only when we came to the llamas. The look of fascination on his face as he stretched out his inquisitive hand toward a big black and white male settled it.

I want to be a farmer. I want to move back up to the foothills, live in the country and see that look on my son's face every day.

My dream is for Jeffrey to know spring is coming because the daffodils are blooming by the barbed-wire fence. I want him to recognize summer by the smell of wild onion and freshly cut hay, autumn by the clash of purple joe-pye weed and yellow black-eyed Susans. I'd like him to spend cold winter afternoons looking at seed catalogs, planning gardens in his head.

Eat Blackberry Cobbler

I'd love to pay Jeffrey a penny for every Japanese beetle he squishes…and bake him a cobbler with the blackberries he picked just 30 minutes earlier. I long to fry fish he caught in our pond (and that his father cleaned). I want him to nibble the ends of honeysuckle blossoms to taste their sweetness.

May the call of the whippoorwill settle him into sleep and the whine of mosquitoes keep him awake. Let the trumpeting of sandhill cranes flying overhead excite him, and the sound of a buck snorting in the woods scare him silly.

I want Jeffrey to grow tomatoes, jump from hay bale to hay bale and dig for worms. I'd like him to herd cows with a good dog.

My hope is he'll have a pasture to run to when he's mad at me. I dream of calling him to supper, my voice ringing out over the land, when I know he's simmered down.

In short, I'd like Jeffry to have my childhood times 10.

I grew up in the country in northern Georgia, on the remnants of what had been one of the largest farms in the county. I watched with the powerlessness of a child as the land was sold off, piece by piece.

My family now owns about 80 acres, only a tiny chunk of what the farm once was. But it is a beautiful chunk. There are

IN THE DRIVER'S SEAT. "My grandson Seth is the fifth generation of our family to roam our ranch," says Bobi Allard of Billings, Montana.

CAT'S CRADLE. "My son Matthew loves to carry the kittens around our farm," explains Sharon Weiss from Red Lake Falls, Minnesota.

deep forests and rolling pastures. There's a little pond that could be expanded for catfish production and a flat piece of land down by the river that would be perfect for a greenhouse or two. With a lot of work, that little piece of land could become a profitable farm.

The life of a farmer is not easy, I know. A farmer is subject to the vagaries of weather, not to mention markets, the economy and government. But people who work the land also have an intimacy with nature, the Earth and the seasons that I don't have in my close-quartered neighborhood and 9 to 5 job.

Satisfaction of Hard Day's Work

And there is my son. I want Jeffrey to grow up with his senses alive. May he know the satisfaction that comes with a hard day's work and eat a meal that he helped produce.

My dream is for him to be a country boy—a farm boy.

That's why I pushed his stroller through every exhibit at the fair while he slept, maybe dreaming of his friend the llama. It's why I talked to alpaca breeders, wondering if the shaggy animals could survive the heat of a north Georgia summer.

I fingered yarn spun from Georgia-bred sheep, thinking the pasture out by the pine grove might suit a flock of woolies. I stopped at the beekeeper's booth, then went home and surfed the Internet looking for information on vineyards and greenhouses until the late hours of the night.

I'd like this life for me, my husband and even for our dog. But most of all, I want it for my son. So I'll keep collecting pamphlets, reading books and surfing the Net…plowing fields in my sleep until my dream for us comes true.

BOY'S BEST FRIEND. "Our son Wade and our new farm dog, 'Cissy,' are just about inseparable," says Wendy Rogers from Gill, Colorado.

2001 OCF Herdsman Award

PROUD MOMENT. "My grandson Jacob had just finished showing his Jersey calf at the fair," notes Martha McReynolds, Danville, Vermont.

COUNTRY HOT TUB. "My grandson Andrew Reiss was cooling off on a hot day at his parents' farm," relates Leesa Shoup, Prospect, Tenn.

Pa's Old Horseshoe May Be Lucky After All

But don't tell Ma, or she'll pitch it away again.

I'VE LIVED 95 years and had a good life. I've seen a lot of changes, but I still have a lot of seeing and living to do.

My grandparents and parents came to America from Austria in 1886. They came to the New World to make a better life—and they realized that dream.

They settled in northern Wisconsin, which was nothing but a wilderness then. They knew it would be a struggle every day just to provide themselves with the necessities, but they were determined to find a spot of land on which to build a good life.

In those days, when a farmer found some land, he only looked at what he

EDITOR'S NOTE: This story was related by Peter Kauer of Rib Lake, Wisconsin and written down by friend Margaret Tauber.

could do with it—never all the work it would take. My grandparents and parents were determined people.

Not far from where they wanted to build their home, they found an old abandoned lumber camp. With the lumber and square nails they salvaged from that old camp, my grandfather and father built a one-room log cabin. They spent $2.50—which was all the money

they had—to buy windows.

My wife, Catharine, and I still live in that cabin. We added on to it, but the old log cabin remains a part of our home to this day.

Believed in Hard Work

My parents' and grandparents' lives were built on faith, hard work and respect. Those ideals have never let me down.

Only once do I remember seeing my mother get really angry and lose her temper. It was over a horseshoe my father found at the old lumber camp.

THE OLD HOMESTEAD. Below is the log cabin Peter Kauer's family built. Peter is the boy wearing the hat and plaid shirt.

Pa insisted on propping the horseshoe over the back door of the cabin, saying it was for good luck. But every time my mother went out the back door with a basket of wash, the horseshoe fell down. And each time, Pa would prop it back up again.

Then one day when the horseshoe fell yet again—missing Ma by inches—she scolded Pa. She said his lucky horseshoe was nonsense—that it was faith, not luck, that had built our house.

Pa replied, "Well, it was luck that the horseshoe didn't hit you."

Ma was so angry, she took that rusty old horseshoe down and stormed out of the house. No one ever knew what she did with it.

Limited Education

My brothers and I didn't get a lot of schooling, but it wasn't because we didn't want it. It was because teachers were hard to come by.

I remember one teacher we had for just 3 months. He wasn't much for teaching us out of a book. Instead, he taught us things like how to whittle. He told some really good stories, too.

It turns out that the man who hired our teacher didn't read well. When he looked at the application and saw that our teacher had spent 2 years at reform school, he thought that was the name of a school where he had taught.

The man lost his teaching job, but he stayed around and went to work in the woods. To the day he died, everyone called him "sir," just as we did when he was our teacher.

Business Was Sweet

We had the first beehives in the area. We made a long, hard drive in our buggy to pick up the hives. As soon as we got them loaded, Pa turned the horses around and started for home. We didn't even stop to sleep because driving at night gave the bees a better chance of survival.

It didn't take long before we were known for our honey. We had more than 100 hives, and we started new hives for many of our neighbors.

My brothers and I would start the new colonies by putting a queen bee on our arm. The worker bees would gather around the queen, and then we would carefully brush them off our arm into the new hive.

I was asked repeatedly why we were

HIDDEN IN TREE. Peter's mother apparently hid his father's horseshoe in the crotch of a tree. When the tree blew down in a storm, Peter found the rusty relic embedded in the trunk.

never stung. I'd explain that even a creature as small as a bee knows if you respect it.

The thing you had to be careful about was not to get two queens in one hive, or the workers bees would swarm, taking one queen and starting a new hive somewhere else.

Made Crown of Thorns

Our family also planted the first honey locust trees in this area. We bought 20, but our rough winters were too much for them. They all died, except for one Ma took care of in the house every winter. She did that for several years, until it got too big, and she had to plant it outside.

The first winter the tree was outside, Ma watched as ice hung on its branches. She was sure that it wouldn't survive. But it did, and a happier woman you never saw.

The blossoms on that honey locust were a wonderful source of nectar and pollen for the bees. And we found many uses for its long, strong needles.

By cutting off the thorns' sharp points, we made knitting needles out of them. They also made great phonograph needles.

Best of all, though, was the crown of thorns Ma made for the church each

Easter. To this day, we still make a crown of thorns for Easter.

Over the years, that tree has withstood some harsh winters. It now stretches clear across the yard and is a lovely sight to see. We have many honey locust trees now, all because of Ma's care for that one tiny seedling.

Keeping Peace in Family

Ma didn't believe in luck, just hard work and faith. But I remembered Pa's horseshoe when a huge white ash tree growing by our back door came crashing down in a storm—missing our roof by inches.

For when that great tree was cut up into firewood, buried in the center of the trunk was that rusty old horseshoe. Ma must have thrown it into the crotch of the tree, and over the next 60 years, the tree grew around it.

I'll bet Pa would have gotten a laugh out of that. As he said, "It must have been lucky—it didn't hit you."

I'm not saying I believe in lucky horseshoes. But to this day, that old horseshoe sits in my living room, still stuck in the center of that log.

It's not hanging over the door, so it wouldn't offend Ma. But it is in the house, and that would please Pa. That way, we keep peace in the family.

You Can't Take the Country Out of This Farm Boy

He's back livin' on the land and lovin' every minute of it.

By Ken Lundeen
Thomasville, North Carolina

I SAT in the loft of the barn, a pile of fresh hay as my mourning bench, and cried as I looked out the back window. My tears blurred the image of the barnyard below, the strawberry patch beyond it and the fenced path to the lake.

It was 1947, and I was 12 and shattered by an imminent tragedy.

No one in our family was dying; no one was even sick. My parents and siblings were excited and even talked happily about the coming event. I was the only one upset by *the move*.

We were leaving the Wisconsin farm that was part and parcel of my earliest memories, and moving 8 miles to a house in town. Sure, it had running water and electricity. But the caves in the woods, the gravel pit by the lake, the saplings I climbed and rode to the ground, and the gooseberry and blackberry patches would be lost to me.

Despite my sadness, the move happened as planned. The emotions of a distraught 12-year-old carried little weight against grown-up considerations.

Our new house was barren of memories. The new school was in "the city" (population 617) with a roomful of kids in each grade, as opposed to the rural schoolhouse with all eight grades in one room.

Endured the Move

I endured the move…moping while coping. Two years later there was another, less traumatic move, then high school, college and a job. The years and places seem to blur after that.

I spent 8 years in and around New York City, marrying a city girl on my passage through. Over the years, we and our three children lived in New York, North Carolina, Arizona, Florida, Pennsylvania and New Mexico. We rented homes, and we owned others, but we never lived on a farm.

Now, after 55 years away from the beloved farm of my youth, my wife and I are settled in our retirement home on 3-1/2 acres in North Carolina. I have land, woods and a creek! I feel like a 12-year-old farm boy disguised as a 67-year-old man, happily resurrecting some of my idyllic past.

When I was a boy, I had a secret glade. It was a clearing in the brush with soft, almost lawn-like grass for my bare feet.

Outside, from a few feet away, I couldn't see it. But as I moved closer, the brush opened up to a sun-caressed, grassy circle about 30 feet across in the middle of 20 acres of woods. It was my own secret place.

New Secret Place

There is no natural glade here. I will create one, though, for my grandchildren's sake. I will clear the stubble and brush from a sunny spot in the woods and plant grass there. I will keep it trimmed, but not too well.

I'll send my grandsons by a "shortcut," while I take the longer, well-worn path. When we meet at the creek, I won't ask them if they found the glade —I want it to be their secret place that will bring them back to Grandpa's farm more often.

As a boy, I dug caves in the woods and the gravel pit. Oh, most never survived more than a few days. After a good rain, they usually fell in, except the ones in the gravel pit.

The gravel pit caves were good. I could dig a horizontal shaft straight into the walls of the pit and sit in the coolness with 10 feet of Mother Earth above me.

Yes, I'll have a cave again. But to my wife and others, I'll refer to it as a root cellar for storing some of my surplus vegetables—lest they accuse me of acting goofy and going through my second childhood. I'll support that premise of a root cellar by storing a few mesh bags of aging onions and potatoes in it. But it really will be my cave.

As a boy, I played "statue." I'd walk into the woods, knowing that my clumsy intrusion stopped the music of life. To bring it back, I sat on the trunk of a wind-toppled tree for 5 minutes, making no movement or sound above my heartbeat.

Soon, the reanimation began. Squirrels, gophers and birds chattered, scurried and sang as before. Still and nonmenacing, I became part of the inanimate backdrop of their lives.

Enjoying Wildlife

Communion with creatures of the wild knows no age limitations. I will sit silently in the woods like I did decades before, but perhaps this time with some corn or apples for the wildlife and maybe a seat cushion for me, and enjoy the melody of life.

When I was a boy on the farm, a few trees had vines. They weren't like the *Tarzan* movie version, where Johnny Weissmuller could swing two stories above the ground and always find another vine waiting at the extremity of the first.

Our vines had roots in the ground. If you cut one off at ground level, you could swing on it, but never far enough to connect to another vine. Still, you could pull it back to a stump, swing for a couple of seconds in an arc above the ground and then drop a few feet to the forest floor.

You could even holler the Tarzan call, provided your mother didn't hear you and think you were in an accident.

There are vines here, some sturdy enough for Tarzan himself. But that's one childhood pastime I won't indulge in. I'm no longer a Tarzan wannabe and wouldn't relish explaining to an emergency room doctor how a 67-year-old man suffered multiple bone fractures after losing his grip on a vine.

But I will share my childhood memories with my grandchildren and set up a swinging place or two where they can fall into a soft pile of leaves.

When I was a boy, we had a big garden, where there was always a stalk of rhubarb or a carrot to snack on. But my favorite spot in the garden was the strawberry patch.

I don't remember how big the patch was, but I know my parents were never concerned about my berry raids. Whenever my mother went to pick dessert for the six mouths in our family, there were always more than enough berries for everyone.

Planting a Garden

I plan to have a small garden and a strawberry patch again. For my New Yorker wife, I'll plant the standards— lettuce, tomatoes, carrots, potatoes and corn.

As a former city dweller, she's not entirely convinced that anything grown in the soil can be natural. But she is willing to accept my seasoned judgement on those staple crops.

Strawberries may be tougher. My wife thinks of them as a dessert that grows only in delicatessens. Little by little, I'll ply her with the natural product until she agrees that they are a reasonable facsimile of the store-bought variety.

But I don't dare dream that she will become a convert to gardening. Near season's end, I see myself bringing in a last bowl of strawberries for each of us, then gazing paternally out the window at the depleted plants and saying, "I need to put some cow manure on the strawberries."

I envision her responding as she reaches into the refrigerator, "Suit yourself. I'm having whipped cream on mine."

He's Staying Put

I've planted flowers, vegetables and trees. Odds are, I'll be here to see the flowers bloom and to bring in the vegetable harvest. The trees are a little iffy at my age. But I'll maintain paths through the woods and check on them frequently.

I will enjoy my little hobby farm and make no plans to leave. I'll tell my wife that if one morning I don't wake up, she should just drag me down to the cave— I mean root cellar—and slide me in.

At long last, I have my farm. I'm not 12 years old anymore, and this time around, I'm not moving. ➤

CATCH OF THE DAY. Like the author of this story, Lee Hopper enjoys pastimes from his childhood, like fishing. The photo was taken by his nephew Steve Bushert of Sullivan, Illinois.

Country Church

By Charles Clevenger, New Boston, Ohio

I remember an old country church
    'Neath the sheltering maple trees;
Where a babbling brook ran crystal clear
    And whispered quiet melodies.

A rusty old bell hung in the spire
    Where its peal rang clear and true.
It called us to come and worship,
    As we each should freely do.

The sermons we heard on Sunday
    Gave us hope for a happier life;
It was there we learned from the Scriptures
    How to deal with trouble and strife.

The weathered old church is silent now—
    Its bell no longer chimes.
It stands as a peaceful monument,
    Where memories recall joyful times.

Photo: Nye Simmons

COUNTRY CHURCHES

Protestants and Catholics Share This Country Church

By Lois Dunwoody, Keystone, Nebraska

WELCOME to Keystone, Nebraska.

Our village of less than 70 people is located along the North Platte River in Keith County. Our claim to fame is The Little Church—the only church in the world that serves both Catholics and Protestants.

In the mid-1800's, much of western Nebraska was the domain of large cattle companies. Then the Homestead Act of 1862 attracted settlers…and bachelor cowboys, many of them emigrants from Denmark and Sweden, married the daughters of these pioneers.

When the Union Pacific brought rail service in 1905, the population of the river valley swelled even more—to several thousand residents. So in 1906, the village of Keystone was platted.

In those early years, Georgia Paxton, wife of one of the town's prominent citizens, organized the King's Daughters—a club to educate the teenage girls of the area in social skills and values.

Started with a Dream

The girls were of an age to dream of love and marriage, and they wanted a church for their weddings. So they set about raising money for a building—undaunted by the fact that several of them were Catholic and others were Protestants such as Presbyterian, Lutheran and Methodist.

The young women raised over $300 from suppers, bake sales and bazaars. When the adults caught the dream, the project quickly became reality. On August 16, 1908, a simple wooden chapel costing a grand total of $1,200 was presented to the community—debt free.

In the meantime, the wheels had been set in motion to obtain special dispensation from the Pope to allow the Catholics to share the building with their Protestant neighbors. Permission was granted on September 15, 1908.

Pews That Flip-Flop

The Little Church has a Protestant altar at the south end of its 18- by 40-foot sanctuary. A Catholic altar, with a confessional nearby, graces the north end. The pews, with seating for 50 to 60 people, have hinged backs that can easily be flipped to allow the congregation to face the appropriate altar.

The only door is in the center of the west wall, directly opposite a wood-burning stove. Kerosene lamps provided lighting in those early days. The church was never wired for electricity.

Many families attended church without concern for who conducted services. When the Catholic priest came, everyone was welcome to attend Mass.

If the Lutheran minister conducted services, the worshipers prayed the Lord's Prayer by saying, "Forgive us our trespasses as we forgive those who trespass against us." The Presbyterian pastor said, "Forgive us our debts"…or was that the Methodist circuit rider?

The ecumenical chapel served the people of Keystone faithfully for over 40 years. Then came automobiles, better roads and the building of denominational churches around the region.

A Historical Site

The last regular church services were conducted in June 1949. Now, The Little Church is maintained as a historical site—a testimony to Keystone's continuing ecumenical spirit.

If you're driving through Nebraska, stop in Keystone. If you'd like to see the inside of the church, drop in at the telephone company and ask Mrs. Wendt for the key.

Or stop by my house a mile north of town. My husband is the local pastor and still officiates at weddings at the church, so we have a key, too. I'll even demonstrate the pump organ for you!

DIVINE INSPIRATION. Rev. E.D. Dunwoody shows the hinged back of a pew so Catholics face their altar and Protestants face theirs on the other end of The Little Church.

COUNTRY CHURCHES

Resurrection of Memories from a Country Church's First Easter

GREENBRIER United Brethren in Christ, my childhood church in Glenmore, Ohio, held its first worship service on Easter Sunday, April 16, 1865.

When members of the congregation gathered that morning, they were unaware that the Civil War had ended and President Abraham Lincoln had been shot 2 days earlier. Jasper McLaughlin was present, and among the church records is a handwritten letter in which he eloquently describes the emotions as parishioners learned the news:

"It had been an unusually early spring. The peach trees were in bloom. A soft fluffy snow had fallen during the night, about an inch deep.

"Easter morning, the millions of bright pink peach blossoms peeping out of the tufts of snow that had lodged in the treetops, together with an unbounded landscape of crystal white, made a picture of resplendent beauty.

"The warm bright sunrise and balmy spring atmosphere rapidly changed the perspective into one of verdant grandeur, much more like the middle of May than the 16th of April."

Church Was Filled

"For weeks, it had been announced that a Sunday school would be organized on Easter Sunday. The house was well filled by 9 o'clock when Elias Dull arrived. This of itself was something very unusual, for he was never known to be late for service or engagements of any kind.

"As he came in the door, it was evident from his haggard appearance that he had met with some dire calamity. With bowed head, he came slowly up the aisle to the front. With trembling voice and broken sentences, he told us he had been to Van Wert the day before and learned that at 10

By Linda Watson, Paoli, Indiana

o'clock Friday night, Lincoln was shot and had died on Saturday.

"Not another word was spoken. Like a funeral pall, everything became as still as death itself. The very air seemed to be charged with some element which made it difficult even to breathe. Had a

"*B*rother Joe opened the service with singing..."

messenger arrived announcing a death in every home there represented, the sorrow could not have been more universal.

"After a length of time, it was decided that reason rather than sentiment should govern the proceedings and that it was best to go on with the organization.

"John Hand, a leading churchman, stated the object of the meeting and nominated Joe Heller for chairman. Brother Joe promptly responded, saying, 'We will open the service with singing and prayer.'

"Taking the pulpit hymnbook, he began to line out a long meter hymn. Then the congregation, all standing,

HALLOWED HALL. The Greenbrier Church closed 5 years ago, but memories remain.

would sing the lines, and so on, alternately, until the hymn was finished.

"Before Joe had finished reading the first two lines, four soldiers coming down the north road in their bright blue uniforms, knapsacks on their backs, carrying their guns, attracted the attention of everyone in the house.

"Singing had scarcely begun when Steve Roberts startled the congregation by crying out, 'Why, it's Pap and John Andrews,' and bolted out the door and down the road to meet them. The other two were soon recognized as Joe Yoder and Lewis Dickerson. They had arrived in Van Wert by an early train and walked the 10 miles out home.

"Lee's surrender, the war ended, Lincoln's death and now these four soldiers, the first in the neighborhood to get home, coming right into church, unannounced and unexpected—with all of these momentous episodes coming in such close proximity to each other, they wrought human emotions up to a degree beyond restraint or control."

Sang Praises

"Good old Aunt Mary Engle, 110 years old, Susan Dull and Polly Johnson were shouting, 'Glory Hallelujah.' Many others with devout unction voiced their praises in joyful thanks and gratitude for the safe return of the soldiers.

"Then came the climax, when with one spontaneous outburst, everyone in the house lustily joined in singing, 'It's the old kind of religion, and it's good enough for me.'

"I am not master of English equivalent to portray the activities which continued for an indefinite period, but if the angels keep record of Pentecostal outpourings here on Earth, that Easter service will be noted among the files."

City Pastor Discovers The Blessings of Country Life

Faith-filled parishioners taught him lessons the seminary couldn't teach.

By Robert Rogers, Bethel, Delaware

I WAS a 20-year-old college student still studying for the ministry when I was assigned to serve a circuit of four tiny churches tucked back in the quiet hills of Tennessee.

These churches were far off the beaten path and even farther from the city where I came from. They were accessible only by rough dirt roads that wound through the valleys and past small farms where my parishioners lived.

Only one of the churches was located in town, the small community of Theta. However, Theta was too tiny to appear on most maps.

The others were simply described as being "down the road" from other equally small and remote hamlets. Union Church was down the road from Santa Fe, Garrison Church was not far from Leiper's Fork and Greenbrier was close to Bending Chestnut.

I was a city boy, not even a real preacher yet. But the congregations welcomed me with quick acceptance. The members' smiles and words of encouragement helped assure me that I really had heard God's call to become a pastor. In return, I loved those people dearly.

The schedule called for me to preach in two of the churches every Sunday. Services were at 10 and 11 a.m., and the schedule alternated so each congregation had one 11 a.m. service a month.

I planned my weeks according to whether it was "first Sunday," "second Sunday," "third Sunday" or "fourth Sunday." The members helped me keep track of when and where I was supposed to be with reminders like, "Theta Church gets the 11 o'clock service on the fourth Sunday."

Tasty Potluck Dinners

On months that had a fifth Sunday, all the congregations came together to worship in one church. Then, following the service, there was "dinner on the grounds," as they called it.

I still remember those outdoor banquets of country ham and fried chicken, biscuits and corn bread, vegetables from members' gardens, glasses filled with iced tea and plates of homemade cakes and pies.

After we ate, the children played, and I quietly listened to the wisdom of the elders, some whose only formal education had been a few years in a one-room schoolhouse.

The services were simple. If I was late getting to the next church, someone would start the singing. Members called this "leading out," and they'd sing until I arrived.

At some of the services, a member would volunteer to play the old upright piano, which was invariably out of tune and pushed against the wall in each of the churches. There was no choir.

Nor was there a restaurant nearby. So nobody was in a hurry to get out of church and beat the rush for Sunday brunch.

In winter, we often gathered around a coal stove instead of the altar. We huddled there for warmth as the cold winds ignored the barrier of thin glass in the windows.

There usually weren't many folks attending services. I will always remember the Sunday when only one person came to the Union Church. But we still had preaching that day anyway.

Simple Weddings

Weddings were beautiful in their simplicity. No one even considered using a florist—flowers came from the meadows or members' own gardens. The wedding party wore their Sunday clothes.

Funerals also had a simplicity about them. Each church had its own cemetery, and after the funeral service, everyone just walked outside for the burial.

When the last verse of *Amazing Grace* drifted out across the valley, the men in the crowd lowered the casket into the earth. Then they took turns shoveling dirt into the grave. With quiet dignity, they seemed to be tucking their beloved friend in for a night of sleep. When the grave was filled, I said a final prayer.

I had never seen burials performed that way in the city. There, we were always quickly escorted back to our cars after the graveside portion of the service, so the cemetery workers could do the burying.

But here in the country, death was a natural part of life. There was no rush, no hurry to escape reality and no mystery about it.

Held Revival Meetings

Once a year each church had a revival. That was as certain as Easter and Christmas Day.

An "outside preacher" was brought in to lead these special evening services, which included lots of singing and earnest appeals for persons to come to the altar to get right with God. Family and neighbors whose relationship to their Maker was in question were urged to attend.

There was always a mason jar of water sitting on the pulpit in case the preacher's throat went dry. Handheld cardboard fans with a printed advertisement from the local funeral home served as air-conditioning.

At least once every sum-

ner, we also had baptisms in
creek near one of the
churches. I had never bap-
ized by immersion before,
much less in a creek.

The congregation gath-
ered on the creek bank and,
as each person was baptized,
someone would lead out in
*What a Friend We Have in
Jesus, The Old Rugged
Cross* or *When We All Get
to Heaven.*

Said Good-Bye

Eventually, the time came
for me to leave Tennessee
and continue my studies at a
seminary in Washington,
D.C. So on a warm fifth Sunday in August after dinner on
the grounds, I said good-bye
to my tiny rural congregations...and to their wonderful, simple way of living.

I already had more formal
education than most of them
and was on my way for
more. Yet, they taught me
lessons I still remember 35
years later.

From them I learned
about the real meaning of
life and death, faith in God,
concern for neighbors, appreciation for even the
smallest blessings and how
a person can be poor, yet
rich. These are all lessons I
never grasped as well in a
classroom.

As I drove off, I saw the
best people in the world in
my rearview mirror, standing silently and watching me
go. I realize now, even more
than then, what a special life
they possessed.

The Pulpit's Yours.

If
you're a pastor (or know of
one) with fond recollections
of a rural parish that you've
served, we'd like to hear
about them and share them
with other readers in future
issues. Send your story to
"God's Rural Realm," *Country EXTRA,* 5925 Country
Lane, Greendale WI 53129.

COUNTRY CHURCHES

Sunday's No Day of Rest for This Preacher

She's dedicated to serving seven country congregations.

By Peg Ratliff, Field Editor, Griggsville, Illinois

IT WAS Sunday morning, and I was on the road again.

I'm a circuit-riding preacher, actually a lay minister associate, for the Bright Star Parish in Pike County, Illinois. We have seven churches in our charge, and this morning I set out to visit three of them.

As the daughter of a career Air Force sergeant, I'd always lived near big cities—Washington D.C., London and St. Louis, Missouri. But in 1984, I accepted a teaching position in the small town of Griggsville. It was a whole new world for me!

The Methodist Church simply doesn't have enough ordained ministers to serve all of its churches. So in addition to teaching, I took courses in lay speaking and servanthood to bring the Gospel to tiny churches in our area. Our charge has an ordained minister and two lay ministers to fill these country pulpits.

No Time to Spare

It was a gorgeous morning as I came down off the bluff and crossed the Twin Eagle Bridges that span the Illinois River. Sometimes I make these trips in rain, fog or sleet, but today the sun was shining.

My first stop was Oxville United Methodist Church (UMC) for the 9 a.m. service. The Oxville church is small and neat, with an average attendance of 12. This morning I was greeted by nine of the faithful.

When the service ended, I headed to Florence for the 10 a.m. service. With such a tight schedule, I must hold my services to 45 minutes. That makes for short and to-the-point messages...which no one seems to mind!

The Florence church sits on the Illinois River, and so far, I've been lucky that the drawbridge has never kept me from starting the service on time. Twice a month, about 12 people worship in Florence and then stay for an adult Sunday school class.

At 11 a.m., I led the service at Detroit UMC. The congregation was founded in

1851, making it the oldest church in Illinois at its original site. With a congregation of about 35, this church has an element that many of our other churches don't have —children.

I have the kids come down to the front for a children's message. This morning I used part of my lighthouse collection to illustrate that Jesus is the light of the world.

By noon, I'd shaken the last hand and headed for home, thinking about the prayer requests of the day.

The following Sunday, I drove to tiny Baylis UMC. A turkey buzzard standing in the road misjudged his takeoff and flew into my windshield. There was no damage to my car, although I couldn't speak for the bird. It's an occupational hazard for those of us who serve in the country.

Seven Faithful Souls

The average attendance at Baylis is seven hearty souls. I'm the youngest person there, and I'm almost 50. But the congregation is faithful as well as grateful.

After the Baylis service, I drove to New Salem UMC, which recently held its 100th annual chicken fry. There's talk of discontinuing the tradition, but many of us are hoping someone will step up and keep it going.

Later in the month, I'll serve in the pulpits of two of our larger churches—Perry UMC and my home church, Griggsville UMC. The Griggsville church is especially blessed right now with many small children. So the children's sermon is particularly lively.

A country church is very special to its parishioners. Most were baptized and married there, and they have loved ones buried in its cemetery. Circuit-riding preachers who drive through God's beautiful countryside on Sunday mornings are dedicated to helping them keep the doors open for as long as they can.

Spread the Word. If you're a member of a country church with an interesting history or unique features, we'd like to spread the word about it. Send your story and sharp color photos to "Country Churches," *Country*, 5925 Country Lane, Greendale WI 53129. Include a self-addressed stamped envelope if you want your photos returned.

ON A MISSION. Peg Ratliff's circuit includes New Salem Methodist Church, built back in 1868.

COUNTRY CHURCHES

They Call Themselves 'Methbaptbyterians'

The Methodists, Baptists and Presbyterians work and worship together in this tiny town.

By Jean Watson, Newbern, Alabama

MOST FOLKS consider themselves Methodist, Baptist, Episcopalian, Catholic or some other denomination. But not me or most of my hometown friends. We're "Methbaptbyterians"—an aggregate of Methodists, Baptists and Presbyterians.

Why such a mixture? Church in Newbern, Alabama is not denominational—it's a community affair. That's because none of the three churches in our town of 231 people can afford a full-time pastor, so we share preachers with surrounding communities.

We all attend a union Sunday school each Sunday, which meets in the educational building of the Baptist church. But worship services are a different matter.

On the first Sunday of every month, we all attend services at Hobson Bethel Methodist Church. Established in 1884, the church originally had a resident pastor and a parsonage. But it now shares a charge with two other congregations, and the pastor can only be here once a month.

The second Sunday of each month finds us worshiping at Newbern Baptist Church. This congregation was organized in 1848, but like the Methodists, today it must also share a pastor with another Baptist congregation.

Presbyterians claim the third Sunday of the month. Their congregation is the oldest in Newbern, having been organized in 1844. Though this church has never had a resident pastor, it has always been very active in the community.

And the Fourth Sunday?

On the fourth Sunday, I guess you could say we're heathens! Just kidding, of course. There's Sunday school, but with no pastor to serve us, we go home afterward. Or we'll use that time for community work days or picnics and commune with each other as well as with God.

Attendance at Sunday school and church varies between 20 and 60 people, depending upon the occasion. Our numbers swell at Easter and

TIDY TRINITY. Tiny Newbern, Alabama (pop. 231) boasts three well-maintained churches—the Baptist (top), Methodist (center) and Presbyterian.

Christmas as well as for family reunions or birthdays, because no one wants to miss seeing members of our community "family" who moved away and are returning for a special get-together.

No one has trouble remembering where church is held on a particular Sunday. All three churches are within sight of each other, and all you have to do is look for the one where all the cars are parked.

Newbern is located in an agricultural region in the west-central part of the state. The town lies along a 1-mile stretch of Alabama Highway 61. In fact, our sidewalk is exactly a mile long.

I was lucky enough to be born and raised in this idyllic place. I grew up going to Hobson Bethel Methodist Church.

Always Late for Church

I married the grandson of a Baptist minister, and we operate a catfish farm outside of town. Byron believed as I did that this was a special place to raise a family, and while our sons were growing up, we lived next to the Baptist church.

Although we lived so close, it seemed we were always the last ones to arrive. The Sunday school superintendent teased us about that, and said, "The Watsons are here, so it must be getting late and time to start."

Here in Newbern, we really don't dwell on our different denominations. What's important is salvation.

We are a community of people working together to promote Christianity and to raise our children in a Christian environment. We love God, and we love our neighbors. It's as simple as that.

Spread the Word. If you're a member of a country church with an interesting history or unique features, we'd like to spread the word about it. Send your story and sharp color photos to "Country Churches," *Country,* 5925 Country Lane, Greendale WI 53129.

Old-Time Religion Is Still Good Enough for Her

Favorite hymns bring back memories of a country church and the congregation that sang them.

By Karen Rasberry, Laurel, Mississippi

LAST SUNDAY as I was sitting in church, I noticed a well-worn Baptist hymnal in the rack on the back of the pew ahead of me. It made me think about Grandma Black and how she loved to sing the old hymns in that book.

In my mind, I could see her swinging on her front porch as she shelled peas and watched the cars coming up the road. She'd hum *What A Friend We Have In Jesus* or *The Old Rugged Cross* as her arthritic fingers worked.

Shelling peas was not my idea of fun. But I would sit there with her, mainly to hear her sing or hum those gospel tunes.

As each car passed by in a cloud of dust, Grandma would ask me who was driving it. Her eyesight was failing, and her glasses were always in desperate need of cleaning. I'd tell her who had driven by, and she would wonder out loud, "Where in the world is he going this time of day?"

To my way of thinking, peas shelled by hand are more valuable than gold because there's so much time and work involved. I'd have to love somebody a whole bunch to sit and shell peas all day and then give 'em to the person.

But that's exactly what my grandmother would do. She'd stand out by the road in front of her house and flag down familiar cars with her friendly wave. "Do you need any purple hulls today?" she'd ask as she leaned in the car window. Nobody ever turned her down.

Giving away shelled peas ought to be worth a few jewels in her heavenly crown.

Pillars of the Congregation

I can't think about Grandma Black without also remembering Bethel Baptist Church up the road where we all gathered for worship. She and my grandfather were there every Sunday and were pillars of the tiny congregation for over 50 years.

The church was a simple, white, wooden building with three rooms. It smelled like musty hymnals and the oil they used to polish the woodwork.

In winter, Papa Black would go to the church about 6:30 a.m. to light the heaters so the congregation could hear about eternal life without freezing to death.

In summer, the funeral home supplied us with cardboard fans. My favorite fan had a picture of Jesus kneeling in the Garden of Gethsemane. The harder the preacher would preach, the faster the fans would go.

Noah's Ark

The congregation was small, but there were always enough of us children to have Bible school each summer. Miss Sue and Miss Alene were in charge one year that I remember in particular.

They planned a program about the flood and Noah's Ark. I had to memorize a very important verse from Genesis 7: "And I will cause it to rain upon the earth 40 days and 40 nights; and every living substance that I have made will I destroy from the face of the earth." I recited this verse over and over until I could say it flawlessly.

After the salute to the American and Christian flags, we sang *Jesus Loves Me* and prepared to recite our verses before the congregation. I was third to do my verse after Diane and Randy. I couldn't even hear myself say it because my heart was pounding so loudly. But I recited it without so much as a stammer.

A boy named Bobby followed me. His verse was about "the beasts and the fowl of the earth, and everything that creepeth upon the earth."

He stood there with his hands in the pockets of his jeans and stared at his shoes for what seemed like an eternity. Miss Alene was trying to get his attention and mouth the words of his verse to him.

He finally looked toward the congregation and blurted out, "The only good bug is a dead bug." At least it had something to do with things that creepeth upon the earth!

After the program, we had Kool-Aid and sugar cookies and teased Bobby until he ran out and hid in the cemetery.

Patent Leather Shoes

The church was less than a half mile from our house, and sometimes my sisters and I would walk. By the time we got there, our patent leather shoes would be dusty and full of gravel. So we'd sit on the church steps and empty them out

Irene Jeruss

before we slipped inside to the back pew.

I remember one Sunday when the crowd was bigger than usual. The flock had been without a shepherd for a good while, and various preachers had been coming to try out for the position.

On that day, the preacher being auditioned was waving his open Bible and yelling loud enough to wake the cemetery. "I tell ye brothers and sisters, ye must turn from your sins and wicked ways or you're gonna bust hell wide open!" he shouted.

Hell is a very serious subject, and the thought of busting it wide open didn't appeal to me at all. But something in all of this struck my sister Phyllis as funny. Soon the whole pew started to shake from her trying not to laugh out loud.

Laughter is contagious, especially in church when you know you're supposed to be very reverent. So when the congregation stood to sing *Just As I Am*, we girls managed to sneak out the door, and once outside, we doubled over and cackled until our sides hurt.

That preacher didn't get the call to minister at Bethel. The deacons finally found someone who could "shell the corn" with a little less fire and brimstone in his messages.

Baptized in New Church

The little white church finally became too outdated for the needs of the congregation. So the year I turned 12, a new church was built, and I was baptized in its modern baptistery.

I was thankful for that because the old church didn't have a baptistery. My sister was baptized in Papa Clark's pond with the snakes and tadpoles while the congregation sang *Shall We Gather At the River*.

Occasionally, I go back to visit Bethel Baptist Church and feel like I've come home. Somehow it seems like I'm a little closer to God in that tiny country church.

Some of the friends from my youth are still there doing the Lord's work and singing the same hymns that I remember so sweetly. As for my grandparents, they've gone on to claim their rewards in the *Sweet By and By* and are buried in the church cemetery. *The Old Rugged Cross* delivered them to a "city that's fairer than gold."

COUNTRY CHURCHES

Church Founders Practiced What They Preached

They showed love toward their enemies—
just like it says in the Good Book.

By Lola Autry, Field Editor, Hickory Flat, Mississippi

PINE GROVE Baptist Church sits high on a hilltop 7 miles from the small town of Hickory Flat, Mississippi. The beautiful white clapboard building is crowned with a tall steeple that can be seen from afar.

The congregation has worshiped at this location since 1845. The first meetinghouse was built of logs and had a humpbacked fireplace made of rocks daubed with mud. It was put up by men in the rural community and soon became the gathering place for the sparsely populated area.

Another one-room church was built later. The building of today was erected across the road from the others in 1913. Land where the first buildings stood was added to the church cemetery.

It was in that third one-room sanctuary that my husband, Ewart, sat in the front pew as a little boy. In the summertime, he wiggled his dusty bare feet, waiting for his preacher father to complete the sermon. His dad, James Autry, became pastor of the church in 1904 and held that position until his death in 1919.

Later, Ewart was pastor there for 33 years. For all those years, his brother Elond was music director.

On a Mission

There are many interesting notations in the church records. One was a vote taken by church members to decide what to do with money left over at the close of the church year. The decision was to give the money to missions. The sum was 50¢.

The pastor's salary around the turn of the 20th century was noted as $6.00.

In 1995, the 150th anniversary of the church was marked by a re-enactment of a time of stress, sorrow and spiritual victory in the church's history. The re-enactment took members back to a cold snowy day during the Civil War. There was a roaring fire in the fireplace of the first log meetinghouse.

The congregation consisted of old men, women and children. The younger men were all away at war.

The worship service had just begun and the congregation was singing the opening hymn, when there was a knock on the door. All became quiet.

Fear played on everyone's face. Women huddled their children close to them. Old men raised questioning eyebrows. Finally one of the deacons said, "We'd better find out who it is and what they want."

At the door stood a group of enemy soldiers. Children, sensing the terror in the hearts of those around them, began to cry.

Then the soldier captain spoke. In a gentle voice he said, "Don't be afraid. We are not here to harm you. We would simply like to worship with you. Will you let us do that?"

The deacon replied, "I'll have to talk it over with those inside. Please wait."

Everyone in the small log building had heard what was said. Finally, the deacon called to a 16-year-old woman. "Betty," he said, "you've suffered more than the rest of us here because of the loss of two of your loved ones in this war. What do you say? Shall we invite these men in to worship with us?"

With a sob in her voice, Betty answered, "If we can't worship with our enemies, then we can't truly worship."

Onward Christian Soldiers

The soldiers entered and joined in the singing of familiar hymns—one even led the group in singing. In addition, there were Scripture readings, prayer and praise. At the close of the service, the soldiers shook hands with each of the old men, then said farewell to all who were there with, "God bless each of you."

Pine Grove church, standing tall on the top of a hill, is still a beacon to anyone who comes to worship. Today, the size of the congregation is greater than it was in 1845. The physical structure is greatly improved, too. But the hearts of those who attend are much the same as those of that long-ago time.

STEEPED IN TRADITION. The steeple of Pine Grove Church not only points heavenward—it's a testimony to the parish's faithful past.

COUNTRY CHURCHES

Church Says Good-Bye to One of Its Own

DURING Sunday morning services at North Fork Baptist Church in Big Pine Valley here in the mountains of western North Carolina, Pastor Gary Fender told the congregation that Leonard Buckner had died early that morning. Most folks had already heard the news when they met friends while coming into church.

It was a moving tribute and simple celebration of the life of "a good man."

By Bill Weber, Field Editor, Marshall, North Carolina

Gary explained that there would be no customary visitation at the funeral home. Rather, the family would be at the church at 10:30 on Tuesday morning for those who wanted to pay their respects.

That would be followed by a funeral at 11:30 and burial in the cemetery on the hill above the church. The men of the church would meet to dig the grave on Monday.

By 10 a.m. Tuesday morning, ladies were carting loads of food into the fellowship hall for the luncheon that was to follow the burial. The women of our congregation are good cooks and take great pride in offering their best casseroles, salads and desserts to their neighbors and friends. The mouth-watering aromas of their efforts filled the hall.

Church Was Filled

My wife, Barbara, and I arrived at the church about 10:45. Cars were parked on the road all around the church, and many folks were standing outside visiting.

As we entered, we could see the open casket in front of the pews and the family grouped to the left. The line of friends offering their condolences filled the center aisle of the church.

In the group were Alma, Leonard's wife of 59 years; sister, Mary Ellen; brother, Robert; his children, Ronnie, Keith, Connie and Kay; and his grandchildren. Barbara and I got a hug from Connie, and I shook hands with her husband. As Bar-

bara embraced Alma, both their cheeks were wet with tears.

I shook Ronnie's hand. He was my friend, and I fumbled for something to say: "I know when my dad died, even though it was expected, it still hurt." With that, I reached for my handkerchief to dry my eyes.

There was a subdued hum of visiting throughout the church, which was filled with Leonard's friends and family. Just before 11:30, the organist began softly playing *Rock of Ages*, and the church got quiet. Those not yet seated found places in the pews.

Two of Leonard's grandsons, Brian, 31, and Brandon, 25, stepped up to the pulpit and began to sing *It Is Well with My Soul*. They sang the duet a cappella, and it was a moving tribute.

Then, Brian, who is an ordained minister, offered his thoughts on his "PaPaw."

"He was a farmer all his life, and he taught me to work beside him in the fields," reflected Brian. "But more importantly, he taught me how to live. He loved this church, and he loved to sing. His life was a testimony to his faith. He gave me the rules to live by."

The quartet sang a hymn, and our former pastor, Bruce, spoke next. "I didn't even know where Big Pine Valley was when I came here 22 years ago to be your minister. But I found good people, a caring community and a great friend in Leonard. He was what we mean when we say someone is 'a good man.' "

Friends Dabbed their Eyes

After he spoke, the quartet sang *He Whispers Sweet Things to Me*. I noticed quite a few folks dabbing their eyes with their handkerchiefs. Of course, the men tried not to be obvious about it.

The last speaker was Pastor Gary. He also didn't speak long, but gave a final tribute to his friend. His voice was husky, and he, too, used his handkerchief.

He read a passage from John 14 and said, "Leonard lived for 81 years. He preached his sermons in this church by the way he lived his life. He was my friend, and his memory will always be part of this church."

The funeral was brief, and the casket was removed. As folks filed out, you knew they were there, not because they had to be. They came because they wanted to say good-bye to their friend.

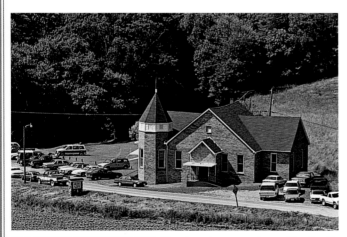

CLOSE-KNIT CONGREGATION. Members become almost like family at small country churches like North Fork Baptist in Big Pine Valley.

SWEET MEMORY. Leonard Buckner taking a break from boiling molasses.

Code of the Country:
Lend a Hand Whenever You Can

We recently asked our Field Editors to list the rules or codes that country folks expect themselves and their neighbors to live by. We figured they'd write about things like keeping their places looking neat, noxious weeds under control and line fences in good repair.

While those things may be important, they weren't what our Field Editors had in mind. Instead, nearly every one who responded to our question described the "Code of the Country" as neighbors coming to the rescue help-ing one another when the need arises.

Here are excerpts from a few of their letters:

"When you live in the country, a neighbor is anyone who lives on your road, or any road that joins it. And you know your neighbors because you rely on them, not only during tragic times, but during good times as well," writes Brenda Vanhorn of Jamestown, North Carolina.

Brenda notes that in the country, neighbors willingly share farm equip-ment and kitchen tools, as well as ad-vice on getting the most out of them.

When Brenda's grandparents bought a farm in 1951, it was a kindly neighbor who helped her grandfather buy his first tractor.

"Grandpa and Uncle Dave had found an old hand plow that they rigged up to Grandpa's Model A truck. Grand-pa was driving the truck, and Uncle Dave was steering the plow when Mr. Wright happened to drive by and see this spectacle. He politely suggested they consider buying a tractor," Bren-da relates.

ter move the cows out of the pasture to higher ground. He went back and got his tractor, drove out in our field in the dark and helped round up our cattle," Liz relates.

Ivan, who has since passed away, told the McCains they could use his pasture anytime theirs was flooded. "He was a good neighbor who lived the Code of the Country," says Liz.

When Peggy Chase's daughter was hurt in a riding accident on their Edison, Ohio farm, neighbors came to help as soon as they saw the ambulance at the Chase home. One neighbor took care of the Chases' younger son until husband Larry arrived home, while others fed their animals. On Thanksgiving Day, neighbors even brought dinner—complete with a turkey—to the hospital for the family.

"Country neighbors," adds Peggy, "will take the long way home from town to drive past the farm of a neighbor who's away, just to make sure nothing is amiss."

Mended Their Fence

Judith Saul and her husband, Henry, were spending a day away from their mini farm near Union Mills, North Carolina when a dead tree fell across the road and landed on a section of their fence.

By the time the Sauls returned home, their neighbors had cut up the tree, cleared the road and patched the fence to keep the couple's goats in until the broken rails could be replaced.

"When I called our neighbors to thank them, they just laughed about trying to mend the fence with the goats already halfway out," Judith writes.

Country folks not only lend a hand when their neighbors need it, but they're fair in their dealings with one another, says Ted Kalvitis from Augusta, West Virginia.

Ted operates a mobile farm tractor repair business, and travels to farms in the northern Shenandoah Valley of Virginia and nearby counties in West Virginia to fix tractors and other farm equipment.

When Ted finishes a job, he notes that his customers have their check-

books ready to pay him even before he has his tools all put away.

"Or, if the client is going to be away, a check for an estimated amount is left behind. That way, at least my expenses are covered until we can settle up," Ted says.

Prompt payment by customers, he says, allows small business owners like him to operate.

Birthday Surprise

Kristie Holsey of Sykesville, Maryland wanted to take her son Andrae to a petting zoo to celebrate his fourth birthday, because he loves animals so much. But there wasn't one nearby within Kristie's price range.

Every day Kristie drove by a farm near her home that had a variety of animals—donkeys, a horse, sheep, cattle, pigs, goats and cats. Although she did not know the owners, she got up the nerve to stop at the farm one day and ask if she could bring Andrae to see their animals.

"When I knocked on the door, a friendly lady—Doris Bell—answered. After I explained my dilemma, Doris said she was a 4-H leader and always happy to educate young people about farm animals," says Kristie.

"Doris' generosity completely overwhelmed me. My son had an unforgettable birthday party, and Doris taught me what the Code of the Country is really about."

Cheryl Espedal of Hauser, Idaho had always heard how country people help each other in emergencies. "Having recently moved to the country, I was surprised—and pleased—to see how they also help each other in the small matters of everyday living," she writes.

Cheryl's family and six others on their road must drive 1-1/2 miles to pick up their newspapers and mail. "The neighbor who goes down the hill first retrieves all the other newspapers and delivers them, saving the rest of us a 3-mile round trip," she writes.

Welcomes New Arrivals

On Cynthia Moran's street in Amherst, Massachusetts, families who move into the neighborhood are welcomed with a bouquet of flowers or fresh-picked vegetables from her garden.

"I always say neighbors ought to be neighborly. It's all part of our Code of the Country," says Cynthia.

The next day Mr. Wright picked up Brenda's grandfather and took him to a farm equipment dealer and helped him select—and bargain for—a 1929 McCormick 1020.

Helped New Neighbors

Liz McCain and her husband, Bob, had just moved to their farm near Florence, Oregon and hadn't yet met their neighbor Ivan Funke. But late one stormy night, Ivan was at the McCains' door to warn them that the creek in their cow pasture was rising fast.

"Ivan came to tell us that we'd bet-

'Looks Like a Bumper Crop, Dad'

"OUR SON Dylon was out in the field during wheat harvest when I spotted him inspecting a head of grain," explains Leslie Niswonger of Wallace, Kansas. "Dylon's daddy, John, is a fourth generation wheat farmer."

Your Turn. If you have a humorous or touching picture like this, send it to "Parting Shot," *Country EXTRA*, 5925 Country Lane, Greendale WI 53129. Be sure to include the details of the photo, your address and daytime phone number. Please include a self-addressed stamped envelope if you want the photo returned.